Department of Health
Welsh Office
Scottish Office Department of Health
Department of Health and Social Services, Northern Ireland

Report on
Confidential Enquiries
into Maternal Deaths
in the United Kingdom
1991-1993

Bryan M Hibbard MD PhD FRCOG
Mary M Anderson FRCOG
James O Drife MD FRCSEd FRCOG
John R Tighe MD FRCP FRCPath
George Gordon FRCSEd FRCOG
Sheila Willatts MD FRCA FRCP
Michael de Swiet MD FRCP
Robert Shaw MD FRCSEd FRCOG
William Thompson MD FRCOG
Gwyneth Lewis MSc MRCGP MFPHM
Beverley Botting BSc HonMFPHM

London: HMSO

CONTENTS

Editorial Board

Statistical Sub-Group

England
Mrs Beverley Botting   Office of Population Censuses and Surveys
Mrs Narupa Dattani

Scotland
Dr Susan Cole   Information Services Division of the
Common Services Agency

Wales
Mr Reginald Kilpatrick   Economic and Statistical Service
of the Welsh Office

Northern Ireland
Mr John Gordon   Registrar General's Office

Departmental representatives
Dr Gwyneth Lewis   NHS Executive, England (from April 1995)
Dr Dawn Milner   Department of Health England
(to March 1995)
Dr Joan Andrews   Welsh Office
Dr Sheila Lawson   Scottish Office Department of Health
Dr Patrick Woods   Department of Health and Social
(from February 1995)
Dr Adrian Mairs   Services Northern Ireland (to January 1995)

Observer
Ms K Partington   Department of Health   England

PREFACE

United Kingdom Confidential Enquiries Into Maternal Deaths Report 1991-93

We are pleased to introduce this, the third combined Report of the Confidential Enquiries into Maternal Deaths, which shows a modest fall in the overall maternal mortality rate from 10.3 per 100,000 maternities in the 1988-90 triennium to 9.8 per 100,000 for the period covered in this Report. In particular the mortality rate for conditions directly due to pregnancy and delivery (*Direct* deaths) has fallen more sharply from 6.0 and 6.1 per 100,000 deaths in the previous two triennia to an overall rate of 5.5 per 100,000 for the period 1991-93.

It is particularly gratifying that this Report has been published nine months ahead of schedule and we hope this will be improved upon for future Reports. However, as we discuss below, there is much that can be done to improve the timely reporting and assessment of these deaths, without which this valuable contribution to raising the standards of maternity care for women with associated clinical problems would not be possible.

We commend the findings and recommendations contained within this Report to all purchasers and providers of maternity services. Fortunately only a small number of women suffer severe complications of what is, for the vast majority, a natural process. Nevertheless, all women are entitled to receive the best available care and this Report should enable those who purchase and provide such services to review their current provision of services and arrangements for audit as well as reassessing local guidelines for the management of the commoner conditions.

In this triennium report forms for 320 deaths were submitted to the Enquiry, covering 99% of known maternal deaths, of which 128 were classified as *Direct* and 100 *Indirect* according to the International Classification of Diseases definitions of maternal deaths. In addition there were 46 *Fortuitous* and 46 *Late* deaths. A detailed description of the definitions used in this Report is given in the section headed " Definitions of maternal mortality and summary of deaths subject to enquiry". During the period 1988-90, 145 *Direct* deaths were reported to the Enquiry compared with 128 for this triennium, representing a decrease in the overall *Direct* death rate from 6.1 to 5.5 per 100,000 maternities. However there was a slight increase in the number of *Indirect* deaths from 93 to 100 over the same period, resulting in a small rise in the *Indirect* death rate from 3.9 to 4.3 per 100,000 maternities. Most of this rise can be attributed to a significant increase in the number of aortic aneurysms reported in 1991-93.

It is heartening to report that the percentage of deaths associated with some degree of substandard care has fallen to 40% compared with 50% in the last triennium, perhaps reflecting that the messages and guidance contained in previous Reports are being heeded, although this proportion continues to remain unacceptably high. We are very grateful to Professor Bryan Hibbard for writing an extremely helpful additional section, Chapter 18, on substandard care which discusses these trends in more detail. However, it is worth noting that 11% of cases of substandard care were due to the woman's own refusal to accept medical advice or treatment based, in many cases, on her personal or religious beliefs. Four women refused blood transfusion and we are grateful to Professor James Drife who has written guidelines for the management of such cases which are annexed to Chapter 3.

In addition we would like to acknowledge the assistance of Dr Sheila Willatts, who, apart from undertaking a very detailed assessment of the anaesthetic causes or contributory factors of death, has also written a further additional section, Chapter 17, on intensive care. Forty per cent of women who died from *Direct* or *Indirect* causes in this triennium required admission to intensive care units and the need for multidisciplinary working and the early involvement of anaesthetists or specialists in other appropriate disciplines when clinical problems are first identified, is highlighted.

When considering the specific causes of *Direct* deaths it is extremely encouraging to report an approximately 50% fall in the number of deaths resulting from ectopic pregnancy and sepsis, a 30% fall in the number of deaths from hypertensive disorders of pregnany and a 25% fall in deaths from antepartum or postpartum haemorrhage. If deaths from women who refused blood transfusion were excluded from the latter cause of death then the decline in the rate would have been even greater.

It is disappointing to report that deaths from thrombosis and thromboembolism, the largest cause of death, have remained obstinately static and that there has been a small rise in the number of deaths following legal abortion. Deaths directly due to anaesthesia also rose from four in the last Report to eight in this. These figures show there can be no complacency in the management of pregnant women. Particularly in relation to anaesthesia, pregnant women may pose specific problems and consultant cover should be immediately available at all times.

Chapter 2 discusses deaths from hypertensive disorders of pregnancy. Although there has been a fall in the number of such deaths, 80% were associated with some degree of substandard care. These deaths occurred before the results of the trials on magnesium sulphate, and although its use is now more commonplace, the recommendations in this Report are that it's wide spread introduction, itself not without risks, will require careful consideration and the development of appropriate guidelines and training. It is helpful that the Scientific Committee of the Royal College of Obstetricians and Gynaecologists (RCOG) are to look at this issue, and their guidance will be given in the next edition of this Report.

The welcome decline in deaths from antepartum and postpartum haemorrhage (Chapter 3) has already been mentioned. However in 33% of cases there was some element of substandard clinical care and in 27% of cases it was due to the actions of the woman herself. Attention is again drawn to the guidelines for the treatment of massive haemorrhage which were contained in the last two Reports and the chapter contains a new annexe, referred to earlier, relating to the management of women who refuse blood transfusion.

Deaths from thrombosis and thromboembolism are discussed in Chapter 4. Some deaths occurred without warning in patients with no risk factors and would have been difficult to prevent. However, other women reported symptoms of breathlessness or chest pain, treated as respiratory infections, one or two days before the embolism occurred. Seventy six per cent of the postpartum deaths occurred in women who had been delivered by Caesarean section and this Report therefore contains the recommendations of the RCOG working party on prophylaxis against thromboembolism in Caesarean section. We can only await the publications of later Reports to see if such measures help to reduce the incidence of deaths from thromboembolism following such deliveries which, to date, have shown no sign of declining.

Chapter 5 deals with amniotic fluid embolism. In this Report the diagnostic criteria have been relaxed to include two deaths in which the assessors conclude that the clinical features were consistent with the diagnosis but the characteristic findings were not present at autopsy. It is considered that including cases where the diagnosis was not histologically confirmed may give a more complete picture of the incidence of this condition.

Early pregnancy deaths are discussed in Chapter 6, which shows that, despite the fall in deaths from ectopic pregnancy, most of these deaths followed misdiagnosis, particularly by deputising doctors and locums tenens. The Chapter contains an extract from the guidelines produced by the RCOG on ultrasound in Early Pregnancy. The small increase in deaths following legal terminations is worrying and will need careful watching in future Reports.

Despite the reduction in the number of deaths from sepsis detailed in Chapter 7, the importance of antibiotic cover for Caesarean section is stressed. Although there were only four deaths from genital tract trauma counted in Chapter 8, there was evidence of inappropriate deputising.

There was a rise in the number of anaesthetic deaths, which are described in detail in Chapter 9. All but one of these was associated with substandard care. In most cases there was a lack of consultant involvement. The recent National Confidential Enquiry into Perioperative Deaths drew attention to the need for greater co-operation between specialities, a recommendation that is equally applicable here.

Two deaths were associated with the use of ritodrine. Complications associated with ritodrine prompted the RCOG to produce guidelines for its' use in delaying the onset of early labour, which are reproduced in Chapter 10. This is a good example of how this Enquiry can prompt the production of appropriate guidelines by the early identification of clinical problems and trends.

A welcome 50% fall in deaths following elective Caesarean sections is reported in Chapter 13, but there was a slight increase in deaths following unplanned emergency Caesarean sections. There were fewer perimortem Caesarean sections, with improved fetal outcome. Overall substandard care related to the operative procedures in 36% of cases.

A new section on deaths from post natal depression and substance abuse, written by Dr Gwyneth Lewis, is annexed to Chapter 15. These are important causes of maternal mortality and will be assessed in more detail and considered further in later Reports.

The standard of maternal autopsies was again poor, as discussed in Chapter 16. We support the recommendations that autopsies should be performed in accordance with the guidelines for maternal autopsy produced by the Royal College of Pathologists, and that, wherever possible, such autopsies should be undertaken by pathologists with a special interest in the area.

Detailed recommendations are contained in Chapter 19, many of which have been mentioned here. We are please to announce that a new UK report form (UK MDR1) was introduced in 1995 but remain concerned about the length of time it takes for maternal deaths to be notified and assessed. The four Health Departments will be issuing guidelines in the near future on how more accurate and timely reporting may be achieved.

This Report could not have been written without considerable assistance from the authors, listed on the front page of the Report, and the members of the Editorial Board, whose names are also given at the beginning. We therefore gratefully acknowledge the time and effort each has given, in their spare time, to it's production. The Editorial board was chaired by Dr Eileen Rubery, Head of the Department of Health's Health Promotion (Medical) Division and latterly by Dr Peter Bourdillion, Head of the Specialist Clinical Services Division of the NHS Executive Health Care Directorate. Dr Dawn Milner acted as medical secretary until April 1995 when the responsibility moved to the NHS Executive and she was succeeded by Dr Gwyneth Lewis.

In particular our thanks go to Professor Bryan Hibbard, retiring as Chairman of the Clinical subgroup, who has not only ably steered the group for the last two triennia, but who has also devoted much time and effort to the successful production of this and the previous Report. He will be succeeded by Professor James Drife who has acted as a Central Assessor for the last six years. We also express our grateful thanks to Professor John Tighe, the Central Pathology Assessor for England, who returned from a well earned retirement late last year to help assess the pathology in each case as well as writing Chapter 16. In addition we are grateful for the invaluable help received from Dr Michael de Swiet who has joined the board as the medical assessor.

Thanks are also due to the Regional and Central Assessors in obstetrics, anaesthetics, pathology and midwifery for all four countries, whose names are listed at the back of this Report. They have worked hard to produce well documented and accurately assessed case reports, as well as offering invaluable contributions to the draft chapters and recommendations of this Report. This is the first Report where case reports, particularly those relating to *Indirect* deaths, have benefited from assessment by a physician with a special interest in medical conditions that may be affected by pregnancy. Finally, given the greater emphasis on team working and following the implementation of Changing Childbirth, we are pleased that for the next Report we will have the benefit of Regional and Central assessors in midwifery.

We are also grateful to all those who contributed to the individual case reports in England, Wales, Scotland and Northern Ireland, which make this Report such a valuable example of professional self-audit. These include obstetricians, midwives, anaesthetists, pathologists, directors of public health or their equivalents, general practitioners, and also coroners and procurators fiscal who made their reports available to the Enquiry.

CMO England   **Sir Kenneth Calman**
CMO Scotland   **Robert Kendall**
CMO Wales   **Deirdre Hine**
CMO Northern Ireland **Henrietta Campbell**

AIMS, OBJECTIVES AND METHOD OF ENQUIRY

The aims and objectives of the Confidential Enquiries into Maternal Deaths

These are:-

- to assess the main causes of, and trends in maternal deaths; to identify any avoidable or substandard factors; to promulgate these findings to all relevant health care professionals,

- to aim to reduce maternal mortality and morbidity rates still further as well as the proportion of cases due to substandard care,

- to make recommendations concerning the improvement of clinical care and service provision, including local audit, to purchasers of obstetric services and professionals involved in caring for pregnant women,

- to suggest directions for future areas for research and audit at a local and national level, and

-to produce a triennial Report for the four Chief Medical Officers of the United Kingdom.

Method of the Enquiry 1991-1993

Historical background

This is the third Report to cover the whole of the United Kingdom, replacing the three separate reports for England and Wales, Scotland and Northern Ireland. The England and Wales reports were published at three-yearly intervals from 1952 - 1984. The reports for Scotland were published at different intervals from 1965 - 1985, the last covering both maternal and perinatal deaths. Northern Ireland reports were started in 1956 and were published four-yearly until 1967; because of the small number of maternal deaths the next report covered ten years from 1968 - 1977, and the last report covered the seven year period 1978 - 1984. The relatively small number of deaths in Scotland and Northern Ireland led to the decision of the four Chief Medical Officers to change to a combined UK Report after 1984. This decision also ensured maintenance of confidentiality. Separate figures for England and Wales, previously included to facilitate comparison with earlier Reports, will, for the most part, no longer be given.

England and Wales

The responsibility for initiating an enquiry into a maternal death rests with the Director of Public Health (DPH) in England, or in Wales with the Director of Public Health Medicine/Chief Administrative Medical Officer (CAMO) of the District in which the woman was usually resident. An enquiry form (MCW97)* is sent to general practitioners, midwives, health visitors, consultant obstetricians and any other relevant staff who had been concerned with the care of the woman.

When all available information about the death has been collected the DPH forwards the form to the appropriate Regional obstetric assessor in England, or the DPHM/CAMO to the Welsh obstetric assessor. The relevant anaesthetic assessors review all cases where there had been involvement of an anaesthetist, and midwifery assessors where the involvement of a midwife may have affected the outcome. In addition every possible attempt is made to obtain full details of any autopsy or pathological investigations which are then reviewed by the appropriate pathology assessors. The assessors add their comments and opinions regarding the cause or causes of death.

Statistical data is supplied by the Office of Population Censuses and Surveys (OPCS).

The MCW97 form is then sent to the Medical co-ordinators, acting on behalf of the Chief Medical Officers of the Department of Health or for Wales, as appropriate. The central assessors in obstetrics and gynaecology, anaesthetics, pathology and general medicine or midwifery as required who then review all available recorded facts about each case and assess the many factors that may have led to death.

Scotland

In Scotland, the system of enquiry is broadly similar except that a single panel of assessors considers all cases. Each obstetric assessor is responsible for a geographical area which includes more than one Health Board. Two anaesthetic assessors cover one half of the country each and all cases are seen by a single pathology assessor. The allocation of cases to diagnostic category is undertaken by the full panel of assessors each year.

On receipt in the Scottish Office Department of Health (SODH) of a certificate of maternal death from the General Registrar's Office (Scotland) an enquiry form (MD1)* is sent to the Chief Administrative Medical Officer (CAMO) of the Health Board of residence of the woman concerned. As in England and Wales, the CAMO takes responsibility for organising completion of the MD1 form by all professional staff involved in caring for the

---

*By the time of publication of this Report these forms will have been replaced by the new United Kingdom form MDR(UK)1, which has been amended in the light of experience to more accurately reflect the concerns of the assessors in light of changing clinical practice.

woman. When this is achieved he passes the form to the appropriate obstetric assessor who determines whether further data are required before the case is submitted for discussion and classification to the full panel of assessors. In cases where an anaesthetic had been given or an autopsy or pathological investigation undertaken he passes the form to the appropriate assessors for their further comments. The form is then returned to the Medical Co-ordinator at SODH, who retains it from that time until it has been fully considered, classified and used for preparation of the Report. As for the other countries at all times each form is held under conditions of strict confidentiality and is anonymised before being provided to assessors compiling the Report.

Additional information is obtained from statistics collected and analysed by the Information and Statistics Division of the Scottish Health Service Common Services Agency. This is available from routine hospital discharge data collected by general and maternity hospitals. The coverage by Form SMR2, the maternal discharge summary, is now almost universal at 98% of registered births. General practitioners and hospital and community medical and midwifery staff assist in ensuring that deaths occurring at home are included in the Enquiry.

Northern Ireland

Maternal deaths are reported to the Director of Public Health (DPH) of the appropriate Health and Social Services Board, who initiates completion of the maternal death form (MCW2 Rev.2, 1981)[*] by those involved in the care of the patient. On completion forms are sent to the Department of Health and Social Services. As in Scotland one panel of assessors deals with all cases. The assessors are asked to consider the report, to give their views on classification and indicate whether avoidable factors were present.

Central Assessment

The assessors review each case thoroughly, taking into account the case history, the results of pathological investigations and findings at autopsy before allotting the case to be counted in a specific Chapter in the Report. Their assessment occasionally varies with the underlying cause of death as given on the death certificate and classified by the Registrars General using the International Classification of Diseases, Injuries and Causes of Death - ninth revision (ICD9). This is because, although the death may have been coded for multiple organ failure as the terminal event, it could have been precipitated by an obstetric cause such as septicaemia from an infected Caesarean section. Although maternal deaths reported to this Enquiry are only assigned and counted in one chapter, they may also be referred to in other chapters; thus a death assigned to hypertensive disorder of pregnancy, in which haemorrhage and anaesthesia also played a part, may be discussed in all three chapters.

Editorial Board

The Editorial Board consists of a clinical subgroup, a statistical subgroup and Departmental representatives of the four countries. The Board is chaired by the head of the Specialist Clinical Services Division in the Health Care Directorate of the NHS Executive, and the clinical subgroup is chaired by a central assessor. The clinical subgroup is responsible for the final classification of the cause of death and evidence of substandard care. Chapters are drafted by members of the Editorial Board. Strict confidentiality is observed at all stages of the Enquiry, and identifying features are erased from all forms. After preparation of the Report, and before publication, all the maternal death report forms and related documents are destroyed.

GLOSSARY OF ABBREVIATIONS

AFE	-	Amniotic Fluid Embolism
APH	-	Antepartum Haemorrhage
ARDS	-	Acute Respiratory Distress Syndrome
ARM	-	Artificial Rupture of Membranes
BEST	-	British Eclampsia Survey Team
BP	-	Blood Pressure
CS	-	Caesarean Section
CEMD	-	Confidential Enquiries into Maternal Deaths
CTG	-	Cardiotocograph
CT (CAT)	-	Computerised Axial Tomography
CVP	-	Central Venous Pressure
D&C	-	Dilatation and Curettage
DGH	-	District General Hospital
DIC	-	Disseminated Intravascular Coagulation
DVT	-	Deep Vein Thrombosis
ECG	-	Electrocardiogram
FH	-	Fetal Heart
GP	-	General Practitioner
Hb	-	Haemoglobin Concentration
HDU	-	High Dependency Unit
HELLP	-	Haemolysis, Elevated Liver Enzymes and Low Platelets
ICD	-	International Classification of Diseases
ICU	-	Intensive Care Unit
IUCD	-	Intrauterine Contraceptive Device
IUD	-	Intrauterine Death
IVF	-	In Vitro Fertilisation
MCW 97	-	Maternal Death Report Form for England and Wales (until October 1995)
MDR UK(1)	-	Maternal Death Report Form for the United Kingdom (from October 1995)
OPCS	-	Office of Population Censuses and Surveys
PG	-	Prostaglandin
PPH	-	Postpartum Haemorrhage
RHA	-	Regional Health Authority
SB	-	Stillbirth
SHO	-	Senior House Officer
SR	-	Senior Registrar
UK	-	United Kingdom of Great Britain and Northern Ireland
WBC	-	White Blood Count

DEFINITIONS OF MATERNAL MORTALITY AND SUMMARY OF DEATHS SUBJECT TO ENQUIRY

Definitions of maternal mortality

There is an international agreement to subdivide causes of maternal deaths into *Direct*, *Indirect* and *Fortuitous*, but only *Direct* and *Indirect* deaths are counted for statistical purposes. The precise definitions for these are given in Table 1.

Table 1

Definitions of maternal deaths	
Maternal deaths[*]	Deaths of women while pregnant or within 42 days of termination of pregnancy, from any cause related to or aggravated by the pregnancy or its management, but not from accidental or incidental causes.
Direct[*]	Deaths resulting from obstetric complications of the pregnant state (pregnancy, labour and puerperium), from interventions, omissions, incorrect treatment, or from a chain of events resulting from any of the above.
Indirect[*]	Deaths resulting from previous existing disease, or disease that developed during pregnancy and which was not due to direct obstetric causes, but which was aggravated by the physiologic effects of pregnancy.
Late[**]	Deaths occurring between 42 days and one year after abortion, miscarriage or delivery that are due to *Direct* or *Indirect* maternal causes.
Fortuitous[*]	Deaths from unrelated causes which happen to occur in pregnancy or the puerperium.

[*] - ICD(9) definition
[**] - ICD(10) definition

Late deaths

The International Classification of Diseases, Injuries and Causes of Death - ninth revision (ICD9) defined a maternal death as "the death of a woman while pregnant or within 42 days of termination of pregnancy, from any cause related to or aggravated by the pregnancy or its management, but not from accidental or incidental causes". However, as shown in Table 1, the latest revision of the ICD codes (ICD10) recognises that some women die as a consequence of *Direct* or *Indirect* obstetric causes after this period and defines *Late* maternal deaths as "those deaths occurring between 42 days and one year after abortion, miscarriage or delivery that are due to *Direct* or *Indirect* maternal causes". For the last triennium *Late* deaths occurring up to 6 months after delivery or abortion were included where possible and for this triennium *Late* deaths occurring up to 1 year after delivery or abortion have been included. These *Late* deaths are considered separately in Chapter 15.

Maternal deaths known to the Enquiry 1991-93

A more comprehensive summary including demographic details can be found in Chapter 1.

In 1991-93, 323 deaths were known to the Enquiry, but despite repeated requests, either no forms or only sketchy details were available in three cases. This compares with 14 outstanding cases in the previous triennium. Of the 320 fully assessed deaths there were 228 *Direct* or *Indirect* deaths, 46 were classified as *Fortuitous* and 46 as *Late*. In this triennium the total number of *Direct* and *Indirect* maternal deaths reported to the Enquiry is slightly lower than the 242 reported in the previous triennium. The number of deaths by the Chapter to which they have been allocated is shown in Table 2.

Table 2.

Maternal deaths counted in the Chapters which relate to main cause of death[*] United Kingdom; 1991-93			
Chapter	**Direct**	**Indirect**	**Fortuitous**
2 Hypertensive disorders of pregnancy	20	-	-
3 Haemorrhage	15	-	-
4 Thrombosis and thromboembolism	35		-
5 Amniotic fluid embolism	10	-	-
6 Early pregnancy deaths**	18	-	-
7 Genital tract sepsis	9	-	-
8 Genital tract trauma	4	-	-
9 Anaesthesia	8	-	-
10 Other *Direct* deaths	9	-	-
11 Cardiac disease	-	37	-
12 Other *Indirect* deaths	-	63	-
Totals	**128**	**100**	
14 *Fortuitous* deaths	-	-	46
15 *Late* deaths (total 46)***	10	23	13

* - in accordance with the ICD(9) definition, see definitions Table 1.

** - Early deaths in this Chapter include those up to 20 weeks gestation, some are counted elsewhere where the main cause of death was ascribed to another Chapter.

*** - *Late* deaths which are classified as *Direct* or *Indirect* according to ICD(9) are not counted for statistical purposes.

A full discussion of trends in maternal mortality rates by those reported to the Registrars General and this Enquiry, together with a comparison of the two can be found in Chapter 1.

Substandard Care

The term substandard care has been used in this Report to take into account not only failure in clinical care, but also some of the underlying factors which may have produced a low standard of care for the patient. This includes situations produced by the action of the woman herself, or her relatives, which may be outside the control of the clinicians. It also takes into account shortage of resources for staffing facilities; and administrative failure in the maternity services and the back-up facilities such as high dependency, intensive care, other anaesthetic services and radiology and pathology. "Substandard" in the context of the Report means that the care that the patient received, or the care that was made available to her, fell below the standard which the authors considered should have been offered to her in this triennium. Chapter 18 discusses these points in more detail.

In this triennium substandard care occurred in 93 (40.1%) deaths, with deficiencies in hospital care in 31.1%, of general practitioner care in 7.0% and of the patient in 11%. Substandard care was most common in deaths due to hypertensive disorders (80%) and haemorrhage (73%). There were eight deaths directly attributable to anaesthesia, seven of which were associated with substandard anaesthetic care.

CHAPTER 1

Trends in reproductive epidemiology and maternal mortality

Introduction

The purpose of this chapter is :-

- to provide an overview of trends in reproductive epidemiology, which help place in context the maternal mortality statistics which follow,

- to review trends in maternal mortality as derived from the Registrars' General official statistics and other official sources,

- to summarise the maternal deaths known to the Enquiry, and

- to identify the main causes of maternal mortality.

Overall trends in reproductive epidemiology

Birth rates and general fertility trends

Birth rates and fertility trends are important in the context of this Enquiry as changes in patterns of childbearing may affect the number of maternal deaths. Since the England and Wales Enquiry started in 1952, joined by Scotland and Northern Ireland in 1985, more than 34 million births have been registered in the United Kingdom. The total number of births and the fertility rate for each triennium since 1973-75 are given in Table 1.1 and Figure 1.1 shows the general fertility rate (births per 1,000 women aged 15-44) over the period 1952-93.

As can be seen in Figure 1.1, fertility increased from 1952 until it peaked in 1964 at 94 births per 1,000 women. This was followed by a steady decrease in the general fertility rate until 1977 when it reached a minimum of 59 births per 1,000 women. The rate then fluctuated, but between 1982 and 1990 there was a small but sustained increase, reaching 64 per 1,000 in 1990. There has been a slight decrease in the three years covered by this Report.

The small fluctuations in fertility rates since 1977 conceal wider medical and social changes affecting reproductive epidemiology. Reduced perinatal and infant mortality means that more children are surviving into childhood. There has also been an increasing proportion of births outside marriage, almost entirely due to an increase in births registered by both parents, which is generally taken to imply that these children are born to parents in a stable relationship. Also women on average are older at childbirth, in part due to older ages at marriage.

Table 1.1

Total number of births (live and still) and fertility rate; United Kingdom 1973-93		
Triennium	**Total births(in thousands)**	**Fertility rate per 1000 women aged 15-44**
1973-75	2,239.2	68.8
1976-78	2,038.3	60.9
1979-81	2,235.4	64.2
1982-84	2,183.2	60.7
1985-87	2,293.7	61.9
1988-90	2,374.8	62.5
1991-93	2,346.8	63.4

Source: England and Wales - Birth statistics series
       Scotland - Registrar General's Annual Report series
       Northern Ireland - Registrar General's Annual Report series

Figure 1.1

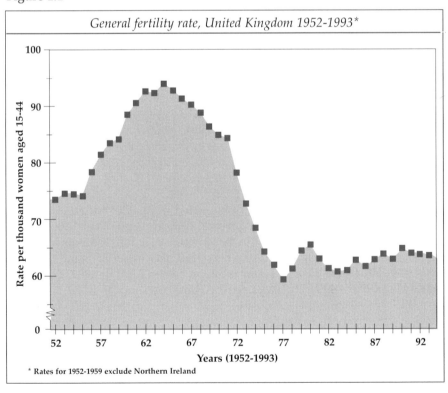

General fertility rate, United Kingdom 1952-1993*

* Rates for 1952-1959 exclude Northern Ireland

Fertility rates in the four countries follow the same pattern but those for Northern Ireland always remain higher than for the other countries. In Northern Ireland the proportion of births occurring outside marriage is lower than in the other countries and it also has the highest mean age at childbirth. This is due at least in part to women having, on average, more children. In 1993 34 per cent of births within marriage in Northern Ireland were the woman's third or higher order birth, compared with 24 per cent of births in England and Wales.

Trends in legal abortion

Since the introduction of legal abortion in 1968, following the Abortion Act 1967 in England, Wales and Scotland, and the end of 1993, over 3.4 million legal terminations of pregnancy have been carried out on residents of Great Britain. The Abortion Act 1967 does not apply to Northern Ireland where only a small number of legal terminations are performed each year on medical grounds under the case law which applied in England and Wales before the Abortion Act 1967. However, some women having legal terminations in Great Britain, of which there were 5204 in 1991-93, gave a usual address in Northern Ireland.

Table 1.2 shows both the number of legal abortions in Great Britain and the rate per 1,000 women aged 15-44 for each of the most recent three triennia. Figure 1.2 shows the legal abortion rate for each individual year over the period 1970 to 1993. From 1983 to 1990 there was a continuing upward trend in this rate, followed by a fall in 1991 and a return to the previous level in 1992 and 1993.

Table 1.2

Legal abortions in Great Britain to women resident in United Kingdom; 1985-93		
Triennia	**Number of abortions**	**Rate per 1000 women aged 15-44**
1985-87	475,330	13.2
1988-90	545,618	15.0
1991-93	520,451	14.5

Source: England and Wales - Abortion Statistics series
        Scotland - Information & Statistics Division

Following the introduction of legal abortion the number of maternal deaths consequent on illegal abortions fell sharply. In 1970-72 (the first full triennium during which legal abortion was available) there were 37 reported deaths from illegal abortion, falling to one in 1979-81, and none have been reported since, including this triennium.

In this Report the deaths of five women following legal abortion were investigated.

Figure 1.2

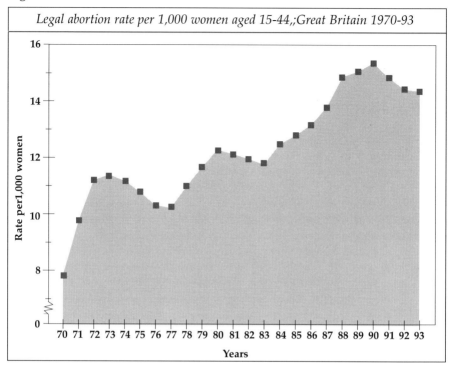

Legal abortion rate per 1,000 women aged 15-44,;Great Britain 1970-93

Maternities and estimated pregnancies

Maternities

Maternities are the number of pregnancies that result in a live birth at any gestation or a stillbirth occurring at 28 weeks completed gestation prior to 1st October 1992 and 24 weeks or later thereafter and are required to be registered by law. However, it is impossible to know the exact number of pregnancies which occurred during this, or any preceding, triennium since not all pregnancies result in a registrable live or still birth. Because of the unreliability of this data, due to the lack of appropriate denominators, most of the succeeding discussions, and maternal mortality rates, will be related to the number of maternities (mothers delivered of live or stillborn infants) rather than to the total number of pregnancies.

Estimated pregnancies

The combination of the number of maternities, together with legal terminations, hospital admissions for spontaneous abortions (at less than 24 weeks gestation) and ectopic pregnancies, with an adjustment to allow for the period of gestation and maternal ages at conception, provide an estimate of the number of pregnancies as shown in Table 1.3. However, the resulting total would still clearly be an underestimate of the actual number of pregnancies since these figures do not include other pregnancies which miscarry early, those where the woman is not admitted to hospital, or indeed those where the woman herself may not even know she is pregnant. Data in previous Reports was given for England and Wales only, and those for 1988-90 are included for comparison. Data for previous triennia were established using a different methodology and, because they are not directly comparable, are not included in this report.

Table 1.3

Estimated number of pregnancies (in thousands); United Kingdom 1991-93.				
Maternities	Legal abortions	Spontaneous abortions	Ectopic pregnancies	Total estimated pregnancies
2315.2	525.7	266.4*	30.2	3137.4

*ICD (9th revision) 634-638
Scottish data for 1993 is provisional

Source: Birth statistics Series FM1
Abortion statistics Series AB
Dept of Health: Hospital Episodes Statistics
Welsh Office: Hospital Activity Analysis
Scottish Morbidity Records (SMR) 1
Inpatients and Daycases Acute
Scottish Morbidity Records (SMR) 2
Inaptients and Daycase Maternity
DHSS Northern Ireland

Using these sources of data, OPCS estimated that 72 per cent of pregnancies in England and Wales between 1991 and 1993 led to a maternity resulting in one or more registrable live or still births. A further 18 per cent of pregnancies were legally terminated under the 1967 Abortion Act. The remaining 10 per cent of known pregnancies were admitted to hospital following a spontaneous abortion or an ectopic pregnancy. Spontaneous abortions which resulted in a day stay or were not admitted to hospital are not included in these data.

Maternities by age and parity

The pattern of fertility in terms of maternal age and age at first birth has changed over recent years. On the other hand figures for parity remain constant. These changes can make an important contribution to maternal mortality because the risk becomes higher with increasing age and parity.

Between 1991 and 1993 fertility rates increased considerably among women in their thirties and forties. In contrast, rates fell among women in their twenties. However, the late twenties remain the peak child bearing years with fertility rates substantially above those for all other age groups.

As a result of a special exercise undertaken in England and Wales, shown in Table 1.4, it is possible to estimate separately, by using the survey data, the changes in the age and parity distribution of live births in England and Wales for each triennium between 1985-87 and 1991-93. More women are delaying childbearing: in 1985-87, 53 per cent of women having their first child were aged under 25 whereas by 1991-93 only 44 per cent were aged under 25. Similar data are not routinely available for Scotland and Northern Ireland.

Table 1.4

Percentage distribution of all live births by parity, age and age at first birth 1985-93; England and Wales only		
1985-87	**1988-90**	**1991-93**

Parity	1985-87	1988-90	1991-93
0	41	41	41
1	34	34	34
2	16	16	17
3	6	6	6
4 and over	3	3	3
Total	**100**	**100**	**100**
Age (years)			
Under 20	9	8	7
20-24	29	27	24
25-29	35	35	35
30-34	20	21	24
35-39	7	7	8
40 and over	1	1	2
Total	**100**	**100**	**100**
Age (years) at first birth			
Under 20	17	16	15
20-24	36	33	29
25-29	32	33	34
30-34	12	14	17
35 and over	3	4	5
Total	**100**	**100**	**100**

Source: Unpublished OPCS fertility tables

Note - Figures may not exactly total 100 due to rounding

Note - Exact parity figures are only available for births inside marriage.

The data in this table are based on estimates of "true" parity order estimated by using information from the General Household Survey

Maternities by marital status

One of the most striking trends in recent years has been the dramatic increase in both the number and proportion of all births occurring outside marriage, which had risen to 32 per cent of births in the United Kingdom by 1993. Nevertheless, this increase has been concentrated in births outside marriage registered by both parents, usually giving the same address. During the period 1980 to 1993 the proportion of all births which occurred outside marriage and were registered by the mother alone remained at 6-8 per cent. The proportion of births outside marriage in England, Wales and Scotland were very similar (32 per cent, 35 per cent and 31 per cent respectively). However, the proportion of births outside marriage in Northern Ireland (22 per cent), was less than in Great Britain, although the rate of increase over the previous decade was similar, as shown in Figure 1.3.

Figure 1.3

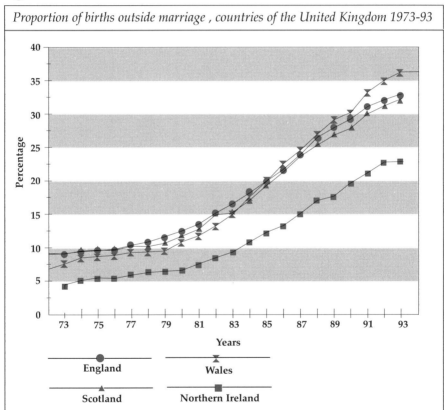

Proportion of births outside marriage , countries of the United Kingdom 1973-93

Maternities by ethnic origin

It has not been possible to present statistics by ethnic origin for this Report as it has not been collected consistently and reliable denominators were not available. Ethnic origin data were collected for the first time in the 1991 Census and from 1994 ethnic origin will be collected on the Enquiry notification forms.

Overall trends in maternal mortality

There are a number of statistical definitions and denominators that can be used to enable comparison of data collected through the Enquiry with data collected by the Registrars General, as shown in Table 1.5. They also enable comparison of trends in maternal mortality over time.

Table 1.5

Maternal mortality definitions used in this Report	
Definition	**Reason for use**
Deaths from obstetric causes per million women aged 15-44	This enables comparison with the other causes of death in this age group
Deaths from obstetric causes per 100,000 maternities*	Maternities are the number of mothers delivered of registrable live births at any gestation or stillbirths of 28 weeks gestation or later prior to 1st October 1992 and 24 weeks or later thereafter, ie these are the majority of women at risk of death from obstetric causes
Deaths from obstetric causes per 100,000 estimated pregnancies	Because the data for spontaneous abortions and ectopic pregnancies are unreliable this denominator is only used when calculating rates of death in early pregnancy

* - Prior to the 1988-90 Report the denominator used was deaths from obstetric causes per 100,000 live and stillbirths.

Deaths from obstetric causes per million women aged 15-44

Maternal mortality data are usually presented in one of two ways. The first expresses maternal deaths per million women aged 15-44. This denominator assumes that all women of childbearing age are at risk of becoming pregnant. However, it has the advantage of enabling comparison with other causes of women's deaths. Maternal mortality rates calculated in this way as shown in Table 1.6 have fallen faster than the death rates from all causes for women in the same age group. Between 1973-75 and 1991-93 the UK mortality rate for women aged 15-44 fell by 25 per cent from 808 deaths per million women to 606, whereas over the same period the maternal mortality rate fell from 9.0 to 3.8 per million females aged between 15-44, a reduction of 58 per cent. In 1991-93 maternal deaths comprised 0.6 per cent of all deaths of women in this age group, compared with 1.1 per cent in 1973-75.

Table 1.6

Mortality rates per million females aged 15-44 years: All causes and maternal deaths; United Kingdom 1973-1993			
Triennia	**All causes**	**Maternal deaths**	**% deaths in age group due to maternal causes**
1973-75	807.9	9.0	1.1
1976-78	763.2	7.5	1.0
1979-81	697.2	6.6	1.0
1982-84	641.7	4.7	0.7
1985-87	622.5	4.2	0.7
1988-90	625.9	4.1	0.7
1991-93	605.6	3.8	0.6

ICD 8th revision: 1970-77, ICD 630-678

ICD 9th revision: 1978-90, ICD 630-676

Source: 1973 The Registrar General's Statistical Review of England and Wales, part 1

      1974-93 Mortality Statistics, cause. Series DH2 Table 2

      1973-93 The Registrar General's Annual Report, Scotland

      1973-93 The Registrar General's Annual Report, Northern Ireland.

Deaths from obstetric causes per 100,000 maternities

The second method of calculating maternal mortality rates is based on the premise that only pregnant women are at risk of contributing to the maternal mortality statistics. The true denominator should be the number of women who had been pregnant during the period of the Enquiry. This would include pregnancies resulting in ectopic pregnancy, spontaneous and legal terminations, stillbirths and live births. As discussed earlier, since the data for some of these outcomes are unavailable or unreliable, the denominator which will be mainly used in this Report will be the number of maternities, the rate being estimated either per million or 100,000. This was first used in the last Report.

The number of maternities is used rather than the total number of births since the latter statistic is slightly inflated by multiple births. Although multiple births form only a small proportion of all maternities, their number has risen steadily over the past ten years from 7,300 maternities in 1983 to over 9,600 in 1993. Part of this increase is due to an increased number of maternities, but the use of ovulation induction drugs and assisted conception techniques is also likely to have played a part. While twin births are quite common, at about one per cent of all deliveries, the higher order births are much less so. Data from the Human Fertilisation Embryology Authority show that in 1992 there were 1430, children born from a multiple birth as a result of in vitro fertilisation (IVF).

Table 1.7 presents maternal mortality and maternity statistics in the United Kingdom for 1985 based on those deaths known to the Registrars General. The maternal mortality rate based on statistics from the Registrars General fell by 22 per cent over the period, from 7.7 per 100,000 in 1985-87 to 6.0 per 100,000 for this triennium. Figure 1.4 shows the maternal mortality rate for each year between 1952 and 1993, also based on statistics from the Registrars General. Data for 1952-72 relate to England and Wales to place in context more recent UK data.

Table 1.7

Maternal mortality rates and maternities as reported to the Registrars General; United Kingdom 1985-93			
	1985-87	**1988-90**	**1991-93**
Maternities	2,268,766	2,360,309	2,315,204
Maternal deaths known to Registrars General	174	171	140
Rate per 100,000 maternities	7.7	7.2	6.0

Source: England and Wales - Mortality Statistics Cause Series DH2
Birth Statistics Series FM1
Scotland - Registrar General Annual Report 1985-93
Northern Ireland - Registrar General Annual Report 1985-93

Figure 1.4

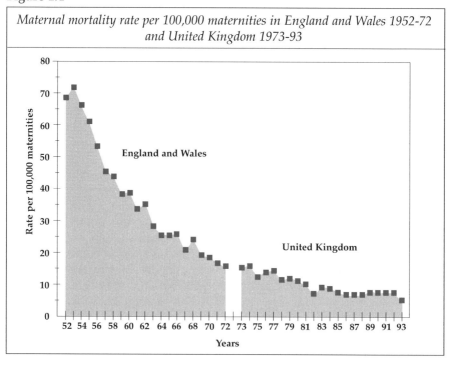

Maternal mortality rate per 100,000 maternities in England and Wales 1952-72 and United Kingdom 1973-93

Maternal deaths known to the Enquiry

In 1991-93 323 deaths were known to the Enquiry, but unfortunately, despite repeated requests, either no forms or only sketchy details were available in three cases. Preliminary details of cases and the Chapters to which they have be allocated were shown in the Summary preceding this Chapter.

Table 1.8

Maternal mortality rates and maternities as reported to the Registrars General* and the Enquiries; United Kingdom 1985-93		1985-87	1988-90	1991-93
Maternities		2,268,766	2,360,309	2,315,204
Maternities known to Registrars General	Number	174	171	140
	Rate per 100,000 maternities	7.7	7.2	6.0
Maternal deaths known to the Enquiry (*Direct* and *Indirect*)	Number	223	238	228
	Rate per 100,000 maternities	9.8	10.1	9.8
***Direct* deaths known to the Enquiry**	Number	137	145	128
	Rate	6.0	6.1	5.5
***Indirect* deaths known to the Enquiry**	Number	86	93	100
	Rate	3.8	3.9	4.3

* - ICD 9th Revision: 630-676

Source: England and Wales Scotland - Registrar General Annual Report 1985-93
　　　Northern Ireland - Registrar General Annual Report 1985-93
　　　Mortality Statistics Cause Series DH2
　　　Birth Statistics Series FM1

Comparison of maternal deaths known to the Enquiry with the Registrars General statistics

It is important to note that, as with preceding Reports, the number of deaths known to the Enquiries exceed those reported in the Registrars' General official statistics. There are a number of reasons for this. The Registrars' General maternal deaths refer to deaths counted from death certificates where the underlying cause of death was "considered to be a complication of pregnancy, childbirth and the puerperium" (ICD9 Chapter XI 630-676). These conditions may have been recorded on death certificates, but the coding rules led to other conditions on the certificate being given precedence when deriving the underlying cause of death.

A number of changes have been made to the cause of death coding rules to bring England and Wales more in line with international practice. In 1993 an automated cause coding system was introduced. One result was a fall in the number of cases where maternal conditions were selected as the underlying cause of death. In the future, however, it will be possible to identify deaths where a maternal condition is mentioned anywhere on the death certificate as all conditions given are now being coded. Also in earlier years, when the information provided by certifiers was unclear or was not final OPCS sent letters to the certifiers asking for further information to help assign an underlying cause of death. This procedure was not used in 1993 as OPCS was unable to deal with these cases in a timely way.

Another reason for the difference in numbers is that the woman may have been transferred to a non obstetric specialist unit when the life-threatening condition arose and may have stayed there for some time. Hence, the death may not have been certified by an obstetrician and the original obstetric event not mentioned. To help identify maternal deaths the International Conference on the International Classification of Diseases (10th Revision) suggested that the pregnancy status of women should be collected at death registration. This currently happens in Scotland and Northern Ireland. A similar question is currently under trial in England and Wales.

Table 1.8 shows that there were 140 maternal deaths in 1991-93 recorded from official sources, 88 fewer than the 228 *Direct* and *Indirect* cases - identified through the Confidential Enquiry. In addition the maternal deaths known to the Registrars General may include *Late* deaths. It is not possible to identify from the death certificate when the delivery or termination occurred.

Category of Maternal Death

Table 1.9 shows that of the 274 maternal deaths (excluding 46 Late deaths) investigated by the Enquiry in 1991-93, 128 (47%) were classified as *Direct*, 100 (36 %) as *Indirect*, and 46 (17 %) as *Fortuitous*. Data given in the previous Report (52 % *Direct*, 34 % *Indirect* and 14% *Fortuitous*) showed proportionately more *Direct* deaths.

Table 1.9

	Direct	Indirect	Fortuitous	Total
Outcome of pregnancy for maternal deaths known to the Enquiry: United Kingdom 1991-93				
Up to 24 weeks completed gestation				
Delivered	3	3	-	6
Undelivered*	24	21	15	60
Over 24 weeks completed gestation				
Delivered	92	53	22	167
Undelivered	8	22	8	38
Not stated	1	1	1	3
Total	128	100	46	274

* Note: includes 8 cases of spontaneous or legal abortion and 8 ectopic pregnancies

Note also that the maternal death may have been subsequent to the end of the pregnancy, and the cause of maternal death may not have been related to the outcome of the pregnancy.

Gestational age at maternal death

On 1 October 1992 the definition of a stillbirth changed from one "born showing no sign of life after 28 completed weeks gestation" to "24 completed weeks of gestation". In 1991-93 66 women were known to have died before twenty-four completed weeks gestation, three of these resulting in a live birth. For comparison with the previous Report, which covered the period before the change in definition of a stillbirth, in 1991-93 89 *Direct, Indirect* or *Fortuitous* deaths (33 %) occurred before 28 weeks completed gestation for this triennium compared with 90 (31%) for the period 1988-90.

Demographic characteristics of maternal deaths known to the Enquiry

Regional variation

The wide regional variation in maternal mortality, by deaths known to the Enquiry, is shown in Table 1.10 and Figure 1.5 .The period 1985-93, the period covered by the UK Reports, is used to increase the number of maternal deaths available for analysis. Over the period 1985-93 in the United Kingdom the ratio of *Direct* to *Indirect* deaths was 1.5:1 but this ratio varied considerably at national and regional level.

Figure 1.10

Direct and indirect maternal deaths reported to the Enquiry and mortality rate calculated by OPCS for English Region or country of residence,1985-93

Area of residence	Total births	Direct deaths*	Indirect deaths	*Direct obstetric mortality rate**	*Indirect obstetric mortality rate**	Total *Direct* and *Indirect* mortality rate
United Kingdom	7,011,780	413	276	5.9	3.9	9.8
England	5,834,735	348	222	6.0	3.8	9.8
Wales	341,220	23	17	6.7	5.0	11.7
Scotland	593,758	38	24	6.4	4.0	10.4
N Ireland	242,067	4	13	1.7	5.4	7.0
Former English Regional Health Authority						
Northern	362,962	23	9	6.3	2.5	8.8
Yorkshire	447,520	24	23	5.4	5.1	10.5
Trent	554,806	34	24	6.1	4.3	10.5
East Anglia	233,004	13	10	5.6	4.3	9.9
NW Thames	451,993	39	6	8.6	1.3	10.0
NE Thames	503,813	31	15	6.2	3.0	9.1
SE Thames	454,493	32	18	7.0	4.0	11.0
SW Thames	349,491	13	14	3.7	4.0	7.7
Wessex	337,289	14	4	4.2	1.2	5.3
Oxford	317,331	13	12	4.1	3.8	7.9
South Western	359,806	20	14	5.6	3.9	9.4
West Midlands	654,016	45	40	6.9	6.1	13.0
Mersey	295,589	18	14	6.1	4.7	10.8
North Western	512,622	29	19	5.7	3.7	9.4

* Includes abortion

** Per 100,000 live and still births

Source: England & Wales: Birth statistics Series FM1
        OPCS Vital statistics
        Scotland: Registrar General's Annual Report series
        Northern Ireland: Registrar General's Annual Report series

Figure 1.5

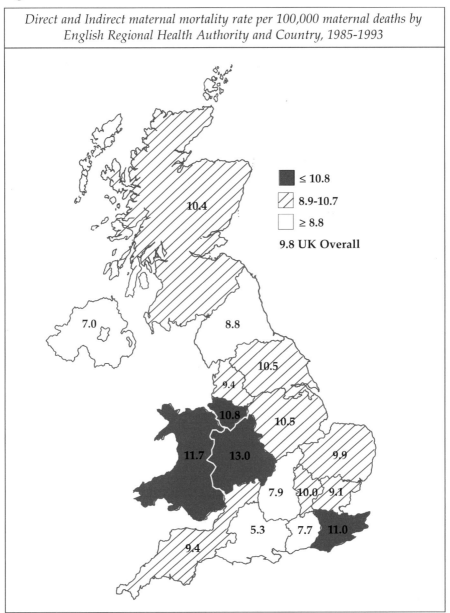

Direct and Indirect maternal mortality rate per 100,000 maternal deaths by English Regional Health Authority and Country, 1985-1993

Age and parity

Maternal mortality is closely related to both maternal age and parity, as shown by the data presented in Tables 1.11 and 1.12. Maternal death rates generally rose with age, as shown in Table 1.11. Published all-cause mortality data for women also show increasing rates throughout the age group 16-45, but the contribution of maternal causes peaked for ages 25-34, being lowest for women aged under 20 or 40 and over. There was a different pattern of maternal mortality with parity (Table 1.12), with lowest rates for *Direct* and *Indirect* deaths being for women in their second pregnancy.

15

Table 1.11

Age	1985-87		1988-90		1991-93	
	n	Rate	n	Rate	n	Rate
<20	15	7.8	17	8.8	7	4.2
20-24	47	7.3	38	6.0	30	5.5
25-29	53	6.8	74	8.8	87	10.6
30-34	60	13.7	57	11.4	61	10.9
35-39	35	23.0	31	18.5	36	19.1
40+	13	41.3	18	57.2	7	20.6
Total	**223**	**9.8**	**238**	**10.1**	**228**	**9.8**

Number of Direct and Indirect deaths by maternal age, and rate per 100,000 maternities; United Kingdom 1985-93

Table 1.12

Estimated parity	1985-87		1988-90		1991-93	
	n	Rate	n	Rate*	n	Rate
0	87	9.3	57	5.3	76	8.0
1	50	6.8	44	6.1	58	7.4
2	30	8.8	10	3.0	51	13.0
3	27	21.1	5	3.8	17	12.2
4+	26	29.6	13	14.2	18	25.59
Not stated	3		109		8	
Total	**223**	**9.8**	**238**	**10.1**	**228**	**9.8**

Number of Direct and Indirect maternal deaths and rate per 100,000 maternities by estimated parity of the mother; United Kingdom 1985-93

[*] - Note: due to the large number of cases for the 1988-90 triennium where parity was not stated it is not possible to draw any significance from the rates in this column

Marital status

Table 1.13 shows the marital status of the women who had a *Direct* or *Indirect* maternal death in 1991-93. Sixty nine per cent of the women were known to be married at the time of death, which is consistent with the 68 per cent of live births born inside marriage in 1993 in the United Kingdom. This suggests that being unmarried is not in itself a risk factor for maternal mortality overall. Therefore, marital status will not be considered in the later chapters of this Report.

Table 1.13

Maternal deaths in relation to marital status; United Kingdom 1991-93			
	Type of death		
Marital status	*Direct*	*Indirect*	**Total**
Married	93	61	154
Single	24	30	54
Divorced	4	5	9
Separated	2	0	2
Not stated	5	4	9
Total	**128**	**100**	**228**

Causes of maternal mortality

Direct deaths

Table 1.14 shows the main causes of *Direct* maternal deaths and the percentage they formed of all maternal deaths in the United Kingdom from 1985 to 1993. Figure 1.7 shows the causes of *Direct* maternal deaths and their percentages for this triennium. The table demonstrates that thrombosis and thromboembolism remain the major direct cause of maternal death accounting for almost one quarter of all *Direct* maternal deaths, the other main causes of death remain the same as in the previous triennium: hypertensive disorders, haemorrhage and deaths in early pregnancy, which together with thrombosis and thromboembolism account for 68 per cent of all *Direct* maternal deaths.

Table 1.14

Causes of Direct maternal deaths, percentage of Direct deaths and rates per 1,000,000 maternities; United Kingdom 1985-93

Triennia		Thrombosis and thrombo- embolism*	Hypertensive disorders of pregnancy	Anaesthesia	Amniotic fluid embolism	Early pregnancy deaths including abortion**	Antepartum and postpartum haemorrhage	Genital tract sepsis (excluding abortion)	Genital tract trauma	Other Direct deaths	All Direct deaths
1985-87	No	32(3)	27	6	9	22(16)	10	6	6	21	139
	%	23.0	19.4	4.3	6.5	15.8	7.2	4.3	4.3	15.1	100
	Rate	12.8[1]	11.9	2.6	4.0	2.6[2] 7.1[3]	4.4	2.6	2.6	9.2	61.2
1988-90	No	33(9)	27	4	11	24(15)	22	7	3	14	145
	%	22.8	18.6	2.8	7.6	16.6	15.2	4.8	2.1	9.7	100
	Rate	10.2[1]	11.4	1.7	4.7	3.8[2] 6.4[3]	9.3	3.0	1.3	5.9	61.4
1991-93	No	35(5)*	20	8	10	18(8)	15	9	4	10	129
	%	27.1	15.5	6.2	7.8	14.0	11.6	7.0	3.1	7.8	100
	Rate	13.0[1]	8.6	3.5	4.3	3.5[2] 3.5[3]	6.5	3.9	1.7	4.3	55.7

Note - Rates are calculated per million maternities
* - Numbers due to thromboembolism other than pulmonary are given in parentheses
** - Numbers due to ectopic pregnancies given in parentheses
*** - Note: one other death assessed as *Indirect*

[1] - Rate for pulmonary embolism only
[2] - Rate for abortion
[3] - Rate for ectopic pregnancies

18

Figure 1.6

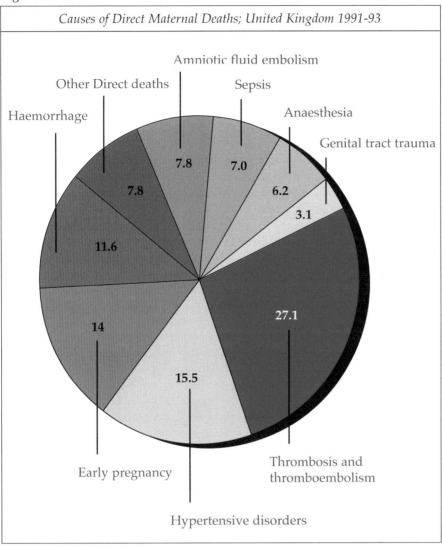

Causes of Direct Maternal Deaths; United Kingdom 1991-93

Amniotic fluid embolism

Other Direct deaths

Sepsis

Haemorrhage

Anaesthesia

Genital tract trauma

7.8

7.0

7.8

6.2

3.1

11.6

27.1

14

15.5

Early pregnancy

Thrombosis and thromboembolism

Hypertensive disorders

Each of the causes of maternal death will be considered in depth in the appropriate Chapters which follow in this Report.

References

Human Fertilization Embryology Authority. Annual Report 1993.

Mortality Statistics: cause. Series DH2. HMSO.

Population Trends, no 67: HMSO, 1992.

CHAPTER 2

Hypertensive disorders of pregnancy

Summary

There were 20 deaths due to hypertensive disorders of pregnancy in the United Kingdom during the triennium 1991 to 1993, a 26% reduction from the 27 cases recorded in each of the previous two triennia. In only one case was there pre-existing hypertension. There were 11 cases of eclampsia.

Substandard care was evident in 80% of cases, the same incidence as in the 1988-1990 triennium. Underlying factors remained similar to those in previous Reports, namely failure to take prompt action and inadequate consultant involvement.

In a number of cases, despite early consultant involvement, care was nonetheless substandard. The assessors consider that an obstetrician-led special interest team of appropriate size and composition should be set up in each unit to formulate and update pre-eclampsia and eclampsia protocols and to advise in difficult cases. Such an arrangement should promote links with a Regional consultant having a special interest in the management of such cases, advice from whom might, on occasion, mean referral of cases. In no case in the present series was there any evidence of advice having been sought from a Regional consultant despite repeated recommendations in these Reports.

In 10 of the 11 cases of eclampsia, the first fit occurred in hospital. Magnesium sulphate was not used in any case in the present series for the management of convulsions. This may change in the light of the findings of the Collaborative Eclampsia Trial (1995) where, in the context of the trial, magnesium sulphate was found to be superior to diazepam and phenytoin. The assessors consider that in units where it is not at present a standard treatment, any change to the use of magnesium sulphate, itself not without danger, should be implemented with caution and following appropriate training.

Five women developed very severe pre-eclampsia within traditional intervals between ante-natal visits. This aspect was also noted among the 383 cases recorded in the British Eclampsia Survey Team (BEST) Report (1994). It may therefore be necessary to treat with caution any local proposals to reduce the intensity of ante-natal screening, in whatever setting, from 24 weeks onwards, even in those women who are normotensive at booking.

Very few of the cases in the present series had appropriate laboratory tests performed despite serious and often deteriorating disease.

Established pre-eclampsia and eclampsia were the sole underlying causes of death in 19 cases, in all of whom the blood pressure was normal in early pregnancy. Eight of these women were primiparous. There was one case of severe pre-eclampsia superimposed on existing hypertension.

In eight other cases, severe pre-eclampsia was a significant factor but the deaths were considered by assessors to have been due to other causes and are therefore counted in the relevant chapters. The causes of death were:- subarachnoid haemorrhage (berry aneurysm), respiratory arrest, cardiac disease, three cases of pulmonary embolism, and two of postpartum haemorrhage. Three others were classified as *Late* deaths, one from myoclonic epilepsy who died a few months after Caesarean section for moderate pre-eclampsia, a second from acute respiratory distress syndrome (ARDS) related to placental abruption, pre-eclampsia and over-transfusion, and a third died from the secondary effects of HELLP syndrome, 6 months after delivery.

Table 2.1 shows the number and rates per million maternities of deaths from pre-eclampsia and eclampsia in the United Kingdom 1985-1993.

Table 2.1

The number of women who died from hypertensive disorders of pregnancy and the death rate per million maternities; United Kingdom 1985-1993						
	Pre-eclampsia		Eclampsia		Total	
Triennium	Number	Rate	Number	Rate	Number	Rate
1985-87	15	6.7	12	5.4	27	12.1
1988-90	12	5.1	14	5.9	27	11.0
1990-93	12	5.3	8	3.4	20	8.6

A comparison of the ages of the women who died of hypertensive disorders of pregnancy in the United Kingdom from 1988 to 1993 is given in Table 2.2

Table 2.2

Number of maternal deaths and the death rates per million maternities from hypertensive disorders by age; United Kingdom 1985-1993

Age in years	1985-87			1988-90			1991-93		
	Maternities total (000s)	No of Deaths	Rate per million	Maternities total (000s)	No of Deaths	Rate per million	Maternities total (000s)	No of Deaths	Rate per million
Under 25	837.8	10	11.9	825.0	8	9.6	714.9	3	4.2
25-29	777.7	5	6.4	836.4	5	5.6	819.9	11	13.4
30-34	437.6	7	16.0	499.9	8	16.0	558.4	4	7.2
35-39	152.1	3	19.7	169.5	4	23.8	188.0	2	10.6
40+	26.6	2	75.1	31.5	2	63.5	34.0	-	-
All ages	2,231.8	27	12.1	2,360.3	27	11.4	2,315.2	20	8.6

Duration of pregnancy

The duration of pregnancy at delivery is shown in Table 2.3

Table 2.3

Duration of pregnancy in delivered patients; United Kingdom 1991-93			
Duration of pregnancy (weeks)	Pre-Eclampsia	Eclampsia	Total
Up to 28	2	0	2
29-32	1	3	4
33-37	4	6	9
38 +	2	2	4
Total	9	11	19

One patient died undelivered. All delivered patients reached 26 weeks gestation or more. Six of the deaths occurred following delivery before 33 weeks gestation, three due to pre-eclampsia and three to eclampsia.

Mode of delivery

Amongst the 19 delivered patients there were 12 Caesarean sections, three of them in twin pregnancies. There were three assisted breech deliveries in two of which the baby was stillborn. There was one vaginal twin delivery and three spontaneous vaginal deliveries in singleton pregnancies.

Eclamptic fits

Eclampsia occurred in 11 patients and severe pre-eclampsia in nine. Of the 11 eclamptics, eight had received no treatment by the time of their first fit, although only one suffered a convulsion outside hospital. Eight patients had single fits.

Immediate cause of death

The immediate causes of death in all cases are shown in Table 2.4. The fall in the total number of deaths compared with previous triennia is attributable to the reduction in deaths from cerebral haemorrhage, with no deaths ascribed to sub-arachnoid haemorrhage. The four deaths classified under other causes were due to cardiac failure, cardiac arrythmia, renal failure and one in which no actual cause of death could be ascertained in the absence of an autopsy. Two women dying from cerebral haemorrhage had the HELLP syndrome underlying. In three cases where pulmonary oedema was considered to be the principal cause of death, ARDS was also present. Poor control of fluid balance with circulatory overload was evident in six cases in this series.

Table 2.4

Cause of deaths due to eclampsia and pre-eclampsia; United Kingdom 1985-93			
Cause of death	**1985-87**	**1988-90**	**1991-93**
Cerebral			
Intracerebral haemorrhage	11	10	5
Subarachnoid	-	2	-
Infarct	-	1	-
Oedema	-	1	-
Total	11	14	5
Pulmonary			
ARDS[*]	9	9	8
Oedema	1	1	3
Haemorrhage	1	-	-
Pneumonia	1	-	-
Total	12	10	11
Hepatic			
Necrosis	1	1	-
Other	3	2	4
Overall total	**27**	**27**	**20**

[*] ARDS - Acute Respiratory Distress Syndrome

Substandard care

In 16 of the 20 deaths (80%) there was evidence of substandard care. In two cases the GP was principally involved while in another two the patient refused treatment. Three of these four women subsequently received substandard care in hospital; one died at home undelivered.

General practitioner responsibility

In the first case the patient's blood pressure at 34 weeks gestation was found to be 140/90 mm Hg at a GP/Midwife Clinic; there was only a trace of proteinuria but very marked oedema. A routine clinic appointment was made for one week later but she required admission the very same evening with a blood pressure of 180/115 mm Hg and 3+ proteinuria. She later suffered eclampsia in hospital.

In the second case the patient was seen by the GP at 38 weeks' gestation with 2+ proteinuria and a diastolic blood pressure, by this time fixed at 80 mm Hg, having been consistently between 40 and 60 mm Hg in early pregnancy. No comment was made. She was admitted, having suffered a convulsion at home 4 days later. She died, after 11 days, in an intensive care unit (ICU) of HELLP syndrome.

Patient responsibility

In one case, rather unusually, the patient totally refused intravenous drug therapy, which was thought to have contributed to her death. In another case the patient returned home despite pre-eclampsia superimposed on pre-existing hypertension which itself was inadequately treated. She died undelivered at home probably as a result of a cardiac arrhythmia.

Consultant unit responsibility

In all 15 cases where there was an element of substandard hospital care, a consultant obstetric unit was involved, and solely so, in 12. In these cases, two principal factors were evident:

- failure to take prompt action, and

- inadequate consultant involvement.

In many cases it was noted that these two often inter-related factors both operated.

Failure to take prompt action

This affected the outcome in two principal ways:

- delay in delivery, and

- delay in transfer to an ICU or appropriate high dependency area.

Delay in delivery

In three cases there were critical delays of 12, 24 and 26 hours respectively, before delivery was effected, which the assessors considered adversely affected the outcome.

In the first, the delay was caused by a shortage of neonatal intensive care facilities. The patient's condition had rapidly deteriorated with severe pre-eclampsia and this case is detailed later in this chapter.

In the second, delivery at 35 weeks gestation was delayed for 24 hours after admission, during which time the patient was not seen by a consultant despite massive proteinuria, raised blood pressure and very marked oedema. Fatal eclampsia resulted.

In the third, despite deteriorating pre-eclampsia, the planned emergency Caesarean section was cancelled because the fetus died in utero. The ensuing induced labour lasted 26 hours during which there was circulatory overload and eventual death from ARDS.

Delay in delivery also occurred on account of efforts to gain fetal maturity. This happened three times in this triennium compared with six in the last. These cases are as follows:-

A patient with a twin pregnancy at 30 weeks gestation was admitted with suspected premature labour, having been seen three days before at the hospital ante-natal clinic when she had 2+ proteinuria and hypertension. For three days corticosteroids and ritodrine were used, with inadequate monitoring of blood pressure and fluid balance. Her pre-eclampsia was meanwhile deteriorating steadily. She had an eclamptic fit and died of a cerebral haemorrhage.

In another case, because of immaturity, delivery at 26 weeks gestation was delayed despite a blood pressure of 170/100 mm Hg and 5.8 g/24h proteinuria. After transfer to the ICU she initially improved but developed hypoxia and became oliguric. She eventually developed disseminated intravascular coagulation (DIC) and she died of multiple organ failure. There is no criticism of the care she received whilst in the ICU.

In the third case, the patient was retained in hospital, undelivered at 29 weeks gestation, with her severe pre-eclampsia being treated with labetalol. The fact that a corticosteroid course had been started indicated an appreciation of the need for early delivery. The pre-eclampsia continued to deteriorate and eclampsia occurred five days after admission when the blood pressure rose very suddenly despite treatment.

The significance of these cases is referred to later in relation to the use of Regional consultants with a special interest in this area.

Delay in transfer

Another form of failure to take prompt action was delay in transfer to an ICU, which adversely affected the outcome in three cases, two of which are described later.

Inadequate consultant involvement

This took the following forms:

- failure to inform consultants,

- failure of consultants to attend, and

- inadequate consultant management.

In a number of cases the consultant, either anaesthetic or obstetric, and sometimes both, should have been informed earlier. Examples are as follows:-

> A young primigravida, with a twin pregnancy at 30 weeks gestation, was admitted in possible premature labour and with moderate pre-eclampsia. Junior staff supervised the prevention of premature delivery without closely monitoring the pre-eclampsia, which was meanwhile deteriorating seriously. Anaesthetic staff had not been informed about this high risk case, only being called to resuscitate her following an eclamptic fit.

> Another woman was admitted with slight vaginal bleeding, severe abdominal pain and absent fetal heart sounds. A consultant obstetrician was only informed of the case by phone at the onset of spontaneous labour. She suffered a rise of blood pressure to 200/150 mm Hg in the late first stage and eclampsia occurred. The consultant was not contacted about her again until after death an hour following delivery. Autopsy showed eclampsia and heart failure, for which she had received no treatment whatsoever.

> A known severe pre-eclamptic at 29 weeks gestation, having received in-patient treatment for 11 days, suffered headache associated with sudden rise of blood pressure to 160/110 mm Hg. A Senior House Officer (SHO), without seeing her, and without informing any senior staff, prescribed co-proximol by 'phone. She had a convulsion an hour and a half later and died eventually of ARDS. This case is referred to earlier.

> A young primigravid patient was without any previous symptoms or signs of pre-eclampsia whatsoever. After completion of perineal suturing she felt unwell and her blood pressure was found to be 170/126 mm Hg with 4+ proteinuria. She developed major respiratory problems and eventually suffered an eclamptic convulsion. Anaesthetic staff were never informed of her presence in the labour ward despite the significant respiratory problem. This case is referred to later under consultant responsibility.

> One patient, whose cause of death is counted in Chapter 3, had labour induced for very severe pre-eclampsia. Because of a fall in blood pressure related to postpartum haemorrhage an SHO, without consulting anyone else, gave her two and a half litres of a crystalloid solution along with four litres of Haemaccel before any blood was transfused. The patient eventually died of ARDS potentiated by the combination of circulatory overload and aggravated by the presence of pre-eclampsia.

Failure of consultants to attend

In two cases the assessors felt that the consultant, although having been informed, should have attended rather than advising by telephone. In another case the consultant attended insufficiently often to supervise the care.

Inappropriate consultant management

In a number of cases, despite close involvement, consultant management was considered by the assessors to be inappropriate:-

> A patient suffered severe breathlessness almost immediately postpartum. She had developed 4+ proteinuria and her blood pressure was 170/126 mm Hg. The consultant diagnosed pulmonary embolism. During transfer back from another department where she had gone for investigation she had a fit, dying eventually of ARDS. There was no evidence of pulmonary embolism.

> In the second case, again a consultant was closely involved. As a result of excessive fluid intake, ordered despite severe postpartum pre-eclampsia and oliguria, the patient progressed to fatal pulmonary oedema.

The following two cases illustrate some or all of the points made previously concerning substandard care:-

> A multigravid patient with a booking blood pressure of 85/60 mm Hg was seen at a GP and Midwife Clinic at 34 weeks. The blood pressure was by then 140/90 mm Hg, with a trace of proteinuria and very marked oedema. No action was taken apart from an appointment made for a week later. She required admission later on the same day with a blood pressure of 185/105 mm Hg, "2+" oedema and 3+ proteinuria, headache, epigastric tenderness, vomiting and hypereflexia. The on-call consultant was contacted, and, without seeing the patient, by telephone advised induction of labour. During early labour and two and a half hours after admission, eclampsia occurred, with the diastolic pressure recorded as 94 mm Hg. No anticonvulsant or antihypertensive therapy had been given. An emergency Caesarean section was performed by an obstetric registrar with an acting up SHO giving the anaesthetic. Neither an obstetric nor anaesthetic consultant had attended during the 11 hours since her admission. When the patient was eventually seen by a consultant anaesthetist no clear instructions about therapy were given and inadequate, if any, treatment was administered. A second fit occurred. The consultant obstetrician again gave instructions by telephone. DIC developed. The patient was retained in the labour ward and was over-transfused, with among other fluids, blood, fresh frozen plasma and platelets. Only 14 hours after delivery was she transferred to an ICU where she eventually died of ARDS.

A multipara required admission at 34 weeks' gestation, three days after her most recent ante-natal attendance when the blood pressure had been normal, but gross oedema had been noted. On admission her blood pressure was 161/104 mm Hg, 2+ proteinuria was present along with severe symptoms and signs suggesting impending eclampsia. Only one hour after admission, in the presence of marked hyperflexia, increasing hypertension and a uric acid level of 470 mmols/l, was hydralazine given. Delivery could not then be carried out immediately because of a lack of neonatal cots, not only in the hospital itself, but in the whole district. As she waited overnight, 3.5 litres of intravenous fluid was given despite oliguria. The central venous pressure (CVP) rose to +7 cm/H_2O. The delayed Caesarean section was eventually carried out 11 hours after admission. DIC and severe postpartum haemorrhage followed. She was only transferred to an ICU 18 hours post-operatively, where she died of multisystem failure. The consultant obstetrician saw her for the first time just before the Caesarean section.

Other aspects of substandard care

In no case in the present series was advice sought from a Regional specialist. The three cases described earlier in this chapter, where there was delay in delivery in an attempt to gain fetal maturity, typify those cases which could benefit from such expert advice.

In six of the hypertensive deaths, along with one ascribed to haemorrhage, and one *Late* death, all of whom had very severe pre-eclampsia, circulatory overload was considered to have occurred, followed by ARDS with or without pulmonary oedema. This is a recurrent theme in these Reports and is caused by a failure to appreciate the reduced intravascular compartment in pre-eclampsia, together with poorly controlled fluid balance. Sometimes the fluids were ordered separately by the obstetrician, the anaesthetist and even the haematologist, each independently using fluid as a vehicle for their particular aspect of therapy without co-ordination.

In two cases a so called "fluid challenge" was ordered inappropriately by an obstetrician in the presence of severe oliguria. Syntometrine was given in four cases where pre-eclampsia was clearly already present; in one it may have been the main precipitating factor in postpartum eclampsia.

There were four cases in this Report in which an SHO was exposed to a situation where, through lack of experience, the gravity thereof was not appreciated. In one, for example, simple analgesia was prescribed by telephone for what was clearly the headache of impending eclampsia. In another, the patient having been successfully treated for eclampsia was nevertheless discharged by an SHO from the ICU as early as the sixth day postpartum despite persisting proteinuria. She required re-admission the following day and died from the effects of severe pre-eclampsia, principally ARDS. However, there appears to be a smaller proportion of cases in this series where such a situation arose compared with previous Reports. Likewise, there were many fewer cases where the GP, midwife and patient herself were involved. In no case was expert domiciliary assistance in the form of a "flying squad", or its equivalent, involved.

Other clinical features

Sixteen of the 20 patients were transferred to an ICU. It is obvious that anaesthetists are playing an ever increasing role in the management of eclampsia.

In at least four cases there was significant delay in the transfer. In two cases the HELLP syndrome supervened but in no other deaths was there liver involvement. Both these cases suffered cerebral haemorrhage as a result.

There were clearly a number of cases where patients were due to be reviewed ante-natally but where severe disease developed between visits planned at orthodox intervals. This matter has been commented on in the BEST Report.

Comments

A welcome fall in the number of deaths from the hypertensive disorders of pregnancy is recorded in this triennium. As there is only a small reduction in the proportion of cases where the assessors felt the care had been substandard, this aspect still remains very unsatisfactory.

There now appears to be more rationale for the standardisation of antihypertensive and anticonvulsant therapy. In five cases hydralazine was used alone. In another six, hydralazine and labetalol were used. In two cases labetalol was used alone, as was oral atenolol in one. Diazepam was used alone as an anticonvulsant in five cases. In four it was used in conjunction with phenytoin, and phenytoin and chlormethiazole were each used alone once.

Nifedipine or magnesium sulphate were not used in any case. However, the use of magnesium sulphate is likely to change in the light of recent publications, particularly those of the Collaborative Eclampsia Trial (1995) where it is clearly stated that in the context of this trial "there is now compelling evidence in favour of magnesium sulphate rather than diazepam or phenytoin for the treatment of eclampsia". The assessors consider that there may be potential hazards in its sudden widespread use for which appropriate training will be required. For this reason the Scientific Committee of the Royal College of Obstetricians and Gynaecologists are to consider the issue and prepare suitable guidelines. The correct place for the use of antihypertensive therapy and the most appropriate drug still await elucidation.

There was little evidence from the actual case reports received by the assessors that additional investigations such as the uric acid level, platelet levels or liver function tests were regularly performed to assess progress and prognosis. As stated in the BEST report "Screening for hypertension and proteinuria has provided a simple and effective way of reducing the dangers of pre-eclampsia in the past, but new methods need to be sought to reduce the impact of the residual problems not detected by these signs".

Many patients deteriorated swiftly despite 1+ or more proteinuria and raised blood pressure not having been recently found together. A similar finding was reported in the BEST Survey of Eclampsia. Full use should be made of day-care facilities, short stay wards and domiciliary midwife visits in cases where either proteinuria or raised blood pressure are present alone.

Once again, as in previous Reports, it must be stated that in severe disease SHOs should not be asked to carry executive clinical responsibilities and appropriate protocols should be established to prevent them being exposed to such potentially dangerous clinical situations.

The mandatory requirement that strict attention be paid to fluid balance needs to be reiterated again in the light of the findings of failure in this respect in this Report. Sometimes too many persons become involved in treatment without co-ordinating their clinical management.

In some cases, despite close consultant involvement, clinical management failed. With a lower number of patients per consultant in the future, and possible progress towards better diagnosis and treatment, one consultant may see an insufficient number of severe cases during professional life to be able to guarantee optimum treatment.

Purchasers must assure themselves that a lead obstetric consultant forms a special interest team of appropriate constitution so that protocols and therapies are fully updated and appropriate staff mobilised. Such a team could more meticulously monitor fluid balance in individual cases. In addition more regular contact should be made with a consultant with a special expertise in the management of such cases. As recommended in earlier Reports, there should be one such consultant in each English Region and for each of the other countries.

Ergometrine either alone or in combination with syntocinon should not normally be used in the presence of any degree of pre-eclampsia unless there is severe haemorrhage.

The number and the standard of the autopsies in this group of cases is very poor, perhaps reflecting the reluctance of staff to request one, particularly after a harrowing period of prolonged intensive care. In some cases, obstetric staff may not be in attendance around the time of death and in others, organs such as heart, lungs, kidney and liver may have been removed for transplantation purposes, thereby vitiating the autopsy findings.

References

Eclampsia in the United Kingdom (British Eclampsia Survey Team BEST Report). *BMJ* 1994; **309**: 1395-1399.

Eclampsia Collaborative Group. Which Anticonvulsant for women with eclampsia? Evidence from the Collaborative Eclampsia Trial. *Lancet* 1995; **345**: 1455-1463.

Redman CWG, Roberts J. Management of pre-eclampsia. *Lancet* 1993; **341**:1451-4 .

CHAPTER 3

Antepartum and postpartum haemorrhage

Summary

Of the 15 deaths directly due to antepartum and postpartum haemorrhage, four were due to placenta praevia, three to placental abruption and eight to postpartum haemorrhage. There were no *Late* deaths. In 11 deaths care was substandard: in four of these 11 cases the cause was attributed to the woman (one had concealed her pregnancy and three refused blood transfusion because of their religious beliefs). In addition to the 15 *Direct* deaths, bleeding was implicated in 12 other deaths (including one *Late* death) which are dealt with in their relevant chapters. The number of *Direct* deaths from antepartum haemorrhage, which had risen sharply in 1988-90, has fallen slightly but is still higher than in 1985-87.

Only deaths due to haemorrhage from the genital tract are included in this Chapter. Deaths due to haemorrhage from other sites (including ectopic pregnancy) are considered in the appropriate chapters.

In 1991-93 there were 15 *Direct* deaths from haemorrhage with a mortality rate of 6.4 per million maternities, compared with 9.2 per million in 1988-90. There were no *Late* deaths. Of these 15 *Direct* deaths eight were caused by postpartum haemorrhage, four by placenta praevia and three by placental abruption. Four of the fifteen women were of Afro-Caribbean or Asian ethnic origin, including all three who died from postpartum haemorrhage after Caesarean section. Care was considered substandard in eleven cases (73%), compared with 14 of the 22 deaths (64%) in 1988-90 and seven of the ten (70%) in 1985-87.

In addition to the *Direct* deaths discussed in this chapter there were 14 from other causes in which bleeding played a significant part. These cases are considered in their relevant chapters, but are also mentioned in the subsequent paragraphs according to the classification of the bleeding. Substandard care was present in nine of these cases. Three of the fourteen women were of Afro-Caribbean or Asian ethnic origin. Four of the 12 deaths were associated with antepartum haemorrhage. There were two deaths from placenta praevia and one from placental abruption. The other case was a *Late* death from cardiomyopathy following a Caesarean section for antepartum haemorrhage complicated by sepsis, and is counted in Chapter 15.

Table 3.1 shows the number of *Direct* deaths from haemorrhage by cause and the death rate per million maternities in the three triennia 1985-93.

Table 3.1

Number and cause of deaths from haemorrhage and rates per million maternities, United Kingdom; 1985-93				
Triennium	Placental abruption	Placenta praevia	Postpartum haemorrhage	Total	Rate per million maternities
1985-87	4	0	6	10	4.5
1988-90	6	5	11	22	9.2
1991-93	3	4	8	15	6.4

The last Report drew attention to the increased risk with age, particularly for those aged 35 and over. This trend is still seen in the present triennium, as shown in Table 3.2.

Table 3.2

The number of deaths from haemorrhage, and death rates per million maternities by age from haemorrhage; United Kingdom 1985-93

Age group	1985-87		1988-90		1991-93		Total 1985-93	
	Number of deaths	Rate per million maternities	Number of deaths	Rate per million maternities	Number of deaths	Rate per million maternities	Number of deaths	Rate per million maternities
Under 20	} 4	} 4.8	0	0.0	1	6.0	} 7	} 0.5
20-24			2	3.1	0	0.0		
25-29	0	0.0	6	7.2	7	8.5	13	5.3
30-34	2	4.6	8	16.2	5	26.5	15	10.0
35-39	3	19.7	4	23.9	1	5.3	8	15.7
40+	1	37.5	2	63.9	1	29.4	4	43.4
All ages	10	4.5	22	9.3	15	6.4	47	6.8

Placenta praevia

Four *Direct* deaths from haemorrhage were caused by placenta praevia. Two of these patients were aged over 35.

Care was substandard in three of these cases. In the first case Caesarean section for placenta praevia was carried out by a senior registrar. Postoperative care was substandard because the blood loss after delivery was underestimated and inadequately treated. This case is discussed in more detail in Chapter 9.

In two cases a routine ultrasound scan had failed to reveal the low-lying placenta but neither case was straightforward.

> In one case the uterine anatomy was distorted by previous Caesarean sections. When antepartum haemorrhage occurred Caesarean section was undertaken by a registrar, but placenta percreta was found in the lower uterine segment and involved the bladder.

> In the other case the placenta, which was later found to be abnormally long and narrow, was thought at the time of the ultrasound scan to be in the upper uterine segment. The woman subsequently had slight uterine bleeding, telephoned the hospital and was told this was a "show". She delivered at home unattended. When the midwife arrived, 20 minutes after being called by a neighbour, the woman was collapsed and unconscious.

Two cases of antepartum haemorrhage due to placenta praevia are counted in other chapters.

> A woman who had necrotising fasciitis after a previous pregnancy underwent Caesarean section for placenta praevia. Abdominal wall necrosis occurred and in spite of repeated wound excisions she died in the intensive care unit from candida myocarditis. The case is counted in Chapter 7.

> An acting registrar carried out a Caesarean section on a woman with two previous Caesarean sections who had a major degree of placenta praevia. Massive postpartum haemorrhage was successfully treated but after the patient was transferred from the Intensive Care Unit (ICU) to a postnatal ward she collapsed and died from pulmonary embolism. The case is counted in Chapter 4.

Although irrelevant to the outcome, in the latter case care was substandard as the Caesarean section should have been carried out by a consultant. The problems of placenta praevia when associated with a lower uterine segment scar have repeatedly been emphasised in these Reports.

Placental abruption

Three maternal deaths were due directly to placental abruption. In one case care was not substandard:

A 26 year old insulin dependent diabetic with Marfan's syndrome and a history of previous mitral valve surgery had a suspected placental abruption at 38 weeks gestation in her third pregnancy and was delivered by emergency Caesarean section. She subsequently developed a coagulopathy, cerebral and pulmonary oedema and acute centrilobular hepatocellular necrosis. She died three days after delivery. Her death was classified as being due to hepato-renal failure of uncertain cause.

In the two other cases care was substandard due to non-co-operation of the woman.

A woman who had two previous deliveries at home after no antenatal care concealed her third pregnancy from her husband, telling him that her GP had diagnosed an ovarian cyst. She collapsed at home. In the ambulance she had a cardiac arrest from which she was resuscitated. She delivered a stillborn baby and died without regaining consciousness.

A woman whose religious beliefs precluded the acceptance of a blood transfusion and who had three previous normal deliveries suffered a severe abruption in the 36th week of pregnancy. She was allowed to labour but continued to bleed and when the haemoglobin level fell to less than 6g/dl Caesarean hysterectomy was carried out by the consultant. The patient, supported by her husband, refused blood transfusion despite repeated warnings about the likely consequences. Heart failure developed the next day and she died 48 hours after delivery, when her haemoglobin was 2.2 g/dl.

In the first case care was substandard because of the concealed pregnancy. In the second care was substandard because the woman, supported by her husband, refused appropriate treatment. The problem of haemorrhage in those refusing blood transfusion for religious or other reasons is discussed in the Annexe to this Chapter.

Two further cases are counted in other chapters. The following is more fully described in Chapter 10.

A woman with a previous Caesarean section and mild ulcerative colitis underwent Caesarean section for placental abruption. She subsequently underwent two laparotomies, first to repair a bowel perforation and then to drain abscesses, and died in the ICU.

In this case care was substandard because the first laparotomy was inadequate. The patient should have been referred earlier to a general surgeon.

The other case, a *Late* death is counted and discussed in Chapter 15.

This case was complicated but care was judged to be substandard: overtransfusion may have contributed to her developing pulmonary oedema and ARDS.

Primary postpartum haemorrhage

Most of the cases of antepartum haemorrhage also involved postpartum haemorrhage but these deaths have not been counted as due directly to postpartum haemorrhage. Eight deaths were due directly to postpartum haemorrhage alone, in the absence of antepartum haemorrhage.

Four of these eight women were aged thirty or over. Their past obstetric histories were: no previous pregnancy (3), one miscarriage (1), one normal delivery (2), two Caesarean sections (1) and three normal deliveries (1).

One death followed laparotomy for extrauterine pregnancy.

> The patient's past history included appendicitis, a pelvic abscess and several laparotomies for adhesions. She had repeated episodes of abdominal pain (and indeed underwent laparotomy for suspected ectopic pregnancy) but subsequent ultrasound scans suggested an intrauterine pregnancy. An elective Caesarean section was planned for an unstable lie, but at operation an extrauterine pregnancy was found. There was heavy bleeding when the placenta was removed. Blood was transfused but cardiac arrest occurred in the intensive care unit.

Transfusion was delayed because blood had been "grouped and saved" but no blood had been cross-matched. Normally in advanced extrauterine gestation the placenta should be left in place after the baby has been delivered at laparotomy. Attempts to detach the placenta can cause uncontrollable bleeding.

Caesarean section

Postpartum haemorrhage followed Caesarean section in three cases counted in this chapter. All three women were of Afro-Caribbean ethnic origin and two were primigravid. Care was substandard in all three cases.

In one case labour was induced for pre-eclampsia but failed to progress and Caesarean section was carried out by a locum registrar. Postpartum haemorrhage was treated by infusion of clear fluid and Haemaccel before blood was transfused. The patient developed respiratory difficulties thought to be due to fluid overload. She was transferred to an ICU but developed acute respiratory distress syndrome.

The severity of the pre-eclampsia was not recognised. The consultant obstetric and anaesthetic staff should have been involved at an earlier stage. There was no intensive care unit on site. The general practitioner was not informed of the woman's death.

A woman who weighed over 90kg and who had two previous Caesarean sections underwent Caesarean section by a locum senior registrar. Bleeding occurred within a few hours and the same doctor carried out laparotomy and hysterectomy. She seemed to recover from the operation but within a few hours collapsed and was transferred to the intensive care unit, where DIC was noted before she died.

The consultant was informed of the postpartum haemorrhage but did not attend when the locum senior registrar carried out the hysterectomy.

A young primigravid woman who had recently come to England from Africa had schistosomiasis treated during pregnancy. Her haemoglobin level remained around 8g/dl and iron-deficiency anaemia was diagnosed. Later in pregnancy she received a transfusion of packed cells. There was poor progress in labour and Caesarean section was carried out. Blood loss at operation was 700ml and she lost a further 1000ml within the next three hours. DIC was suspected and treated and she was transferred to the ICU. Her condition appeared to stabilise but the next morning she had a seizure and died. Autopsy showed no clear cause of death, despite a search for signs of amniotic fluid embolism.

Instrumental delivery

There was only one case in which postpartum haemorrhage followed instrumental delivery.

A primigravid woman had a "physiological cardiac murmur" checked by a cardiologist during pregnancy. Later in pregnancy she was admitted with dark brown streaks of blood on a vulval pad and an ultrasound scan showed a fundal placenta. She was admitted in spontaneous labour at term. Progress was rapid and fetal distress developed during the second stage, with the mother developing cyanosis. Vacuum extraction was performed: the baby had an Apgar score of 0 at delivery but was resuscitated. The mother continued to bleed but no source of the bleeding could be found. The bleeding was not dramatic but an hour after delivery the mother became shocked. Her condition deteriorated despite attempted resuscitation and she died two hours after delivery. Autopsy was inadequate because there was no report on histological examination of the lungs.

Several features of this case suggest a diagnosis of amniotic fluid embolism but on balance it was felt the death could not confidently be ascribed to this cause.

Spontaneous delivery

There were three cases in which death from postpartum haemorrhage followed uncomplicated spontaneous delivery. In one case, care was not substandard.

> A woman who had an atonic postpartum haemorrhage after her first normal delivery had a small antepartum haemorrhage in her second pregnancy. Labour was induced at 38 weeks gestation and she had a spontaneous delivery. This was followed by postpartum haemorrhage and retained cotyledons were removed from the uterus under anaesthesia soon after delivery. In spite of transfusion she died three hours after the uterine evacuation.

The religious beliefs of two other women were such that they refused blood transfusion in spite of clear and repeated warnings to both them, their partners and in one case the elders of their church, that they would die without transfusion. Apart from the refusal of treatment, in only one of these cases was there any other substandard aspect of the care.

> Eight days after a normal vaginal delivery a woman underwent uterine curettage for retained products of conception. Three days later she was readmitted with secondary postpartum haemorrhage and a further uterine evacuation was carried out. She continued to bleed during the operation. The consultant anaesthetist attended and the consultant obstetrician carried out a hysterectomy. She died four hours after the hysterectomy.

The patient's refusal to accept blood transfusion was the only aspect of substandard care.

> A woman aged over 40 had a splenectomy as a child for thrombocytopenia. After her fourth normal delivery heavy bleeding began within an hour of delivery. The consultant obstetrician carried out hysterectomy an hour after bleeding started. Her haemoglobin level fell to 1.6 g/dl and she died seven hours after delivery.

The consultant anaesthetist handed care over to a colleague during the resuscitation because of distress at the patient's refusal to accept treatment. A consultant haematologist was not contacted. Care was therefore substandard but this did not affect the outcome.

Cases counted in other chapters

Five cases of primary postpartum haemorrhage are counted in other chapters. Care was substandard in four of these cases.

> In the first case the woman died after postpartum haemorrhage for which she refused blood transfusion due to her religious beliefs. The cause of death was amniotic fluid embolism (AFE) and the case is counted in Chapter 5.

Care was substandard: Despite the poor prognosis of AFE her life may have been saved by blood transfusion, which she, supported by her husband, refused.

> In a further case Caesarean section for fulminating pre-eclampsia was followed by postpartum haemorrhage and disseminated intravascular coagulation (DIC). The case is counted in Chapter 2.

Care was substandard: The woman was not transferred to the intensive care unit until 18 hours after delivery.

> The third woman had spontaneous labour augmented with syntocinon. This was followed by forceps delivery, manual removal of the placenta and a postpartum haemorrhage. Blood was transfused. Within a few hours the patient was noted to be "yellow" and oliguric. She died in a liver unit and the most likely diagnosis is a transfusion reaction. The case is counted in Chapter 12.

Care was substandard: There was delay in transfer to an intensive care unit, which was on another site.

> In the fourth case postpartum haemorrhage occurred after an emergency Caesarean section for pre-eclampsia. The case is counted in Chapter 9.

Care was substandard: Attempts to insert a central venous pressure cannula caused a haematoma in the neck and the patient died from obstruction of the airway.

In the fifth case care was not substandard.

> A woman with a twin pregnancy was admitted with mild hypertension and then with a flu-like illness. Spontaneous labour was followed by vacuum extraction of the first twin and Caesarean section for the second because of cord prolapse. Antibiotics were given at the time of the Caesarean section. She had a postpartum haemorrhage of 800ml and was pyrexial afterwards. A week later the uterus was explored. She developed DIC and was transferred to the intensive care unit where she died a month later.

Postpartum haemorrhage due to uterine rupture

Two cases of uterine rupture associated with postpartum haemorrhage are counted and discussed in Chapter 8.

A woman weighing over 100kg who had one previous Caesarean section died of postpartum haemorrhage after a rapid spontaneous labour.

Care was substandard: The haemorrhage was inappropriately treated by a locum registrar and the consultant did not attend.

In a general practitioner unit labour was induced with prostaglandin in a woman aged over 35 who had four previous deliveries. The pregnancy had continued two weeks past the expected date of delivery. A normal delivery was followed by postpartum haemorrhage due to rupture of the uterus.

Care was substandard for a number of reasons which are discussed in Chapter 8.

Secondary postpartum haemorrhage

There was one death following secondary postpartum haemorrhage. Care was not substandard.

An overweight woman who had six previous deliveries underwent elective Caesarean section for twin pregnancy. She required a blood transfusion after the operation and seven days later she developed secondary postpartum haemorrhage, DIC and septicaemia. She underwent hysterectomy and further laparotomies and suffered cardiac arrest. The case is counted in Chapter 7.

Coagulation failure

Fatal obstetric haemorrhage is usually thought of as involving coagulation failure. However, in this triennium coagulation failure complicated less than half the cases. Of the 15 cases, coagulation failure was demonstrated in four and may have been present in another two (in one the laboratory results were equivocal and in one case of abruption clotting studies were not performed). This total is smaller than in previous reports. As several of these cases demonstrate, obstetric haemorrhage can occur so rapidly, either before or after delivery, that it can be fatal even in the absence of coagulation failure.

Substandard Care

Some aspect of care was substandard in 11 of the 15 cases counted in this chapter. In four cases this was due to the woman: one had concealed her pregnancy and three refused blood transfusion. In two cases of placenta praevia the diagnosis had not been made on ultrasound scan, but neither case was straightforward. In a third case of placenta praevia, blood loss after delivery was underestimated and inadequately treated. In three cases of postpartum haemorrhage consultant involvement should have been more prompt. In another case, blood was not immediately available for transfusion.

Comments

The number of *Direct* deaths from haemorrhage has fallen from 22 in the previous triennium, but it is still higher than the total of 10 in 1985-87. The proportion in which there was substandard care shows less variation, 73% in the present report compared with 64% in 1988-90 and 70% in 1985-7.

The importance of older maternal age is confirmed in this triennium. The older woman of low parity deserves as much vigilance as has been traditionally given to the "grande multipara".

The previous Report drew attention to cases of placenta praevia in which Caesarean section had been inappropriately carried out by registrars, contrary to repeated recommendations in earlier Reports. It is probable that these recommendations are being followed more widely; elective Caesarean section for placenta praevia by a registrar did not occur in any of the *Direct* deaths in this triennium. It did occur in one of the *Indirect* deaths, however, and the time-honoured recommendation is repeated here in case it is forgotten:-

Placenta praevia, particularly in patients with a previous uterine scar, may be associated with uncontrollable haemorrhage at delivery and Caesarean hysterectomy may be necessary: the presence of a consultant at operation is essential.

The fifteen cases in this triennium fall into two approximately equal groups. In seven cases death occurred within seven hours after bleeding began, and in the other eight haemorrhage began a cascade of complications, mainly DIC or respiratory problems, which led more slowly to death.

The "rapid" group included one concealed pregnancy, one case of placenta praevia and three cases of postpartum haemorrhage after normal delivery. In four of these cases death occurred within four hours of the onset of haemorrhage.

Obstetricians and midwives should be aware of the speed with which collapse can occur with obstetric haemorrhage.

In five of the cases care was substandard because of underestimation of blood loss, delay in transfusion or delay in referral to a consultant. These factors have been referred to in previous Reports, and previous recommendations are summarised again here. Previous Reports have emphasised:

    -accurate estimation of blood loss,

    -prompt recognition and treatment of clotting disorders,

    -early involvement of a consultant haematologist,

    -involvement of a consultant anaesthetist in resuscitation,

    -the use of adequately sized intravenous cannulae, and

    -the importance of monitoring central venous pressure.

All units should have a blood bank on site and a protocol for the management of massive haemorrhage. Attention is drawn to the Guidelines for the management of massive obstetric haemorrhage, published in previous Reports. Because such emergencies are infrequent, staff may become unfamiliar with hospital procedures and regular "fire drills" are recommended.

The great majority of births in the United Kingdom in this triennium took place in hospital where blood transfusion is normally readily available. However, the importance of prompt and adequate treatment is underlined by the higher mortality rate amongst women who refuse blood transfusion because of their religious beliefs. The management of such cases is discussed in the Annexe to this chapter.

If in future there is an increase in the proportion of home deliveries, it will be important to ensure that facilities are available for rapid treatment and transfer of women to hospital if postpartum haemorrhage occurs.

ANNEXE TO CHAPTER 3

The treatment of obstetric haemorrhage in women who refuse blood transfusion

Introduction

The vast majority of women accept blood transfusion if the clinical reasons for it's necessity are fully and appropriately explained. However, a few women may continue to refuse transfusion because of specific personal or religious beliefs. The main group of women who may refuse for religious reasons are members of the Jehovah's Witnesses, who believe that the Bible forbids the consumption of blood or blood products. There are about 125,000 Jehovah's Witnesses in Britain. In 1991-3, assuming normal fertility rates, the death rate from haemorrhage in this group would be approximately 1 in 1000 maternities compared with an expected incidence of less than 1 in 100,000 maternities.

Massive obstetric haemorrhage is often unpredictable and can become life-threatening in a short time. In most cases blood transfusion can save the woman's life and very few women refuse blood transfusion in these circumstances. If it is thought likely that a woman may do so, the management of massive haemorrhage should be considered in advance.

The management of women refusing blood transfusion

Booking

1.   At the booking clinic all women are normally asked their religious beliefs, and should also be asked if they have any objections to blood transfusion. If a woman is a Jehovah's Witness or likely to refuse blood transfusion for other reasons, this should be noted in the case notes. She should be asked if she is willing to receive blood transfusion if necessary, and her reply should be noted.

2.   If she asks about the risks of refusing blood transfusion, she should be given all relevant information. This must be done in a non-confrontational manner. She would be advised that if massive haemorrhage occurs there is an increased risk that hysterectomy will be required (see para 23-24), and the woman and her partner should be offered the opportunity to read and discuss the treatment guidelines in this Annexe.

3.   If she decides against accepting blood transfusion in any circumstances, she should be booked for delivery in a unit which has all facilities for prompt management of haemorrhage, including hysterectomy, as outlined in this Annexe.

Antenatal Care

4.   The woman's blood group and antibody status should be checked in the usual way and the haemoglobin and serum ferritin should be checked regularly. Hematinics should be given throughout pregnancy to maximise iron stores.

5.   An ultrasound scan should be carried out to identify the placental site.

6.   There are well-described procedures for elective surgery in Jehovah's Witnesses: some Witnesses will donate blood before surgery for subsequent auto-transfusion if necessary though others consider that this too is forbidden by their religion. Blood storage should not be suggested to pregnant women, as the amounts of blood required to treat massive obstetric haemorrhage are far in excess of the amount that could be donated during pregnancy.

7.   If any complication is noted during the antenatal period the consultant obstetrician must be informed.

Labour

8.   The consultant obstetrician should be informed when a woman who will refuse blood transfusion is admitted in labour. Consultants in other specialities need not be alerted unless complications occur.

9.   The labour should be managed routinely, by experienced staff.

10.   Oxytocics should be given when the baby is delivered. The woman should not be left alone for at least an hour after delivery.

11.   If Caesarean section is necessary it should be carried out by a consultant obstetrician if possible.

12.   The great majority of pregnancies will end without serious haemorrhage. When the mother is discharged from hospital, she should be advised to report promptly if she has any concerns about bleeding during the puerperium.

Haemorrhage

13.   The principle of management of haemorrhage in these cases is to avoid delay. Rapid decision-making may be necessary, particularly with regard to surgical intervention.

14.   If unusual bleeding occurs at any time during pregnancy, labour or the puerperium the consultant obstetrician should be informed and the standard management should be commenced promptly. The threshold for intervention should be lower than in other patients. Extra vigilance should be exercised to quantify any abnormal bleeding and to detect complications, such as clotting abnormalities, as promptly as possible.

15. Consultants in other specialties, particularly anaesthetics and haematology, are normally involved in the treatment of massive haemorrhage. When the patient is a woman who has refused blood transfusion the consultant anaesthetist should be informed as soon as possible after abnormal bleeding has been detected. The consultant haematologist should also be notified, even though the options for treatment may be severely limited.

16. Dextran should be avoided for fluid replacement because of its possible effects on haemostasis. Intravenous crystalloid and artificial plasma expanders such as Haemaccel should be used.

17. In cases of severe bleeding, vitamin K should be given to the woman intravenously. Other drugs which have been recommended include desmopressin, methylprednisolone, and fibrinolytic inhibitors such as aprotinin (Trasylol) and tranexamic acid. The advice of the haematologist should be sought before considering the use of heparin to combat disseminated intravascular coagulation.

18. The woman should be kept fully informed about what is happening. Information must be given in a professional way, ideally by someone she knows and trusts. If standard treatment is not controlling the bleeding, she should be advised that blood transfusion is strongly recommended. Any patient is entitled to change her mind about a previously agreed treatment plan.

19. The doctor must be satisfied that the woman is not being subjected to pressure from others. It is reasonable to ask the accompanying persons to leave the room for a while so that the doctor (with a midwife or other colleague) can ask her whether she is making her decision of her own free will.

20. If she maintains her refusal to accept blood or blood products, her wishes should be respected. The legal position is that any adult patient (ie 18 years old or over) who has the necessary mental capacity to do so is entitled to refuse treatment, even if it is likely that refusal will result in the patient's death. No other person is legally able to consent to treatment for that adult or to refuse treatment on that person's behalf.

21. The staff must maintain a professional attitude. They must not lose the trust of the patient or her partner as further decisions - for example, about hysterectomy - may have to be made.

22. Massive obstetric haemorrhage usually occurs in the form of postpartum haemorrhage. In the case of life-threatening antepartum haemorrhage in which the baby is still alive, the baby should be delivered promptly, by Caesarean section if necessary.

23. Hysterectomy is normally the last resort in the treatment of obstetric haemorrhage, but with such women delay may increase the risk. The woman's life may be saved by timely hysterectomy, though even this does not guarantee success.

24. When hysterectomy is performed the uterine arteries should be clamped as early as possible in the procedure. Subtotal hysterectomy can be just as effective as total hysterectomy, as well as being quicker and safer. In some cases there may be a place for internal iliac artery ligation.

25. The timing of hysterectomy is a decision for the consultant on the spot. when making this decision it may be helpful to note that the shortest time from delivery to death recorded in these Reports was in 1985-87, when a woman died within 3 hours of delivery with a haemoglobin concentration of 3.4g/dl. Survival without hysterectomy has been recorded with a haemoglobin concentration of 4.9g/dl (Reid et al 1986).

26. With the use of hyperbaric oxygen, survival has been reported with a haemoglobin concentration of 2.6g/dl (Hart 1974). However, it would be unrealistic to recommend that these women should only be booked for delivery where such a specialised facility was available.

27. If the woman survives the acute episode and is transferred to an intensive care unit, the management there should include erythropoetin, parenteral iron therapy and adequate protein for haemoglobin synthesis. The reports by Mann et al (1992) and Buscuttil and Copplestone (1995) may be helpful.

28. If, in spite of all care, the woman dies, her relatives require support like any other bereaved family.

29. It is very distressing for staff to have to watch a woman bleed to death while refusing effective treatment. Support should be promptly available for staff in these circumstances.

References and sources

Bonakdar MI, Eckhous AW, Bacher BJ, Tabbilos RH, Peisner DB. Major gynaecologic and obstetric surgery in Jehovah's Witnesses. *Obstetrics and Gynecology* 1982; **60**: 587-90.

Boyd ME. The Obstetrician and Gynaecologist and the Jehovah's Witness. *Journal of the Society of Obstetricians and Gynecologists of Canada* 1992; **14**: 7-9.

Reid MF, Nohr K, Birks RJS. Eclampsia and haemorrhage in a Jehovah's Witness. *Anaesthesia* 1986; **41**: 324-5.

Mann CM, Votto J, Kambe J, McNamee MJ. Management of the severely anaemic patient who refuses transfusion: lessons learned during the care of a Jehovah's Witness. *Annals of Internal Medicine* 1992; **117**: 1042-8.

Thomas JM. The worldwide need for education in nonblood management in obstetrics and gynaecology. *Journal of the Society of Obstetricians and Gynaecologists of Canada* 1994; **16**: 1483-7.

Hart, GB. Exceptional blood loss anaemia, treatment with hyperbaric oxygen. *JAMA* 1974; **228**: 1028-29.

Buscuttil D, Copplestone A.Management of blood loss in Jehovah's Witnesses. *BMJ* 1995; **311**: 1115-1116

CHAPTER 4

Thrombosis and thromboembolism

Summary

There are 35 deaths from thrombosis and/or thromboembolism counted in this chapter: 30 from pulmonary embolism and 5 from cerebral thrombosis. In addition there were 5 *Late* deaths from pulmonary embolism occurring beyond the 42nd day which are counted in Chapter 15. There is known to be one further death from pulmonary embolism in a postpartum patient but no details were available.

There were 12 antepartum deaths, one intrapartum death and 17 postpartum deaths from pulmonary embolism. In seven cases symptoms suggestive of thrombosis or embolism had not been investigated fully during prior contact with medical services.

Of the 17 post partum deaths, 13 (76%) occurred in women who had been delivered by Caesarean section.

The five deaths from cerebral thrombosis all occurred in the puerperium, and four patients had been delivered by Caesarean section.

Deaths from thromboembolism and cerebral thrombosis are counted as *Direct* causes of maternal death and are discussed in this chapter. Whilst with massive pulmonary embolism the patient may suddenly collapse and die, increasing numbers of patients survive for varying periods of time and are transferred to intensive care units (ICUs), ultimately dying from other contributory causes, such as acute respiratory distress syndrome (ARDS), and multiple organ failure. In this Report the date of the initial major pulmonary embolism is recorded (rather than ultimate date of death) since the timing of the risk factor is important in endeavouring to develop any strategy of prevention via prophylaxis.

Pulmonary embolism

Comparison of the number of cases of death from pulmonary embolism in this triennium with other years is shown in Table 4.1.

Table 4.1

Deaths from pulmonary embolism (excluding Late deaths); United Kingdom 1985-93						
	Total	**Deaths after abortion/ ectopic**	**Antepartum deaths**	**Deaths in labour**	**Deaths after vaginal delivery**	**Deaths after Caesarean section**
1985-87	**30**	1	16	0	6	7
1988-90	**24**	3	10	0	3	8
1991-93	**30**	0	12	1	4	13

Antepartum

A total of 12 patients died from pulmonary embolism during the antenatal period. The periods of gestation were as follows:

Up to 12 weeks	-	3 deaths
13 to 27 weeks	-	5 deaths
28 weeks to term	-	4 deaths

The salient features of these 12 deaths are given in Table 4.2. Whilst in previous reports a significant proportion of first trimester deaths had occurred following abortion or ectopic pregnancy, none did so in this triennium. The youngest woman was aged 25 and four of the 10 were aged over 35. The worrying feature in several of the cases was their prior contact with doctors who they attended complaining of symptoms of chest pain or breathlessness but which were not identified by the GPs as potential pointers to pulmonary thromboembolism. In three instances patients were inpatients at the time, undergoing investigation or treatment for other conditions.

Bed rest and immobilisation in women who are pregnant, even in early pregnancy, should be recognised as a risk factor for development of deep vein thrombosis (DVT) and prophylaxis should be considered.

Table 4.2

	Antepartum venous thrombosis; United Kingdom 1991-93	
Age	**Gestation in weeks**	**Features**
Under 35	8	Grandmultipara, flu-like illness treated with antibiotics from GP. Developed chest pain, admitted to medical ward and died within 12 hrs. Not known to be pregnant.
	14	In-patient on medical ward with history of breathlessness. Treated for upper respiratory tract infection and metabolic acidosis for 3 days. Collapsed and died.
	15	Inpatient several weeks for treatment of medical condition. 2 day history of breathlessness and chest pain before collapse. Treated with antibiotics. Had labour induced for intrauterine death with prostaglandin but then deteriorated and died 2 weeks later in ICU. Autopsy revealed 2 week old pulmonary embolus.
	26	Poor past obstetric history. Developed severe intrauterine growth retardation and admitted for investigation. Breathless, tests suggested pulmonary embolism. Heparin commenced but deteriorated and required admission to ICU. Autopsy showed familial cardiomyopathy and pulmonary embolism.
	28	Chest pain, seen by GP ? Flu. Collapsed and died 2 days later.
	30	Uncomplicated pregnancy. Suddenly collapsed and died. Right deep vein thrombosis found at autopsy.
	34	Obese, varicose veins, otherwise uncomplicated pregnancy. Suddenly collapsed and died.
	36	Primigravida. Uncomplicated pregnancy. Admitted to A&E having collapsed. Died from massive pulmonary embolism.
Over 35	6	Chest pain and flu like symptoms. On medical ward for 5 days. Died 1 day after discharge.
	8	Obese. Not known to be pregnant. Admitted having collapsed. Died 2 days later. Autopsy showed pulmonary embolism and left deep vein thrombosis.
	13	Inpatient for 2 weeks, hypertension and impacted retroverted uterus. Died 3 days after attempted (failed) correction of retroversion under anaesthesia.
	15	Obese. Unbooked. Seen 3 days previously in A&E with chest pains.

For abbreviations see Table 4.3

Tables 4.3

Postpartum venous thrombosis following Caesarean section; United Kingdom1991-93

Postpartum Day	Features
1	Collapsed within 14 hrs of C/S for failed induction.
*1	In-patient pre C/S for placenta praevia.
2	Obese. General anaesthetic for C/S.
2	Obese, Anaemic antenatally. Emergency C/S.
11	Past history retinal thrombosis, on low dose aspirin antenatally. Repeat C/S - subcutaneous heparin for 3 days only post op.
12	Obese, smoker, C/S for PIH - on bed rest preoperatively.
12	Emergency C/S, severe PPH with DIC. Required second operation and hysterectomy. Not given prophylaxis until 4th day, slow recovery. Still in-patient at time of pulmonary embolism.
12	Uncomplicated C/S. Home day 5.
13	Emergency C/S ? Abruption. Severe asthmatic. Collapsed day 3 - thought due to asthma. Compromised brain function in ICU. Diagnosed DVT day before death. Autopsy revealed pulmonary embolism.
14	In-patient for 7 days with severe PIH. C/S at 31 weeks and slow to mobilise. Sudden collapse when visiting baby.
20	Known ovarian tumour. C/S at 28 weeks for worsening maternal condition. Died 20 days post C/S of pulmonary embolism.
21*	Emergency C/S. Slow recovery post op. Anaemia.
25	C/S for breech. Obese. Wound infection.

* - patient over 35 years old
C/S - Caesarean section
ICU - Intensive care unit
PIH - Pregnancy induced hypertension

PPH - Postpartum haemorrhage
DIC - Disseminated intravascular coagulation
IUD - Intrauterine death
A&E - Accident and Emergency Department

Intrapartum

There was only one death which occurred during labour.

> This young patient, who spoke no English, apparently had an uncomplicated pregnancy and was admitted near term in labour. She collapsed in labour, became unconscious and Caesarean section was performed because of fetal distress. The mother failed to regain consciousness and death was found to be due to massive pulmonary embolism. This case is discussed in more detail in Chapter 9.

In this patient lack of command of the English language may have meant that preceding symptoms of her deep vein thrombosis (DVT) were not passed on to her medical or nursing attendants.

Postpartum

There were seventeen deaths due to pulmonary embolism in the puerperium (up to 42 days post delivery), an increase from the 11 deaths in the 1988-90 report. Thirteen of the women had Caesarean sections and brief details of the indications, potential risk factors and timing of the pulmonary embolisms are shown in Table 4.3. In only one case was prophylactic subcutaneous heparin administered, to a patient with a past history of retinal thrombosis. Unfortunately treatment was ceased on the third post operative day and the patient died on the eleventh day. In another case prophylactic heparin was only started four days after a second operation.

Following Caesarean section deaths predominantly occurred after the first week of delivery in contrast to the four deaths after vaginal delivery, three of which occurred within the first seven days of delivery, as shown in Table 4.4. Only three of these 17 puerperal women were aged 35 years and over. Comparison of the timing of events is shown in Table 4.5.

Table 4.4

Postpartum venous thrombosis following vaginal delivery; United Kingdom 1991-93		
Days postpartum	**Delivery**	**Features**
5[+]	Breech	Premature stillbirth. Pre-eclampsia. Delay in starting heparin. Died of multiple organ failure and pulmonary embolus.
7	SVD	Postpartum haemorrhage, anaemic on discharge day 5.
7	SVD	Seen by GP re back pain day before death - treated as urinary tract infection.
24	SVD	Seen 2 weeks post delivery having become breathless with a cough, presumed viral infection. Increasing shortness of breath 3 days before death.

[+] - denotes timing of pulmonary embolism and not date of death in this instance

SVD - Spontaneous Vaginal delivery

Tables 4.5

Interval between delivery and pulmonary embolism; United Kingdom 1991-93					
Days postpartum	**0-7**	**8-14**	**15-42**	**(Late)[*] 42+**	**Total**
Vaginal delivery	3	0	1	4	**8**
Caesarean section	4	6	3	1	**14**
Total	**7**	**6**	**4**	**5**	**22**

* - deaths counted in Chapter 15

There were five *Late* deaths occurring beyond the 42nd day of delivery (7 to 13 weeks) which resulted from pulmonary embolism, as shown in Table 4.6. Four of these followed vaginal deliveries and one followed Caesarean section. This latter patient developed a cerebral infarct 10 days post Caesarean section. Although discharged home she had marked reduction in mobility and several weeks later developed a DVT. She was admitted to hospital and was commenced on heparin but died 2 days later of pulmonary embolism. In the remaining four cases it is difficult to know to what degree the recent pregnancy and delivery was the cause of the thrombosis and embolism although no other precipitating factors appeared to have been present in these women.

In one case, counted in Chapter 7, pulmonary embolism, together with mesenteric thrombosis, was diagnosed 19 days after Caesarean section. The patient was treated with heparin but subsequently died of septicaemia following complications of the bowel surgery. The mesenteric thrombosis thus, whilst not the direct cause of death, necessitated the surgery, the complications of which resulted in eventual death.

Table 4.6

Late deaths, counted in Chapter 15, from pulmonary embolism, potentially pregnancy related; United Kingdom 1991-93		
Weeks postpartum	Delivery	Features
7	SVD	Premature labour.
8	C/S	Cerebral infarct on day 10. Immobile at home. 2 days prior to death deep vein thrombosis diagnosed and commenced on heparin.
12	SVD	Postpartum haemorrhage, transfused - suddenly collapsed at home three months later.
12	SVD	Obese, postpartum haemorrhage, transfused.
13	SVD	Obese. Seen in A&E with chest pain. Discharged. Readmitted ? urinary tract infection. Discharged and died 2 weeks later.

C/S - Caesarean section
SVD - Spontaneous Vertex Delivery

Substandard care

Care was considered substandard to varying degrees in 5 cases of pulmonary thromboembolism, 3 antenatal and 2 postpartum cases.

Amongst the antenatal deaths:

A young woman was undergoing inpatient treatment for an unrelated medical condition requiring bed rest for some 4 weeks. She complained of breathlessness and chest pain two days before collapse. She underwent a prostaglandin induced midtrimester termination for a dead fetus with evacuation of the uterus the day before collapsing. She was then treated in an ICU for 2 weeks, but her condition deteriorated and she died. Autopsy revealed pulmonary emboli deemed to be at least 2 weeks old. She had not had a diagnosis made antemortem.

This case highlights the fact that any pregnant patient on prolonged bed rest is at increased risk of thromboembolism and this diagnosis should be amongst the possibilities considered in anyone who suddenly collapses.

> A previously fit young woman, just entering the third trimester, called out her GP because of chest pain. She was apyrexial but was told she had flu. Two days later she died following a massive pulmonary embolism.

If this patient's symptoms had been investigated more fully a diagnosis might have been possible before the major pulmonary embolism occurred.

> An older patient was in the gynaecology ward being investigated for hypertension and an impacted gravid uterus with fibroids. An unsuccessful attempt was made under general anaesthesia to correct the uterine position. An ultrasound scan of the pelvis several days prior to death had reportedly shown reduced flow in the pelvic vessels. Three days later she died from embolism from pelvic vein thrombosis.

In this case there was delay in attempting to disimpact the uterus and failure to take cognisance of the ultrasound report which indicated an increased risk of pelvic vein thrombosis from compression of the vessels by a pelvic mass.

Caesarean section has been identified in the past to increase the risk of pulmonary embolism, particularly in the presence of other risk factors.

> A woman was booked for elective Caesarean section. She had a past history of retinal vein thrombosis and had been treated antenatally with low dose aspirin. She was given prophylaxis with subcutaneous heparin, but only for 3 days. She was readmitted 11 days after Caesarean section, collapsed and died from pulmonary embolism.

It could be argued that in such a case more prolonged prophylaxis should have been instituted with a recognised increased risk factor of past history of thrombosis.

> An older patient underwent elective Caesarean section for a breech presentation. Some 9 days post operatively she had a cerebral infarct. Because of lower limb paralysis she remained relatively immobile during the ensuing weeks but was discharged home. Several general practitioners saw her in the few days prior to readmission with chest symptoms, shortness of breath and pain, which were treated as infection. Two days following readmission for treatment of a DVT she died from pulmonary embolism.

Patients who have paralysed lower limbs or marked restriction of mobility are particularly at risk of thromboembolism following surgery and during pregnancy and appropriate thromboprophylaxis should be instituted.

Cerebral thrombosis

There were five cases of cerebral thrombosis, all of which occurred postpartum. Four cases occurred in women who had been delivered by Caesarean section. The onset of the problems were between 8 and 17 days post delivery and the cases are summarised in Table 4.7. There appears to be no identifying risk factors in these cases other than delivery by Caesarean section to enable prediction of these uncommon thromboses. The fifth case followed spontaneous delivery. No autopsy was performed

Table 4.7

Postpartum cerebral thrombosis; United Kingdom 1991-93		
Day following delivery	**Type of Delivery**	**Summary**
8	C/S	C/S at 31 weeks for pregnancy induced hypertension. Readmitted 2 days after discharge with cerebral venous thrombosis.
10	C/S	Developed cerebrovascular accident 10 days following C/S. Died on the 35th day following C/S.
17	C/S	Obese patient discharged home on 8th day post C/S but readmitted with headache and vomiting on 17th day. Cerebral venous thrombosis diagnosed, died next day.
17	C/S	Discharged home 5 days after C/S. Readmitted on 17th day with headaches. Sagittal sinus thrombosis diagnosed, died 2 days later.
3	Spont	Sudden collapse. Died same day in I.C.U.

C/S - Caesarean section

Comments

As in previous Reports thrombosis and thromboembolism has again been found to be a major cause of maternal death in the United Kingdom. Some deaths occurred without prior warning and in patients with no apparent risk factors and were thus difficult to prevent. However a significant number of patients had been seen with symptoms of breathlessness or chest pain, often treated as respiratory infection, in the day or two before the pulmonary embolism occurred. In the majority of instances the presence of a deep vein thrombosis had not been detected before embolism occurred.

It is recommended that close attention is paid to any woman with chest symptoms who is currently pregnant or recently delivered, to exclude the presence of deep vein thrombosis or potential small pulmonary embolism.

In antenatal patients no relationship between parity or gestation emerged, but the incidence is higher in older women.

Clinicians are advised to be particularly vigilant of pregnant women admitted and on prolonged bed rest whilst undergoing investigation or treatment. The use of compression stockings in such patients should be considered particularly if other risk factors such as age, smoking or obesity exist.

Caesarean section and prophylaxis against thromboembolism

Caesarean section is clearly a risk factor for development of venous thrombosis and hence risk of pulmonary embolism.

This has been identified in previous Reports. The value of prophylaxis against thrombo-embolism has been raised in the review of deaths following surgery conducted by the National Confidential Enquiry into Perioperative Deaths (NCEPOD) 1995. This report highlighted the need to extend the use of prophylaxis within gynaecological surgery.

Prompted by the NCEPOD report and the Confidential Enquiries into Maternal Deaths Report (1988-1990), published in 1994, the Royal College of Obstetricians and Gynaecologists set up a Working Party to review these issues. The working party reported, along with it's recommendations, in March 1995. It was recommended that patients undergoing Caesarean section be categorised into low, medium or high risk as shown in the Annexe to this chapter. Various methods of prophylaxis were reviewed which could be used. Subcutaneous heparin (unfractionated or low molecular weight) may well be the method of choice in many patients undergoing Caesarean section. Appropriate dosage, monitoring if used longer than 5 days and commencement prior to surgery are important in achieving the desired effect of reducing the incidence of deep venous thrombosis. The available data from general surgery indicates the need to administer regimens for 5 days, or longer if the patient is not fully mobilised.

We can only await the outcome of later triennial Reports to establish whether such prophylactic measures help to reduce the incidence of deaths from thromboembolism following Caesarean sections which have shown no sign of reduction in the last decade.

ANNEXE TO CHAPTER 4

Prophylaxis against thromboembolism in Caesarean section

The following recommendations, taken from the RCOG Working Party Report on Prophylaxis against Thromboembolism, are of relevance to patients requiring Caesarean section.

A risk assessment of all patients undergoing elective or emergency Caesarean section should be performed and prophylaxis instituted as appropriate. See box below.

Risk Assessment Profile for Thromboembolism in Caesarean Section

LOW RISK - Early mobilisation and hydration
Elective Caesarean section - uncomplicated pregnancy and no other risk factors

MODERATE RISK - Consider one of a variety of prophylactic measures

- Age >35 years

- Obesity (>80 kg)

- Para 4 or more

- Gross varicose veins

- Current infection

- Pre-eclampsia

- Immobility prior to surgery (>4 days)

- Major current illness, eg heart or lung disease, cancer, in flammatory bowel disease, nephrotic syndrome

- Emergency Caesarean section in labour

HIGH RISK - Heparin prophylaxis +/- leg stockings

- A patient with three or more moderate risk factors from above

- Extended major pelvic or abdominal surgery, eg Caesarean hysterectomy

- Patients with a personal or family history of deep vein thrombosis, pulmonary embolism or thrombophilia; paralysis of lower limbs

- Patients with antiphospholipid antibody (cardiolipin antibody or lupus anti-coagulant)

Management of different risk groups

Low risk patients

Patients undergoing elective Caesarean section with uncomplicated pregnancy and no other risk factors require only early mobilisation and attention to hydration.

Moderate risk patients

Patients assessed as of moderate risk should receive subcutaneous heparin (doses are higher during pregnancy but not following Caesarean section) or mechanical methods. Dextran 70 is not recommended until **after** delivery of the fetus and is probably best avoided in pregnant women.

High risk patients

Patients assessed at high risk should receive heparin prophylaxis and, in addition leg stockings are beneficial.

Prophylaxis until the 5th postoperative day is advised (or until fully mobilised if longer).

The use of subcutaneous heparin as prophylaxis in patients with an epidural or spinal block remains contentious. Current evidence from general and orthopaedic surgery does not point to an increased risk of spinal haematoma. (Berquist et al 1992, Wildsmith and McClure 1991).

Prophylaxis against Thromboembolism in Pregnancy

The RCOG Working Party also made recommendations for prophylaxis against thromboembolism in pregnancy, which are summarised in the box below.

Prophylaxis against Thromboembolism in Pregnancy

Patients with a previous history of venous thromboembolism in pregnancy or the puerperium and no other thrombotic risk factor should receive thromboprophylaxis for up to 6 weeks post partum (subcutaneous heparin and then oral warfarin if desired).

Patients at higher risk, eg those having had multiple episodes of thromboembolism, may require heparin throughout the pregnancy.

References

Bergqvist D, Linblad B, Matzsch T . Low molecular weight heparin for thromboprophylaxis and epidural/spinal anaesthesia - is there a risk? *Acta Anaesthesiol Scand* 1992; **36**: 605-9.

Wildsmith J A W, McClure J. Anticoagulant drugs and central nerve blockade. *Anaesthesia* 1991; **46:** 613-4.

Report on Confidential Enquiries into Maternal Deaths in the United Kingdom 1988-1990. London; HMSO 1994.

Report of the National Confidential Enquiry into Perioperative Deaths 1991/2. London: HMSO 1993.

CHAPTER 5

Amniotic fluid embolism

Summary

There were ten deaths due to amniotic fluid embolism in the United Kingdom in 1991-93 compared with eleven in 1988-90 and nine in 1985-87. All the women were aged over 25, but none was of high parity. Induction or augmentation of labour has been thought to be a risk factor for amniotic fluid embolism but in this triennium only one case was associated with induced labour and only two with augmented labour. In three cases maternal collapse occurred during spontaneous labour which had not been augmented. Research into the pathophysiology of this condition is required.

Ten *Direct* deaths were attributed to amniotic fluid embolism (AFE) and classified under ICD(9) 673.1. In eight cases the diagnosis was confirmed by the finding of squames or hair in the lungs on histological examination. The other two were deaths in which a clinical diagnosis of AFE was made without confirmation of the diagnosis at autopsy. The clinical features of these cases are shown in Table 5.1.

The acceptance of these cases marks an important change for this Report in the diagnostic criteria for AFE. Previous Reports have accepted only deaths where autopsy provided histological evidence of squames in the lungs. The clinical basis of the diagnosis in the two additional cases was as follows:

> A woman aged under 30 with a previous normal pregnancy underwent serum screening for Down's syndrome followed by amniocentesis, with a normal result. She developed polyhydramnios and went into preterm labour before 28 weeks gestation, for which she received ritodrine, dexamethasone and insulin for raised blood sugar. Labour continued and Caesarean section was performed because of a transverse lie. Within 20 minutes of the operation she was noted to be bleeding from the abdominal wound. Disseminated intravascular coagulation (DIC) was diagnosed and postpartum haemorrhage developed. It was controlled by hysterectomy, during which high airway pressure was noted along with suffusion of the face and neck, central cyanosis and pulmonary oedema. She died five days later in the intensive care unit (ICU). Careful histological examination of the lungs showed no squames.

The second case is summarised later in this chapter, under the heading "Substandard care".

Table 5.1

Clinical features of deaths from amniotic fluid embolism ; United Kingdom 1991-93

Parity	Antepartum complications	Labour		Intrapartum complications	Mode of delivery	Baby	Postpartum complications
		Induced	Augmented				
Histologically confirmed							
0	Multiple pregnancy	Spon	No		Spon	Live	PPH
1+0	None	Spon	No	Collapse	CS	Live	
2+0	None	PGX2		Collapse	VE	NND	DIC/ARDS
3+1	Multiple pregnancy	Spon	No	Collapse	CS	NND	
0	APH, praevia	CS before labour			CS	Live	DIC
1+0	RTA collapse	CS before labour			CS	SB	
2+3	Amniocentesis	Spon	ARM	Fetal distress / cyanosis	CS	Live	DIC
0+1	None	Spon	Synt	Collapse	CS	Live	DIC/ARDS
Clinical diagnosis							
1+1	Amniocentesis Polyhydramnios	Spon preterm	No	Convulsion	CS	Live	DIC
3+0	Obesity (120 Kg)	Spon	No		FD	NND	PPH

APH = antepartum haemorrhage ARM = artificial rupture of the membranes CS = Caesarean section
DIC = disseminated intravascular coagulation FD = forceps delivery NND = neonatal death PG = prostaglandins for induction or augmentation of labour
PPH = postpartum haemorrhage Synt = intravenous infusion of syntocinon (oxytocin) VE = vacuum extraction

62

A further case suggestive of AFE is mentioned here but counted in Chapter 8.

> A woman aged over 35 who had one previous delivery had labour induced with prostaglandins because of postmaturity. The labour was subsequently augmented with oxytocin and fetal distress developed, requiring a forceps delivery. The patient collapsed very quickly afterwards; postpartum haemorrhage occurred and the patient died despite hysterectomy. Autopsy revealed a tear in the lower uterine segment. The speed of collapse suggested AFE but the case is counted in Chapter 8.

In the opinion of the assessors, having reviewed all available evidence, the diagnosis of AFE was a distinct possibility in all these cases.

Age

Table 5.2 shows the age groups of the women with proven amniotic fluid embolism for 1985-93 inclusive. The risk of this condition increases with age. In the present triennium as in 1988-90, no case of amniotic fluid embolism occurred in a woman under the age of 25.

Table 5.2

All maternal deaths with amniotic fluid embolism present by age and estimated rates per million maternities; United Kingdom 1991-93			
Age	**Number**	**Maternities (x000)**	**Rate/million maternities**
Under 25	0	714,9	0.0
25-29	4	819,8	4.9
30-34	4	558,4	7.2
35-39	2	188,0	10.6
40+	0	34,0	0.0
All ages	**10**	**2,315.2**	**4.3**

Parity

As in 1988-90, no association was seen between amniotic fluid embolism and high parity. Three patients had never had a previous pregnancy proceeding beyond 24 weeks, three had one previous delivery, two had two previous term pregnancies and a further two had three.

Ethnic origin

Three of the ten *Direct* deaths were in women of Afro-Caribbean or Asian origin, as was one of the two deaths in which AFE occurred but which are counted in other chapters.

The role of induction or augmentation of labour

Table 5.1 shows the number of cases in which prostaglandin or oxytocin had been given. Of the ten patients counted in this chapter, two had undergone Caesarean section before the onset of labour. Only one of the remaining eight had labour induced, with prostaglandin pessaries. Only two of the seven patients who went into labour spontaneously had labour augmented: one received an intravenous infusion of oxytocin, the other had artificial rupture of the membranes.

Mode of delivery

Only one of the patients had a normal delivery. Seven were delivered by Caesarean section, one by vacuum extraction and one by forceps. In six cases the indication for operative delivery was maternal collapse (or, in one case, maternal convulsion) which was presumably the first sign of amniotic fluid embolism. In one of these cases maternal collapse occurred before labour (after a road traffic accident) and in the other five cases collapse or convulsion occurred during labour.

In one case the indication for operative delivery was fetal distress associated with maternal cyanosis, again, presumably the first sign of amniotic fluid embolism. In one case Caesarean section was performed because of preterm labour. This patient had undergone amniocentesis and had subsequently developed polyhydramnios. In the remaining case postpartum haemorrhage occurred after spontaneous delivery of twins conceived after fertility treatment.

Speed of collapse

In four cases the mother collapsed before delivery. In another four cases maternal collapse occurred between 20 and 45 minutes after delivery. In one case maternal cyanosis was noted before delivery but collapse occurred immediately after delivery. In the remaining case an atonic postpartum haemorrhage of four litres occurred within an hour of delivery. Hysterectomy was carried out but death occurred within seven hours of delivery.

With regard to the interval between delivery and death, patients fell into two equal groups. One group comprised five cases in which death occurred within seven hours of delivery: this group included two cases in which postpartum haemorrhage led rapidly to death and three in which attempts at resuscitation were started before and abandoned soon after delivery. In the other group of five cases, resuscitation was successful enough to allow transfer to an ICU. In these cases the interval between delivery and death was between 2 and 14 days.

In three of the cases admitted to an ICU the interval between delivery and death was 12 days or more. In all of these the diagnosis of AFE was confirmed histologically, in one case by the identification of squames and in the other two by the identification of hair. The clinical picture in ICU was of difficult ventilation, complicated in one case by sepsis.

Pathology

All cases came to autopsy and in eight cases the diagnosis was confirmed by histological examination of the lungs. The presence of fetal squames was taken to confirm the diagnosis although it was not always clear whether special staining had been done. The two cases in which histological examination of the lungs did not confirm the diagnosis are summarised elsewhere in this Chapter.

Substandard care

In two cases there were elements of substandard care. Amniotic fluid embolism is a condition with a high mortality, and treatment, however rapid and efficient, is often unsuccessful. The clinical and administrative deficiencies revealed in these two cases may not have affected the outcome but nevertheless attention is drawn to them.

> A patient with sickle-cell trait, who weighed over 80kg, was admitted in spontaneous labour at term. Epidural analgesia was established by an anaesthetist SHO; the patient became hypotensive and this was corrected with Haemaccel. Fetal distress developed and whilst the patient was being positioned for forceps delivery she complained of difficulty in breathing. She became cyanosed and regurgitated gastric contents and cardiac arrest occurred. Cardiopulmonary resuscitation was started and although an endotracheal tube was correctly placed ventilation proved to be extremely difficult. The anaesthetic registrar attended and a Caesarean section was carried out. It became clear that the woman had suffered brain damage and she died twelve days later in the intensive care unit. Autopsy showed squames in the lungs.

Senior staff should have been involved at an earlier stage. There is no record of consultant involvement in the delivery.

> A woman weighing over 100kg, who had previous normal pregnancies, went into spontaneous labour at term. Artificial rupture of the membranes was carried out. During the second stage of labour she had a fit and a forceps delivery was carried out quickly. Postpartum haemorrhage occurred after 45 minutes, associated with DIC. Haemaccel was infused but the patient became severely hypotensive. Blood transfusion was started two hours after delivery but cardiac arrest occurred. Resuscitation was abandoned three hours after delivery. The autopsy was inadequate and there is no report on histological examination of the lungs.

In this case the facilities were inadequate, with the obstetric unit being several miles away from the nearest intensive care unit.

Comment

The number of maternal deaths from amniotic fluid embolism in England and Wales has fallen only slightly over the last twenty years. The total of ten deaths in the UK in the present triennium is similar to the totals of nine in 1985-7, and eleven in 1988-90 and comprise approximately 10% of *Direct* maternal deaths.

Successive Reports have drawn attention to apparent risk factors for AFE but only one of these, maternal age over 25, has been consistently present from triennium to triennium. As in the previous Report, none of the women in 1991-93 was of high parity.

Strong uterine contractions have been thought to be a risk factor for AFE and previous Reports have drawn attention to the use of oxytocic agents to induce or augment labour. However in the present triennium only one patient had labour induced, one had labour augmented with oxytocin and one had the membranes artificially ruptured. By contrast, in three cases maternal collapse or convulsion occurred in a spontaneous labour which had not been augmented. In none of these three cases had labour been noted to be rapid.

The clinical presentation of AFE is that of sudden collapse, followed rapidly by cyanosis and then by the development of coagulopathy and bleeding. A clinical diagnosis of AFE can now be accepted if these features are present and no other explanation can be found.

Of the two cases which this Report has accepted on clinical grounds, one presented in this way. In the other case, which was associated with Caesarean section, cyanosis followed the development of coagulopathy but the presence of high airway pressure supported the diagnosis.

The change of definition of AFE in this Report to include cases in which the diagnosis was not histologically confirmed may give a more complete picture of the incidence of the condition. However, there is a danger in accepting this diagnosis on clinical grounds alone because, since AFE is known to be associated with a poor prognosis, such a diagnosis may be used to excuse a poor outcome in a case which might have been more effectively treated. On the other hand, insistence on too rigid criteria for inclusion in this chapter might lead to misclassification of some cases. On balance the new approach is considered to be more helpful and will be continued in further Reports.

Nevertheless, the recommendation in previous Reports is repeated here, that women dying after labour of causes other than suspected amniotic fluid embolism should have their lungs examined for amniotic squames to check whether amniotic fluid can enter the circulation without a fatal outcome.

Because the definition of AFE used up till now has depended on autopsy findings it is not known how many women have been successfully resuscitated after amniotic fluid embolism. The 1988-90 Report recommended that if postpartum haemorrhage occurs in an older woman in whom labour had been induced, consultant staff should be promptly involved in the management and the patient should be rapidly transferred to an intensive care unit. Although the significance of induction of labour is now questioned, the importance of consultant involvement and rapid transfer is reiterated.

At first sight it is disheartening that the number of deaths from AFE has not fallen since 1985. However, in 1991-3, for the first time, more than 50% of the cases survived long enough for transfer to an ICU. Previous Reports have focused on identifying risk factors with a view to preventing AFE, but this approach has not proved useful. Attention should now be paid to improving our understanding of the pathophysiology of the condition with a view to improving treatment. Identification and reporting of suspected cases which have survived could be helpful in identifying successful treatment protocols.

CHAPTER 6

Early pregnancy deaths

Summary

As in previous Reports all deaths from ectopic pregnancy and abortions have been considered under the title Early Pregnancy Deaths, defined for the purposes of this Report as deaths up to 20 weeks gestation. Eighteen such deaths, all classified as *Direct*, are counted in this Chapter, compared with 35 in the previous triennium. Of these 8 were due to ectopic gestation (compared with 15 in the previous Report) and 5 deaths followed legal and 3 followed spontaneous abortion (compared with 14 in 1988-1990). Evidence of substandard care was found in all cases except for one woman who died following a spontaneous abortion and another who died of *Clostridium Welchi* infection following a legal abortion. Two other deaths which occurred before 20 weeks gestation are also included in this chapter, one from ovarian hyper-stimulation syndrome, the other following apparent spontaneous uterine rupture.

Apart from the 18 deaths counted in this chapter there were 8 other deaths occurring in connection with early pregnancy which are counted in other chapters. These are: Chapter 4 (3 cases), Chapter 12 (2 cases) and one case each in Chapters 3, 9, and 10.

As in previous Reports, deaths from ectopic pregnancy and deaths from abortion are considered separately. Deaths from abortion are divided into deaths following spontaneous abortion and deaths following legal abortion.

Ectopic pregnancy

There were nine reported ectopic pregnancy deaths in this triennium representing 4.2% of all *Direct* and *Indirect* deaths. Of these deaths, eight were directly due to the rupture of the ectopic pregnancy and are counted in this chapter. This compares with 15 deaths for the previous triennium. One woman who died from acute respiratory distress syndrome (ARDS) following operation was assessed as an anaesthetic death and her case is counted in Chapter 9.

Table 6.1 shows deaths from ectopic pregnancies and rates per 1000 estimated ectopic pregnancies. The figures for 1991-93 include all UK countries, but similar data was not available in the last triennium for Scotland and Northern Ireland. Data produced in earlier reports is no longer comparable as it was based on a 10% sample of hospital admissions, not all hospital admissions as currently available.

Table 6.1

	Deaths from ectopic pregnancies and rates per 1000 estimated pregnancies; England and Wales 1988-1990 and United Kingdom 1991-93				
	Total estimated pregnancies in thousands	Total estimated ectopic pregnancies	Ectopic pregnancies per 1,000 pregnancies	Deaths from ectopic pregnancies	Death rate per 1,000 estimated ectopic pregnancies
England and Wales					
1988-90	2886.9	27,750	9.6	15	0.5
United Kingdom					
1991-93	3137.4	30,160	9.6	9*	0.3

* One death from anaesthesia

Sources: 1982-90 England HIPE/Hospital Episode Statistics (HES)
Wales Hospital Activity Analysis (HAA)
1991-93 England HES, Wales HAA
Scottish Morbidity Records (SMR) 1 Inpatients and Daycases Acute
Scottish Morbidity Records (SMR) 2 Inpatients and Daycase Maternity
DHSS Northern Ireland

Substandard Care

Of the 8 counted cases of deaths from ectopic pregnancy, all were considered to be associated with substandard care. These are described in detail.

Patient responsibility

In one case the patient was considered to have contributed to the outcome. Nevertheless clinical responsibility also played a part.

> A primigravida in her thirties was a frequent attender at the GP's surgery complaining of abdominal pains. On this occasion she attended the surgery on a routine appointment, but gave no history of abdominal pain or of amenorrhoea. Two days later she telephoned the GP on duty and described intermittent abdominal pains with vomiting and diarrhoea but no other symptoms. The GP provided advice but did not visit. The patient's partner claimed that a further telephone call was made to the surgery that evening but there was no record of this. The patient was found dead at home next day and at autopsy a ruptured ectopic pregnancy with massive haemorrhage was found.

The substandard care in this case was considered doubtful. The case also illustrates the need for GP surgeries to have unequivocal arrangements for patients to obtain a doctor's assistance out of hours.

Clinical responsibility

In seven cases there were features of substandard care in clinical management.

> A grande multipara in her twenties was admitted under the care of the surgeons with a history of lower abdominal pain. A provisional diagnosis of ectopic pregnancy was made and she was transferred to the care of the gynaecologists. A diagnostic laparoscopy was performed by a senior registrar with some experience of laparoscopic surgery, although not as applied to ectopic pregnancies. An ectopic pregnancy was confirmed and an attempt made to remove it via the laparoscope. Problems were encountered, the procedure became prolonged and the patient suddenly collapsed. She died during the laparotomy which followed. Gas embolism was considered to be the cause of collapse and of the fatal outcome, although it was not possible to confirm it at autopsy. No senior experienced surgeon was informed that the procedure was being undertaken or when difficulties arose.

The substandard element in this case is the not uncommon situation of a junior surgeon undertaking a procedure for which he or she has no or inadequate experience and persisting with the procedure in spite of difficulties without informing a senior colleague.

Three cases involved failure of diagnosis by GPs.

> A woman with a history of abdominal pain, vomiting, fainting and a short period of amenorrhoea was attended by a deputising doctor who diagnosed gastroenteritis. Five hours later she collapsed and was taken to hospital by emergency ambulance. She was severely shocked and died in the intensive care unit (ICU) after laparotomy and salpingo-oophorectomy. Massive haemorrhage was found at laparotomy.

The history of ectopic pregnancy in this case was classical but the doctor who first saw her did not seem to consider the diagnosis.

> A woman in her thirties with a history of 8 weeks amenorrhoea, bleeding and abdominal pain was seen by a deputising doctor. Examination revealed tenderness in the left iliac fossa and a diagnosis of "colonic colic" was made. The next day she was admitted to the Accident and Emergency (A&E) department in a state of profound shock and attempts to resuscitate her failed. At autopsy no actual ectopic was found and only a 1.5 cm corpus luteum cyst which had bled was identified. It was felt, however, that ectopic pregnancy was the likeliest diagnosis, the specimen having got lost in the massive haemorrhage.

This case, in spite of an unsatisfactory autopsy raising doubt over the diagnosis, nevertheless again demonstrates the dangers of ignoring a significant history and clinical signs which, if identified would have lead to earlier hospital admission and investigation.

> A woman in her late twenties had 8 weeks amenorrhoea. She had been seen by two GPs at 5 and 6 weeks of amenorrhoea with slight bleeding and persistent lower abdominal pain. The night before her admission to hospital a third GP saw her, again complaining of abdominal pain, diarrhoea and vomiting. Gastroenteritis was diagnosed. The following morning she collapsed, was resuscitated by the ambulance crew and taken to hospital. At laparotomy massive haemorrhage from a ruptured ectopic pregnancy was found and she died shortly afterwards in the ICU.

These three cases demonstrate clearly the need for primary care doctors, especially those working for deputising services, to be aware of the diagnosis of ectopic pregnancy. A suggestive history in a woman of reproductive age must lead to earlier admission to hospital where the final diagnosis can be made and acted upon.

The remaining three cases demonstrate different aspects of management which were considered to be substandard.

> A gravida 2 with a history of pelvic inflammatory disease and with about 10 weeks amenorrhoea was seen and examined in the antenatal clinic by a consultant. An ultrasound scan performed by the consultant obstetrician revealed a 10 week fetus "within the pelvis" but it was not clear whether it was intra- or extrauterine. No further action

was taken, presumably because the woman was asymptomatic at the time. Some days later she collapsed and died in the ambulance on her way to hospital. Massive haemorrhage from a ruptured ectopic pregnancy was found at autopsy.

The doubtful substandard care here lies in an equivocal scan finding from a possibly substandard portable machine. It is emphasised that in such situations repeat scanning should be carried out using adequate equipment and a further opinion obtained in cases of doubt.

> A grande multipara in her thirties was admitted to an A&E department as an emergency with a history of abdominal pain and was shocked. She was not seen by the casualty officer until 75 minutes later and during examination cardiac arrest occurred. Resuscitation was successful and when laparotomy was carried out a ruptured ectopic pregnancy was found. The consultant was not informed by the registrar until the patient was transferred to the ICU. The next day a second laparotomy was performed because of secondary bleeding. Disseminated intravascular coagulopathy (DIC) developed and the patient subsequently died. At autopsy cerebral necrosis secondary to massive haemorrhage was found.

On arrival at A&E the patient was first seen by a nurse who failed to recognise the severity of her condition. This case raises the question of the efficiency of the triage system in A&E departments. It also raises yet again the problem of failure by junior staff to involve senior consultant assistance at an early stage in the management of seriously ill patients.

The third case demonstrates a managerial problem involving split sites.

> A woman in her twenties was admitted as an emergency to the A&E department with severe abdominal pain. The A&E department was in a general hospital and when the diagnosis of ectopic pregnancy was suspected she was transferred to the gynaecological hospital where she arrived in a state of collapse. Immediate laparotomy took place and massive haemorrhage from a tubal pregnancy was found. There was some delay in receiving cross matched blood. Two hours after surgery the patient collapsed and required a further laparotomy for secondary bleeding. There was no ICU in the hospital and she had to be transferred back to the general hospital, where she died next day.

Isolated obstetric and gynaecological units without intensive care facilities continue to exist in spite of repeated highlighting of the risks. Other aspects of management in this case, especially the delay in transfusion, confusion of information from one hospital to another and the need for transfer, on more than one occasion, of a very ill patient are all, directly or indirectly, related to the difficulties of split sites.

Comments

Ectopic pregnancy continues to be an important cause of maternal deaths and the need for early diagnosis is paramount. Awareness of the possibility of an ectopic pregnancy in any woman of reproductive age is essential and the emphasis is again placed on the importance of the history in the diagnosis as well as suggestive signs on examination. Primary care doctors in particular must be constantly aware of the possibility of this diagnosis.

When a woman presents either to her GP or to an A&E Department with unexplained abdominal pain, with or without vaginal bleeding, every means available must be used to exclude an ectopic pregnancy. The ready availability of sensitive ß-hCG kits for the detection of early pregnancy means that the diagnosis of pregnancy can be made in GPs surgeries or A & E Departments. If the diagnosis of ectopic pregnancy is likely then vaginal examination is best deferred until the patient is in hospital.

Ultrasound scanning, and specifically transvaginal scanning, revealing an empty uterine cavity in the present of a positive pregnancy test in a woman with even vague symptoms should lead to early laparoscopy which remains the cornerstone of diagnosis. Ultrasound scans must be carried out by an experienced sonographer and high resolution equipment used.

The Royal Colleges of Radiologists and Obstetricians and Gynaecologists recent guidance on Ultrasound procedures for Early Pregnancy (1995) are helpful and relevant sections are reproduced below:-

Extracts from the RCOG/RCR Guidelines for Ultrasound Screening in Early Pregnancy

"A special clinic, usually operating for five days a week, should be established for early pregnancy and gynaecological emergencies. GPs should be able to refer patients to such a clinic on a daily basis. The clinic should be staffed appropriately. Facilities for same day ß-human chorionic gonadotrophin (ß-HCG) testing should be available in the clinic. Immediate admission for surgery should be possible for patients with unequivocal diagnosis of fetal loss or with acute conditions such as ectopic pregnancy.

Protocols should be defined for dealing with emergency cases of complications of early pregnancy which present outside the normal working day, and it is essential that those personnel who provide the "on call" service in obstetric ultrasound are appropriately trained."

The management of the collapsed patient bleeding from a ruptured ectopic pregnancy must be swift and expertly carried out. Team work is essential and gynaecologist, anaesthetist and haemalogist should all be involved. In every case an adequately experienced doctor must be in charge, and senior consultant colleagues informed at an early stage. There is no place for the inexperienced doctor in the care of such patients. The availability and early use of ICU facilities are essential in these cases.

Abortion

In this section deaths related to both spontaneous and legal abortions are considered. This is the fourth Report in which no identified deaths from illegal abortion are reported. It is disappointing to record five deaths from legal termination in this triennium, one more than the previous triennium. Table 6.2 contains data on abortion deaths for the United Kingdom since 1985. "Estimated pregnancies" includes conception data discussed in Chapter 1; this was not available for Scotland or Northern Ireland for 1985-90

Table 6.2

	Direct abortion deaths by type of abortion per million maternities and rates per million estimated pregnancies; United Kingdom 1985-93					
	Spontaneous	Legal	Illegal	Total	Rate per million maternities	Rate per million estimated pregnancies
1985-87	5[1]	1[2]	0	6	2.7	N/A
1988-90	6	3	0	9	4.0	N/A
1991-93	3	5	0	8	3.5	2.5

[1] Includes one death from missed abortion.

[2] Does not include one unexplained death associated with legal abortion.

Spontaneous abortion

Three women died in association with spontaneous abortion. These are reported in detail.

> A woman in her first pregnancy suffered from severe Von Willebrand's disease. She was first seen by the consultant in the antenatal clinic at the end of the first trimester. Two weeks later she was admitted with an inevitable abortion. At that time she was pyrexial, but this finding was not followed up immediately. She was given Factor VIII on the advice of the haematologist but continued to bleed and an evacuation of the uterus was carried out. Blood transfusion because her Hb concentration was 9.4g/dl was begun and Augmentin was given empirically, her temperature having risen again. Following operation she suffered a cardiac arrest from which she was initially resuscitated, but DIC developed and severe haemorrhage resulted including haematemesis. In spite of further attempts at resuscitation, including clotting factor administration, she died.

This case was complicated by the medical condition which meant that concern was concentrated on the bleeding and inadequate attention was paid to the fact that infection was present. No blood cultures were done and inadequate antibiotic therapy was given in a case which was almost certainly septicaemic shock. In her management the advice and help of the anaesthetist was sought late and no help was obtained from a physician or haematologist. In such complex seriously ill patients the need for team work in management is again stressed.

> A woman in her thirties had a normal antenatal course until 19 weeks when spontaneous rupture of the membranes occurred. The option of termination of pregnancy was offered, but in the absence of infection she wished to continue with the pregnancy. Two days later, she became pyrexial and rigors developed in spite of prophylactic antibiotics. An oxytocin infusion had begun and delivery of the fetus took place about 8 hours thereafter. The placenta was retained and formal evacuation had to be carried out later. In the meantime DIC and renal failure developed and she became profoundly shocked. Transfer to the ICU was arranged and full invasive resuscitative measures initiated. There was therefore considerable delay (12 hours) before evacuation of the uterus was carried out. During the operation she was virtually moribund and died shortly after. No autopsy was allowed.

The management of this patient was correct in the initial stages in that in the absence of a pyrexia she was given the choice as to whether the pregnancy be allowed to continue or not. In retrospect this was wrong as it was unlikely that such a conservative policy would be successful and when infection ensued it was severe. Correctly, oxytocin was used but when the placenta was retained urgent emptying of the uterus should have been performed, whereas a prolonged period of time elapsed during which the patient developed multiple fatal complications. The management of sepsis in such cases is discussed in Chapter 7.

> A young primigravida had recurrent episodes of bleeding in early pregnancy. Ultrasound scanning showed the placenta covered the internal os. At approximately 18 weeks gestation a spontaneous abortion occurred with severe haemorrhage. DIC developed and although appropriate treatment was given her condition deteriorated. Laparotomy was performed but she did not recover and died shortly afterwards.

This was an unusual outcome to a spontaneous abortion even where severe bleeding occurs. It was considered that there was no evidence of substandard care.

Two other cases of spontaneous abortion are mentioned in this chapter although they are counted elsewhere. One patient, counted in Chapter 4, who suffered from a long standing medical condition aborted at 15 weeks and required evacuation of the uterus. Following this she developed ARDS, had a pulmonary embolus and died in the ICU. The other patient, counted in Chapter 10, developed Wernicke's encephalopathy following severe hyperemesis gravidarum. There was intrauterine fetal death and extra amniotic prostaglandin was used to induce abortion. She collapsed and after resuscitation was transferred to the ICU where she later died.

Legal abortion

There were five deaths following termination of pregnancy.

> A multipara in her thirties at 8 weeks gestation had a termination performed by a registrar. Thirty six hours later she was re-admitted with severe abdominal pain and uterine perforation was diagnosed at laparoscopy. Laparotomy was carried out because of bleeding. She was given broad spectrum antibiotics but collapsed after surgery and was transferred to the ICU where she had a cardiac arrest and died. *Beta haemolytic streptococci Group A* were identified and the cause of death was given as endotoxic shock.

The operation of termination of pregnancy must not be underestimated and surgeons of appropriate seniority and training must carry out these procedures. An experienced registrar was the operator in this case. Perforation of the uterus is a known complication and if recognised must be adequately managed (laparoscopy proceeding to laparotomy and repair if necessary). To miss or ignore perforation may have fatal consequences, as here. The next case also illustrates this point.

> A multipara in her twenties at 8 weeks gestation had a suction termination of pregnancy performed by a senior house officer (SHO). During the operation the SHO suspected that perforation had occurred. He called the senior registrar who took over the procedure and decided that no perforation was present. Overnight, increasing abdominal pains with signs of peritonitis developed. Laparotomy showed perforation of the uterus and small bowel damage requiring bowel resection. Her condition deteriorated over the next few days and a further laparotomy was carried out because of a suspicion that other unidentified damage might have occurred but this was not found to be the case. Her condition continued to deteriorate in spite of full intensive care and she later died.

The problem in this case lay in the failure of the senior registrar to follow up adequately the concern of the SHO. If laparoscopy had been done at that early stage complications might have been avoided.

> A young woman at 10 weeks gestation had a suction termination of pregnancy carried out by a SHO. The procedure was apparently uneventful and she was discharged from hospital on the same day. Three days later she was re-admitted with septicaemia, having previously seen her GP who failed to appreciate the seriousness of the situation and admit her to hospital earlier. Her condition deteriorated and she died two days later. The autopsy showed adult respiratory distress syndrome, DIC and infection with *bacteriodes melaminogenicus*.

A multiparous woman had a scan revealing a female fetus. At 18 weeks gestation she sought a termination but did not give the true reason for her request. A week later, after Cervagem preparation, a dilatation and evacuation was performed by a registrar supervised by the consultant. Four hours later she had a cardiac arrest. Following resuscitation a laparotomy was carried out where a perforation of the uterus with a large broad ligament haematoma was found. Hysterectomy was performed but the patient never recovered and irreversible brain damage ensued.

Although no substandard care was considered to have occurred in this case it clearly demonstrates the risk of the operation of termination of pregnancy.

A woman in her twenties underwent a mid trimester termination because of fetal abnormalities incompatible with life. Abortion was successfully induced by Cervagem pessaries but was followed, four hours after delivery, by an evacuation of the uterus for a retained placenta. Later the same evening she developed pyrexia and complained of pain in her thigh. There were no obvious clinical signs. The pain worsened and she rapidly developed jaundice and disseminated intravascular coagulation (DIC). She was started on antibiotics. Three hours later a consultant surgeon made a presumptive diagnosis of *Clostridium Welchi* infection but she died shortly afterwards before her leg could be amputated. Autopsy confirmed *Clostridium Welchi* at an injection site.

This is a very unusual case of *Clostridium Welchi* infection, "gas gangrene", from which the patient died less then twelve hours after initially complaining of pain in her thigh. It is considered possible, although not proven, that the injection site was contaminated by faeces as she had suffered faecal incontinence during her termination. At autopsy no infection was found in the uterus or genital tract. Care was not considered to be substandard.

Comments

The need for strict supervision of these cases, the awareness of potential problems, the competence of medical staff and the adequacy of available facilities are all highlighted. In particular since day surgery for these cases is so common, general practitioners should be aware of the later complications. Early therapeutic intervention could avert some of these fatal outcomes.

Other cases

The two remaining cases do not fall into the preceding categories.

Spontaneous uterine rupture

A woman in her late twenties was 20 weeks pregnant. She had one previous normal delivery and one spontaneous miscarriage at 6 weeks. Two days previously she had been admitted to hospital with what was thought to be a urinary tract infection but settled and she was discharged on the following day. On the night of readmission she had more severe abdominal pain and became shocked in spite of intravenous infusion. There were apparently no definite signs of intra-abdominal or intrauterine haemorrhage. She had a cardiac arrest and failed to respond to resuscitation by the emergency team. Autopsy revealed an apparently spontaneous rupture of the fundus of the uterus.

It is possible that this case was one of cornual pregnancy and therefore to be regarded as ectopic. It was a most unusual case and it is considered no substandard care occurred.

The other case is also unusual but demonstrates the need for clear instructions to be given to patients and, in cases where it is possible to check compliance, to follow up the patient.

Ovarian hyper-stimulation syndrome

A nulliparous patient was having treatment for infertility. Prior to in vitro fertilisation (IVF) induction of ovulation with Pergonal was carried out with a resultant very high oestrogen level and a large number of follicles. Three oocytes were collected and transferred in the usual manner. Some days later she became ill with abdominal pain and vomiting but failed at first to contact the hospital or her GP. Ultimately she was admitted to hospital as an emergency with severe ovarian hyper-stimulation syndrome and a positive pregnancy test. In spite of resuscitation measures in the ICU she failed to response and died. At autopsy there were pleural and pericardial effusions with evidence of early implantation within the uterus.

Evidence of hyperstimulation was present from the start and it could be argued that the treatment cycle should have been abandoned.

Comments

Most of the cases in this chapter demonstrate continuing problems which have unfortunately all been highlighted in previous Reports. With ectopic pregnancy the need for awareness of the possible diagnosis is paramount. In all critically ill patients team work is essential and gynaecologist, anaesthetist, pathologist and physician if necessary must all be involved. Again the need for junior staff to turn at an early state to more senior experienced staff is essential. Protocols and guidelines should reiterate this advice. Inexperienced surgeons should not operate without supervision and the availability of a comprehensive ICU on site is vital.

Reference

Royal College of Radiologists, Royal College of Obstetricians and Gynaecologists. *Guidance on Ultrasound Procedures in Early Pregnancy*. Royal Colleges; London: September 1995.

CHAPTER 7

Genital tract sepsis excluding abortion

Summary

There were 15 deaths directly due to genital tract sepsis in this triennium; a similar number to that which occurred in the previous triennium. Nine of the deaths are counted in this chapter and the other six occurred in early pregnancy and are counted in Chapter 6.

Four other cases associated with sepsis but where the underlying cause of death was ascribed to another condition are counted in Chapters 2, 5, 10 and 11 respectively.

The number of *Direct* deaths from sepsis compared with the previous two triennia are shown in Table 7.1.

Table 7.1

Maternal deaths from genital tract sepsis including abortion and ectopic pregnancy with rates per million maternities; United Kingdom 1985-1993							
Triennium	Sepsis after abortion	Sepsis after ectopic pregnancy	Puerperal sepsis*	Sepsis after surgical procedures	Sepsis before or during labour	Total	Rate per million maternities
1985-87	2	1	2	2	2	**9**	4.0
1988-90	7	1	4	5	0	**17**	7.2
1991-93	4	0	4	5	2**	**15**	6.5

Note - This table includes only those deaths directly due to sepsis counted in Chapters 6 and 7.
*   Puerperal sepsis includes deaths following spontaneous vaginal delivery. Deaths following Caesarean section are included in "Sepsis after surgical procedures".
** Two cases counted in Chapter 6.

The nine cases counted in this chapter have been divided into sepsis after surgery and sepsis after vaginal delivery.

Sepsis after surgery

Five women died from genital tract sepsis following Caesarean section. A further four cases, counted in other Chapters, were also associated with delivery by Caesarean section. The details of the five cases are as follows:

A multiparous woman in her twenties died from complications of necrotising fasciitis having been delivered by elective Caesarean section at 33 weeks gestation for placenta praevia. In a previous pregnancy this patient had developed a serious postpartum infection following an intramuscular injection necessitating an excision of necrotic tissue from an abscess site on the buttock. She developed extensive cellulitis of the Caesarean section wound 48 hours after the operation which did not respond to antibiotics. Debridement of the anterior abdominal wall was undertaken on 4 occasions. Despite intensive treatment she continued to deteriorate and died from myocardial necrosis, endocarditis and diffuse alveolar damage. The only organism grown from the wound site was *candida albicans*. An extensive immunological investigation was inconclusive.

An older primigravida with an uncomplicated pregnancy was admitted at 39 weeks gestation in spontaneous labour. Fetal distress was diagnosed and an emergency Caesarean section performed. She subsequently developed a coagulopathy and bled from the abdominal wound. This was followed by renal failure with a probable diagnosis of the HELLP syndrome. Following transfer to the intensive care unit (ICU) she developed necrotising fasciitis of the abdominal wall which did not respond to antibiotic therapy or surgical debridement. She had several laparotomies but finally infarcted the whole of her gut and died a month after the Caesarean section.

Necrotising fasciitis is extremely rare and exceptionally so in relation to Caesarean section; in spite of this two cases have been reported. A similar case was recorded in the last triennial Report.

In a further case, in which only an autopsy report was available to the assessors, a woman developed signs of septicaemia two days after Caesarean section and laparotomy revealed serosanguinous pus in the peritoneal cavity. There had been a history of skin blisters on the abdominal wall during pregnancy. Despite antibiotic treatment her condition continued to deteriorate and she developed disseminated intravascular coagulation (DIC). She was transferred to an ICU but died five days after delivery. No causative organism appears to have been isolated.

A grande multipara had an elective Caesarean section and tubal ligation at 38 weeks gestation. The indication was a twin pregnancy with the first fetus presenting as a footling breech. She had a significant secondary postpartum haemorrhage with evidence of disseminated intravascular coagulation (DIC) on the 7th day after delivery. A total abdominal hysterectomy was performed and a further laparotomy was undertaken within 24 hours to secure haemostasis because of persistent intra-abdominal bleeding and a broad ligament haematoma. She remained in the intensive care unit following this surgery and her initial progress was satisfactory. She then developed evidence of sepsis which did not respond to antibiotic therapy. A further laparotomy was performed because of a suspected pelvic abscess. However, no site of sepsis was identified and her general condition deteriorated. She died from septicaemia some three weeks following the Caesarean section.

A young primigravida was admitted to hospital at 37 weeks gestation with pyrexia and a two day history of herpetic ulcers on the vulva. Spontaneous labour commenced 3 days later and a Caesarean section was performed for fetal distress in the first stage of labour. Shortly after delivery she became drowsy and developed acute renal failure, DIC and severe liver dysfunction. In spite of intensive treatment for systemic herpes infection her condition deteriorated with multiple organ failure and she died 48 hours post partum. An autopsy confirmed hepatic necrosis due to herpes viraemia.

Sepsis after spontaneous delivery

Four women died from sepsis of the genital tract following spontaneous delivery. One of these women had a concealed pregnancy and delivered unattended at home.

A woman was admitted to hospital as an emergency with severe shock, claiming that she had heavy menstrual blood loss for five days. She was uncooperative and denied any possibility of pregnancy. On examination she was found to have an abdominal mass and an ultrasound scan confirmed an enlarged uterus with evidence of retained products of conception. There was evidence of coagulopathy. Despite the patient's continued denial of pregnancy it was concluded that she had septic shock and DIC secondary to retained products of conception. Antibiotic therapy was commenced and she was transferred to theatre for evacuation of retained products. However, she died prior to the operation. An autopsy confirmed that the cause of death was puerperal sepsis. Following this patient's death the police were informed and after a search of her home the body of a newborn baby, together with the placenta, were found in a dustbin. Autopsy of the infant suggested that it had been born alive but died shortly after birth.

This was an extremely difficult clinical problem, exacerbated by the patient's refusal to provide any information about the pregnancy or delivery. This led to a 12 hour delay before the decision was taken to evacuate the retained products of conception. Earlier intervention may have saved her life. However, the failure of cooperation on the part of the patient was clearly the most important factor contributing to her death.

A woman in her late twenties had a previous history of a premature delivery at 25 weeks gestation. In this pregnancy she had a twin gestation and was admitted at 22 weeks with a show. Spontaneous rupture of the membranes occurred 24 hours later and she developed a pyrexia with associated tachycardia 2 days later. Blood and vaginal swabs were negative on culture and she was commenced on antibiotics. The following day she developed generalised abdominal pain and rigors. Labour was induced with syntocinon and she was delivered with forceps of stillborn twins under general anaesthesia. During the operation she developed severe coagulopathy requiring massive blood transfusion. She was transferred to an intensive care unit but, despite intensive treatment, she developed liver and renal failure. She died 2 days post-partum. E. Coli were isolated from placental tissue and from a post-mortem swab of the uterine cavity. The cause of death was E. Coli septicaemia due to chorioamnionitis.

A parous woman had a raised alpha feto protein (AFP) level at 13 weeks gestation and an ultrasonic scan at 17 weeks confirmed that the fetus was abnormal. She was offered termination of the pregnancy but refused. She was admitted to hospital at 28 weeks with spontaneous rupture of the membranes, refused induction, and was treated conservatively without antibiotic cover. Four days later she developed rigors and lower abdominal pain. There was an associated intrauterine death. She was commenced on antibiotics. Induction of labour with prostaglandins was attempted but failed. A clotting screen disclosed a developing coagulopathy and it was decided to deliver the patient by Caesarean section. Prior to the operation the patient "collapsed" but a general anaesthetic was administrated, following which she had a cardiac arrest. Despite intensive resuscitation measures she did not recover. The autopsy confirmed that the cause of death was due to septicaemia from chorioamnionitis. Culture showed a mixed growth of *proteus* and coliform organisms. The stillborn infant had multiple congenital abnormalities.

This fetus was unlikely to survive if it had been born alive and the advice to terminate the pregnancy at 17 weeks was sound but refused by the patient. She should have been fully resuscitated prior to anaesthesia; there was no urgency to perform this operation as the fetus was dead. In addition antibiotics were not started until labour was induced and there may have been inadequate screening for infection.

A parous woman in her late twenties had an uncomplicated pregnancy and was admitted in spontaneous labour at 36 weeks' gestation. She had a forceps delivery for delay in the second stage of labour. Four days post partum she complained of lower abdominal pain and was treated with antibiotics for a presumed pelvic infection. Although her general condition remained well she had further abdominal pain and vaginal discharge 10 days post partum and received a further course of antibiotics; *B. proteus* was cultured from a vaginal swab. She collapsed at home 23 days following delivery and was dead before admission to hospital. An autopsy suggested that death was a result of a gram negative septicaemia.

Comments

These cases demonstrate, once more, that infection must never be underestimated and that it continues to be an important cause of maternal mortality.

It must be pointed out that the onset of infection, particularly after spontaneous rupture of the membranes, can be insidious and can rapidly progress to a fulminating septicaemia. As noted in the previous Report, consensus opinion, which we endorse, appears to be in favour of prophylactic antibiotics for Caesarean section.

When infection develops and the patient is systemically ill, urgent and repeated bacteriological specimens, including blood cultures, must be obtained. The advice of a microbiologist must be sought at an early stage to assist with the use of appropriate antibiotic therapy.

CHAPTER 8

Genital tract trauma

Summary

As in previous Reports, this chapter is concerned with maternal deaths directly due to genital tract trauma including vaginal, cervical and uterine lacerations. There were four such deaths in this triennium compared with three in the previous Report. All were due to uterine rupture. There was evidence of sub-standard care in all of these cases. In addition two further cases of uterine perforation occurred in association with termination of pregnancy and these are discussed and counted in Chapter 6.

Spontaneous uterine rupture

This occurred in three cases. In one case prostaglandins and in another both prostaglandins and syntocinon had been used. In the third case a previous lower segment Caesarean section scar had ruptured.

> A grande multiparous woman was booked for confinement in a General Practitioner maternity unit; her past obstetric history had been uneventful. Labour was induced with prostaglandin pessaries as the pregnancy was post-term. She had a normal vaginal delivery. Approximately one hour later she complained of breathing difficulties and collapsed and failed to respond to resuscitative measures. At autopsy a large quantity of blood was present in the abdominal cavity and there was a rupture on the left side of the lower uterine segment.

This grande multiparous woman should not have been booked for confinement in a GP Unit. In any event, she should have been transferred to a consultant unit when it was decided to induce labour. Although the doctor must assume primary responsibility for these decisions, midwives should not have agreed to supervise the labour under these circumstances. No medical staff were present at the delivery nor were they available in the building when the patient collapsed. It is unclear from the notes who took the decision to use prostaglandin to induce labour in this high parity patient.

> A parous woman in her late thirties was admitted to a consultant unit for induction of labour at 42 weeks gestation. She received prostaglandin pessaries and when labour was established it was augmented with a syntocinon infusion. Because of fetal distress in the second stage of labour a forceps delivery was performed. She collapsed shortly after delivery and a laparotomy and subtotal hysterectomy were performed because of a ruptured uterus. In spite of adequate transfusion she developed severe disseminated intravascular coagulation (DIC), her general condition deteriorated and she died within 24 hours of delivery.

Although there was no evidence of an amniotic fluid embolus at autopsy, it was difficult to explain the cause of this patient's death on the basis of blood loss and DIC which were adequately and promptly treated. A review of the labour ward records suggest that this woman received an excessive dose of syntocinon which probably resulted in fetal distress and uterine rupture. In this regard there was an element of substandard care.

> A considerably overweight woman who had a previous delivery by Caesarean section for a non-recurrent indication was admitted to a consultant unit in early labour at 41 weeks gestation. She proceeded to a normal vaginal delivery and approximately one hour later had a massive postpartum haemorrhage of at least 3 litres. Following blood transfusion the duty registrar sutured a cervical laceration under general anaesthesia. Further blood transfusion was given but the patient collapsed and was transferred to an intensive care unit where she suffered a cardiac arrest. She was resuscitated but, in spite of further transfusion, she died several hours later. At autopsy there was a tear extending from the ruptured Caesarean section scar through the left uterine artery with massive intra- and retroperitoneal haemorrhage. There was no evidence of a cervical rupture and the anterior and posterior lips of the cervix had been sutured together.

The locum registrar, who was on his first night on call, informed the consultant about this case but was allowed to continue with the management in what was obviously a serious situation given the amount of blood loss. An exploration of the uterine cavity was not performed prior to the attempts to suture the cervix. This was clearly substandard care.

Traumatic uterine rupture

This occurred in one case following a failed vacuum extraction and forceps delivery with laceration extending into the upper vagina and uterus.

> A parous patient was admitted to a consultant unit in spontaneous labour at 39 weeks gestation. She progressed rapidly to full dilatation with strong uterine contractions which virtually stopped in the second stage of labour. A syntocinon infusion was commenced and the duty registrar attempted to deliver the fetus with a vacuum extractor. During the course of this procedure the patient became distressed, with clinical evidence of blood loss. The delivery was completed with Kielland's forceps but the infant was stillborn, in spite of a report that the fetal heart was normal shortly before delivery. It was incorrectly assumed that the patient had an amniotic fluid embolus and heparin was given, thus precluding the insertion of a central venous pressure (CVP) line. The patient's condition deteriorated without adequate transfusion and she failed to respond to resuscitation following a cardiac arrest. At autopsy there was a large quantity of blood in the peritoneal cavity and a spiral tear in the left lateral vaginal wall extending to the Pouch of Douglas.

The care in this case was considered substandard as the registrar failed to appreciate the serious nature of the problem or alert senior staff. Heparin was given to a woman with obvious signs of concealed blood loss, even before an adequate assessment of her condition was established. The severe laceration of the vagina was due to the vacuum extractor as there was evidence of blood loss before the application of the Kielland's forceps. The fact that the infant was unexpectedly stillborn would suggest a lack of adequate monitoring of the labour.

Comments

These cases emphasise the need for a team approach to the management of severe haemorrhage. All obstetric units should have a written protocol and staff should be aware of their contingency plans to cope with sudden unexpected haemorrhage. In two of the cases junior staff assumed or were given too much responsibility in dealing with the emergency.

CHAPTER 9

Deaths associated with anaesthesia

Summary

There were 14 deaths associated with anaesthesia in this triennium. Retrieval of records for their adequate evaluation has been a problem. Eight deaths were directly attributed to anaesthesia and substandard care was present in seven of these. Hypoxia and airway obstruction were responsible for five deaths, the acute respiratory distress syndrome for two and failure of tissue perfusion for one. In six further deaths anaesthesia contributed, and these are discussed later in this chapter. Two each are counted in Chapters 3 and 11 and one each in Chapters 4 and 7.

Lack of consultant involvement, inadequate diagnosis and assessment of severity of illness, aspiration of stomach contents, hypovolaemic shock and availability of intensive care facilities were the main factors associated with mortality.

The cases are presented in some detail in order that anaesthetists may evaluate the problems and deficiencies in care that led to death and make provision for improved consultant supervision in the future. It is notable that despite the changing trend towards regional anaesthesia for operative delivery, all *Direct* anaesthetic deaths which were associated with Caesarean section occurred in women who had general anaesthesia. In some cases information is limited. Attention is again drawn to the importance of good record keeping. In particular evidence of monitoring and recording of physiological variables is very limited.

Deaths directly attributable to anaesthesia

Table 9.1 summarises deaths directly attributed to anaesthesia compared with previous triennia and a summary of the deaths discussed in this Report is shown in Table 9.2.

Table 9. 1

Deaths directly associated with anaesthesia (excluding Indirect and Late deaths), estimated rate per million maternities and percentage of Direct maternal deaths; United Kingdom 1985-93			
	Number of deaths directly associated with anaesthesia	**Rate per million maternities**	**% of maternal deaths**
1985-87	6	2.6	4.3
1988-90	4	1.7	2.7
1991-93	8	3.5	6.5

Table 9.2

Summary of Direct anaesthetic deaths : United Kingdom 1991-1993

Operation	Indication	Deficient features	Cause of death
Emergency laparotomy	Ruptured tubal pregnancy	No pulse oximetry, HDU, fluid balance chart or CVP monitoring.	ARDS, multiple organ failure.
Planned emergency C/S	Fetal distress	Poor communications.	Cerebral hypoxia and airway obstruction.
C/S	Pre-eclampsia	Premature extubation, no neuromuscular monitoring available. No tracheostomy skills.	
Elective C/S	Unstable fetal lie Previous Caesarean section	Induction without monitoring. No capnography.	Aggregate anaphylaxis and hypoxia.
Unplanned emergency C/S	Severe pre-eclampsia	No consultant input. No pulse oximetry. Insertion of CVP in neck in presence of DIC.	Tracheal compression and asphyxia.
Insertion of epidural catheter	Post-delivery perineal pain	No intravenous infusion.	Hypoxia, poor tissue perfusion due to extensive epidural block.
Planned emergency C/S	Fetal distress	No pulse oximetry or CVP.	Aspiration of gastric contents. ARDS.
Planned emergency C/S	Failure to progress in labour	No consultant input.	Hypoxia, cardiac arrest.
Planned emergency C/S	Fetal distress	None.	Anaphylaxis to suxamethonium.

C/S - Caesarean section DIC - Disseminated intravascular coagulation CVP - Central venous pressure line
ARDS - Acute respiratory distress syndrome HDU - high dependency unit

This patient required surgery for ruptured ectopic pregnancy. The anaesthetist, a senior house officer (SHO), whose first language was not English, had skilled assistance. The consultant anaesthetist on call was not informed because the patient was not considered to be at special risk although pale and poorly perfused.

The anaesthetic record is poor, but what evidence there is suggested a straightforward anaesthetic. Monitoring was probably used but there is no record of a single pulse rate or blood pressure during the entire operation; the non-invasive blood pressure record has been lost. Pulse oximetry showed oxygen saturation (SaO_2) of 100%. The fluid chart records that Hartmann's solution 1000ml, gelofusine and 4 units of blood were transfused.

The anaesthetist was called to another case immediately after the operation. The patient's condition was poor, with the possibility of septicaemia, as she had a raised white blood cell count (WBC) and a fever. She remained drowsy and oliguric. She was not then seen by an anaesthetist for the next 30 hours, when a consultant was contacted and requested her admission to the intensive care unit (ICU), by which time she was moribund with severe hypoxia and described as having marked fluid overload. She was ventilated, given antibiotics and her renal failure was treated by haemofiltration. She died 11 days after Caesarean section in cardiopulmonary failure. The autopsy described 'shock lung' (presumable acute respiratory distress syndrome (ARDS)) but there is no histology to support this.

In this case profound hypotension alone could have precipitated ARDS. Pyrexia may have arisen from endotoxaemia due to poor gut perfusion, another situation which is known to cause ARDS. Young healthy patients commonly maintain their blood pressure initially at the expense of profound peripheral vasoconstriction and impaired organ blood flow. Only invasive monitoring reveals the true situation.

Clinical detection of post-operative cyanosis may have been difficult as she had dark skin. She would clearly have benefited from pulse oximetry.

The hospital did not have high dependency facilities and the need for urine output or central venous pressure (CVP) monitoring on the ward was not appreciated. Assessment of fluid balance is impossible owing to the absence of records.

This is a serious case of substandard anaesthetic care. The SHO was inexperienced, failed to detect the severity of the situation, failed to institute appropriate invasive monitoring or to arrange for admission to an intensive care unit (ICU) in time and above all failed to seek senior assistance until it was too late to benefit the patient.

The patient was an immigrant who underwent Caesarean section. Her husband acted as her interpreter. She refused permission for the procedure under the existing successful epidural block. The anaesthetist was a registrar who had skilled assistance from an operating department assistant (ODA) and informed the consultant on call.

In addition to oedema due to pre-eclampsia the patient was obese, with mouth opening limited to 2 fingers. She was therefore at high risk for general anaesthesia. There was no difficulty with the anaesthetic. She developed post-extubation obstruction of the airway and attempted re-intubation failed. Neither the vocal cords nor the epiglottis could be seen. Some respiratory effort was occurring and two attempts were made to insert a laryngeal mask airway (LMA). Suxamethonium was given and repeated attempts at reintubation were made with a variety of endotracheal tubes, stilettes and bougies. Ventilation via the LMA was also to no avail. A mini-tracheostomy was performed 5 minutes after extubation but the neck was oedematous and a second attempt was required. Following this there was a rise in SaO_2 to 90%. Bilateral air entry was recorded and some CO_2 registered on the capnograph. Slight surgical emphysema developed and despite further attempts to improve air entry adrenaline and external cardiac massage were needed. The patient was reintubated with difficulty by the consultant anaesthetist. However oxygen saturation remained at 70-80% and end-tidal CO_2 <0.3k Pa. Bradycardia was resistant to inotropic agents and resuscitation was discontinued.

The autopsy revealed collapsed lungs with no evidence of aspiration of stomach contents. There was mild cutaneous emphysema but remarkably no evidence of a tracheostomy entry site into the larynx or trachea. Death was attributed to cerebral hypoxia due to airway obstruction after Caesarean section.

Communication with the patient was clearly a problem although she appeared to have understood the need for surgery. She was at high risk for general anaesthesia and a consultant should have been present, particularly as delivery took place in an isolated maternity unit.

Extubation was probably premature. The use of a peripheral nerve stimulator to ensure adequate reversal of neuromuscular blockade might have prevented the post-extubation respiratory difficulty. There was lack of resident expertise in performing a tracheostomy. It is essential to confirm the intratracheal position of the needle by aspirating air. There is no evidence from the autopsy that the minitracheostomy was in fact in the airway.

However, the major problem in this case was lack of adequate consultant supervision.

This woman was of high parity, short and obese. Her consultant obstetrician recommended Caesarean section because of an unstable lie and previous Caesarean section. The anaesthetist was an experienced consultant. She was offered regional anaesthesia but strongly preferred general anaesthesia. Routine preparation took place beforehand. No nasogastric tube was passed.

Induction occurred in the anaesthetic room with no apparent monitoring. An 8.0mm Oxford endotracheal tube was passed with the aid of a bougie. The anaesthetist was sure the tube was correctly placed in the trachea but hand ventilation proved difficult. The pulse was satisfactory but there was hypotension although no anaphylactic rash. Air entry could not be heard on auscultation. The inspired gas was changed to 100% oxygen with halothane. Ventilation became more and more difficult and the patient became cyanosed. The anaesthetist again considered a misplaced endotracheal tube and checked its position. With the aid of a bougie the endotracheal tube was replaced with another Oxford tube but there was no improvement in ventilation and although the pulse was still strong the pupils were dilating.

The anaesthetist checked the equipment and treated this as a case of anaphylaxis, with intravenous adrenaline and hand ventilation. The ODA went into theatre to fetch the monitoring trolley and aminophylline and hydrocortisone were given over the next few minutes. An accurate blood pressure could not be recorded. The SaO$_2$ read 60% when first recorded but it fell within 2 minutes to 40%. Assistance was summoned and a further dose of suxamethonium given. The endotracheal tube was changed to a Magill tube without benefit. Caesarean section was undertaken. Hand ventilation was continued. Atropine and isoprenaline were required for bradycardia. After 10 minutes hypoxia the consultant anaesthetist called an end to the resuscitation. The anaesthetic registrar arrived and confirmed the position of the tracheal tube through the larynx and the impossibility of ventilation.

Autopsy revealed haemorrhage into both lungs and collapse of the right lung with pneumothorax on that side. Histology of both lungs and kidneys showed fibrin aggregation which the pathologist considered supported a diagnosis of aggregate anaphylaxis. The problem with the right lung was believed to be secondary to resuscitation. The endotracheal tube was seen extending beyond the carina into the right main bronchus.

The anaesthetist performed the correct actions such as checking the position of the endotracheal tube, checking the equipment, using 100% oxygen and considering the diagnosis of anaphylaxis.

It is inappropriate to induce anaesthesia in an area without monitoring equipment. The patient should have been anaesthetised in the operating theatre itself. The initial position of the endotracheal tube could have been readily ascertained by capnography. It seems likely that the endotracheal tube was too long throughout the procedure and this could have initiated bronchospasm, particularly in a smoker.

The suggested diagnosis of aggregate anaphylaxis is rare and contentious. The dose of adrenaline was not recorded; these patients often require a large amount. The second dose of suxamethonium is very difficult to justify in view of the preliminary diagnosis of anaphylaxis.

Against these criticisms the patient was insistent upon having a general anaesthetic.

Tracheal and laryngeal compression causing asphyxia/hypoxia and cardiac arrest

This patient is also mentioned in Chapters 2 and 3. She had sickle cell trait and had a previous Caesarean section. She required emergency Caesarean section due to worsening pre-eclampsia. The anaesthetist was a registrar who reported no problems. After surgery the uterus was poorly contracted so a syntocinon infusion was set up and the patient was transferred to the high dependency area.

There was continuing blood loss and coagulopathy. The wound was explored under general anaesthesia and bleeding was found to be from the wound itself. An hour later there was very little urine output so the registrars in anaesthesia and obstetrics decided that CVP monitoring was indicated. The internal jugular route was chosen. There was difficulty with insertion of the CVP line. At the second attempt neck swelling developed and further attempts were abandoned, particularly as her urine output had improved. Digital pressure was applied to the neck followed by a pressure dressing. The haematoma extended and four hours later she complained of tightness in her neck and inability to breathe. When the anaesthetic registrar arrived the patient was cyanosed and could not breathe at all so an attempt was made to intubate her trachea. Direct laryngoscopy showed an oedematous larynx and pharynx. Several attempts at intubation were made using a bougie but bradycardia developed and cardiopulmonary resuscitation was required. A senior colleague was called, 100% oxygen was administered, with external cardiac massage and intravenous adrenaline and atropine, but all resuscitation efforts were to no avail.

This patient should have been monitored with oximetry: she was a sickle-cell trait Afro-Caribbean woman being nursed in a darkened room at night. She had just had a Caesarean section followed by exploration of the wound, both under general anaesthesia. Oximetry would have allowed adjustment of her inspired oxygen to deal with worsening hypoxia and alerted the nursing staff to impending respiratory difficulties.

It was reasonable to consider monitoring the CVP. However the extent of the coagulopathy would be a contraindication to insertion of a neck line and a long line from the antecubital fossa would have been safer. In any event treatment at this time should have been discussed with both obstetric and anaesthetic consultants.

In view of all the problems presented by the patient it would have been appropriate to transfer her to an ICU at this stage. It is doubtful that monitoring equipment and nursing staff in the area where she was managed fulfilled the criteria for high dependency care.

There is evidence of substandard care. The registrar failed to appreciate the requirement for pulse oximetry, the need to watch for airway difficulties after development of the haematoma and above all to notify the consultant on call.

Epidural analgesia (and pulmonary embolism)

> Thirty six hours after forceps delivery this patient complained of perineal pain and epidural analgesia was established to control this. It appears that the patient was insistent that she did not want an intravenous infusion. She was dehydrated and oliguric and shortly after epidural insertion she was found to be pale and vasoconstricted. There is no blood pressure record.

> The dose of local anaesthetic given is unknown but it appears that she had an extensive block with numbness in her hands. This would have been accompanied by a very extensive sympathetic block which is poorly tolerated by patients with depleted intravascular volume. The records state that the patient was agitated and restless but no attempt was made to exclude hypoxia as a cause before giving sedation. Administration of frusemide had no effect on the urine output. No vasopressor medication was given, and no oxygen until an ECG abnormality developed. Hypotension progressed to cardiac arrest. Resuscitation attempts were unsuccessful.

A likely explanation of events is that the extensive epidural block resulted in reduced perfusion producing reduced blood flow to the brain and heart and tissue hypoxia. There may have been additional respiratory depression due to the large dose of epidural opiate.

At autopsy the lungs were found to be congested and oedematous and there were 2 minute emboli in the right lung. There were multiple areas of collapse associated with patchy pulmonary oedema and traces of aspirated vomit in the bronchioles and some alveoli.

It is standard practice to set up an intravenous infusion in all patients having an epidural block because of the risk of a fall in blood pressure. Care was substandard because the epidural analgesia was mis-handled as the patient refused to have an intravenous infusion. The anaesthetist should have either insisted or refused to go ahead with the regional technique.

This patient required emergency Caesarean section for fetal distress. The anaesthetist was of subconsultant grade and skilled help was available. The consultant anaesthetist was not informed because no special abnormalities were recognised preoperatively. Standard preparation and induction occurred although ranitidine was not given exactly in accordance with the unit protocol. There was a note of secretions in the pharynx before intubation. These secretions were removed by suction and the endotracheal tube was passed initially into the right main bronchus (SpO$_2$ 90%). This was corrected and SpO$_2$ rose to 97-98%. Thereafter the operation was uneventful except for excess blood loss. Saline and Haemaccel were administered. Blood was not available during the operation as the haematologist was involved elsewhere. Uncrossmatched blood was held in the maternity unit but was not given, although the patient was group B positive with no significant antibodies present.

The patient had a period of serious hypotension beginning shortly after induction of anaesthesia. Despite this she was transferred after delivery to the postnatal ward where a blood transfusion was commenced. She was visited by the on-call obstetrician, her blood transfusion was speeded up, syntocinon was given because of a poorly contracted uterus and oxygen by mask was prescribed but poorly tolerated. Her pulse rate was 160 bpm and additional analgesia was given. Antibiotics were started as it had been noted that she had a cough and was drowsy. She had been febrile preoperatively. Six hours later she was oliguria and hypoxic. Frusemide was given and it was considered that she had aspirated stomach contents either at induction of anaesthesia and/or whilst hypotensive and obtunded on the postnatal ward. Hydrocortisone was given and the associate specialist in general medicine was consulted. She was transferred to another hospital to receive intensive therapy and from there transferred to a teaching centre for extra-corporeal membrane oxygenation (ECMO) for her ARDS. She died 21 days after delivery.

A very thorough autopsy described the death as due to intrapulmonary haemorrhage due initially to aspiration of stomach contents producing ARDS. Fatty liver of pregnancy was also detected.

Secretions in the pharynx before intubation suggest regurgitation of stomach contents until proved otherwise.

There was inadequate monitoring and the extent of the haemorrhage at Caesarean section warranted insertion of a CVP line. There were no pulse oximeters available and detection of cyanosis would have been difficult as the patient had dark skin.

Cross-matched blood was not available intraoperatively but it is difficult to understand why Group O-Rh negative blood was not given. Blood was finally given, but too little and too late.

The patient required care at least in a high dependency unit (HDU) but preferable an ICU post-operatively. No consultants were involved in this case until it was too late for the patient to benefit. This is a serious case of sub-standard care for all the reasons given above.

Hypoxia after extubation

> The patient was obese. Emergency Caesarean section was performed for failure to progress in labour. She refused epidural analgesia. Her general anaesthetic was given by a sub-consultant grade anaesthetist. Intubation was not difficult but at surgery her blood was noted to be dark. Low SpO_2 had been noted during the pre-oxygenation and fell to 75-80% shortly after induction. Aminophylline was given intra-opera-tively. There was a typical capnograph trace with end-tidal CO_2 30mm Hg. Airway pressure was high and she required 100% oxygen throughout. The endotracheal tube was changed once. There was no evidence of inhalation of gastric contents. She could not be extubated until an hour after delivery and was then transferred to the recovery room where she developed stridor requiring reintubation. She then had a cardiac arrest (ventricular fibrillation), was resuscitated and transferred to the HDU for controlled ventilation. The consultant anaesthetist was not informed until resuscitation was underway. In the HDU she developed multiple organ failure, including clinically assessed cerebral anoxia. She died 10 days after delivery after a diag-nosis of brain stem death.

> Autopsy failed to establish a cause for the death but the lungs did show changes of ARDS which the pathologist recorded as likely to be due to resuscitation and not the cause of the initial episode. Hypoxia was a major contributing factor.

There was an unconfirmed suggestion of anaphylaxis to suxamethonium. Care was clearly substandard as the consultant anaesthetist was not informed until it was impossible to have an effect on outcome.

Anaphylaxis to suxamethonium, acute myocardial ischaemia

The patient's parents both had hypertension and heart disease. She was a primigravida, admitted in labour and fetal distress developed. She was taken to theatre for a Caesarean section. Both a consultant anaesthetist and an SHO were present. Shortly after endotracheal intubation she developed bron-chospasm which was resistant to treatment with adrenaline, hydrocortisone and promethazine. She required 100% oxygen but despite this she deterio-rated, developed bradycardia and required external cardiac massage. Ventricular fibrillation followed and defibrillation was unsuccessful. Subsequent investigation showed raised IgE antibodies against suxametho-nium and it seems very likely that she had an anaphylactic response to the drug. Autopsy showed moderate coronary atheroma with some left ventric-ular hypertrophy. The pathologist felt that acute myocardial ischaemia was precipitated by the anaphylactic response.

Care was not considered substandard as she was appropriately monitored and treated before and after the episode of acute bronchospasm and circulatory collapse.

Deaths to which anaesthesia contributed

There were six deaths to which anaesthesia contributed. They have been counted in other chapters and are summarised in Table 9.3.

Caesarean section for major placenta praevia, haemorrhage and multiple organ failure.

This case in counted and discussed in Chapter 3.

> The patient's last pregnancy had required emergency Caesarean section for placenta praevia. In this pregnancy onset of labour occurred spontaneously and blood was cross-matched for emergency Caesarean section. There is no record by the anaesthetist concerned nor by the consultant anaesthetist responsible for the service.
>
> At operation the placenta appeared morbidly adherent but was removed piecemeal, possibly leaving small fragments. The patient appeared cold and 'shut-down' and the obstetrician ordered further blood to be cross-matched and transfused. The estimated blood loss was at least 3 litres. The anaesthetist was asked to insert a central venous pressure line and to transfuse more blood. Four units of fresh frozen plasma were requested but the anaesthetist was apparently satisfied with the patient's condition. The patient became hypotensive, tachycardiac and developed acute renal failure. The obstetric registrar requested that the anaesthetic registrar become more involved and call the consultant anaesthetist. Two hours after this it was decided that hysterectomy should be performed but the patient's condition was extremely poor. Glucose and insulin were required to reduce her potassium and the operation could not proceed. She became anuric and a decision was taken to transfer her to the ICU in the main hospital but meanwhile she sustained a cardiac arrest from which she could not be resuscitated.

Essential records for this patient are missing but it is clear that consultant anaesthetic involvement was absent.

A major degree of placenta praevia in a patient who had a previous Caesarean section has a high risk of placenta percreta. More blood should have been cross matched when the extent of the bleeding was apparent. The registrar under-estimated the gravity of the situation and failed to replace blood loss adequately or to treat her hypovolaemic shock. This is a case of substandard care where the consultant anaesthetist should have been involved much earlier.

Table 9.3

Cases counted in other Chapters to which anaesthesia contributed to the woman's death; United Kingdom 1991-93

Type of Caesarean section	Counted in Chapter	Cause of death	Deficient features
Planned emergency for placenta praevia.	3	Acute renal failure, blood loss, coagulopathy.	No consultant input. Inadequate blood replacement.
Planned emergency for maternal cardiac hypertension.	4	Pulmonary embolism.	No consultant input.
Planned emergency for pulmonary hypertension.	11	Acute on chronic heart failure, pulmonary hypertension, systemic sclerosis, intrapartum haemorrhage, thrombocytopaenic purpura.	No physician input.
Planned emergency for failure to progress in labour.	3	Postpartum haemorrhage, amniotic fluid embolism.	None, although difficult reintubation.
Planned emergency for failed induction for intrauterine death.	7	Septicaemia.	Antibiotics given late, poor timing of delivery.
Planned emergency for fetal distress.	11	Acute right heart failure, primary pulmonary hypertension.	Inadequate antenatal investigation.

This case is counted and discussed in Chapter 4.

> The patient spoke no English. She was admitted in labour distressed, vomiting and difficult to examine. Epidural analgesia was suggested. The anaesthetist was a registrar who made a good appraisal of the situation via an interpreter before giving a fluid load and inserting an epidural. Until this time Entonox had been used to supplement analgesia. A 3ml test dose of 1.5% lignocaine was followed by 10 ml bupivacaine 0.375%. Subsequent doses of 4+6 ml of 0.25% bupivacaine were given.

> After the establishment of epidural analgesia the patient fell asleep and developed an obstructed airway and paradoxical respiration. She was turned into the full lateral position and given incremental doses of naloxone, after which she woke up. The fetal heart rate fell but recovered after oxygen and fluids were administered. A syntocinon infusion was started. She was seen half-hourly by the anaesthetic registrar and, although sleepy, she awoke to verbal command. Five and a half hours later she collapsed in the presence of the obstetric registrar who found her to be pulseless. She was given naloxone and oxygen and an attempt at forceps delivery confirmed cephalo-pelvic disproportion. Resuscitation and immediate Caesarean section were performed with delivery of a live 4 kg baby with a low Apgar score who responded well to resuscitation. Excessive bleeding from the vagina began. It was assumed that she was developing disseminated intravascular coagulopathy. She developed terminal asystole and was declared dead.

> Autopsy showed that both pulmonary arteries and both pelvic veins contained thrombi.

The consultant anaesthetist in charge of obstetric services should have been informed as soon as difficulties arose but this would have been unlikely to have made any difference to the outcome. Only 2 sessions each week were available for obstetric anaesthesia in this hospital which has a very busy obstetric unit warranting 5-6 sessions.

Earlier consideration of the likelihood of thromboembolic disease might have allowed thrombolysis but this would have presented considerable risk. Pulmonary embolectomy would have been a possible heroic treatment that just might have saved the patient's life.

Cardiac arrest due to acute on chronic heart failure

This case is counted and discussed in Chapter 11.

> The patient had systemic sclerosis with pulmonary hypertension and idiopathic thrombocytopenic purpura. A previous pregnancy had been complicated by pre-eclampsia and delivered by Caesarean section. She was admitted to hospital because of severe hypertension and reduced urine output. Because of continuing dyspnoea she was transferred to a teaching hospital where she was found to have severe pulmonary

hypertension. Labour began at 27 weeks gestation. An emergency Caesarean section was agreed. The anaesthetist was a consultant. Intubation was difficult because of the limited mouth opening but was successful on the third attempt. A 1.1 kg live baby was delivered after which the blood pressure and pulse fell. The placenta was delivered and significant retroplacental clot was found. Cardiac arrest occurred. Resuscitation attempts included DC shock, use of adrenaline, atropine, calcium, sodium bicarbonate and isoprenaline but all attempts failed.

The major problem with this case was lack of physician input into her care and lack of early discussion with the anaesthetic department regarding her management in the peri-delivery period.

The anaesthetic technique was logical although a case could be made for intubation under local anaesthesia with the fibre-optic bronchoscope. However this is stressful and may have resulted in greater cardiac decompensation than the three attempts at intubation using the bougie under general anaesthesia. More invasive central venous and pulmonary artery pressure monitoring might have led to changes in therapy but were extremely unlikely to have changed the outcome. The low platelet count could have been corrected provided there were no anti-platelet antibodies.

Difficult reintubation

This case is counted and discussed in Chapter 3.

> This patient had schistosomiasis in the second trimester of pregnancy. She was brought to hospital at term with a history of 12 hours of abdominal pain, subsequently requiring a Caesarean section for failure to progress in labour. After delivery there was postpartum haemorrhage and early disseminated intravascular coagulation (DIC). After administration of blood and fresh frozen plasma her oxygenation deteriorated and she became oliguria. The possibility of amniotic fluid embolus was considered and she was transferred to the ICU where she had a grand mal convulsion. Attempted tracheal intubation failed, after which she developed bradycardia, was then intubated, but became asystolic and could not be resuscitated.

It is difficult to comment in the absence of more detail but consultant management on the ICU might have led to successful intubation although this was unlikely to have affected the outcome. Anaesthetic difficulties contributed to this death but it is not a case of substandard care.

Endotoxic shock - inadequate resuscitation

This case of spontaneous rupture of membranes in mid-trimester is counted and discussed in Chapter 7.

> The anaesthetic involvement started when a decision was made to undertake Caesarean section following failure of a prostaglandin induction of labour. The first anaesthetist was a registrar who recog-

nised that the patient was in septic shock, sent for the consultant anaesthetist and resuscitated the patient, attached monitoring equipment including a CVP line and proceeded to induce anaesthesia. The anaesthetic chart shows that Hespan, Haemaccel, FFP and syntocinon were given during the procedure. Five minutes after induction asystole occurred. Active resuscitation continued for 30 minutes without success.

Death was due to endotoxic shock with gram-negative septicaemia due to ascending infection after rupture of membranes.

The decision to undertake a Caesarean section having been made by the consultant obstetrician placed some pressure on the anaesthetic registrar to proceed. Caesarean section was unlikely to have helped. Transfer to ICU for pulmonary artery (PA) catheterisation and haemodynamic monitoring and organ support was an alternative.

The anaesthetist should not have started without the consultant as there is no urgency when the fetus is known to be dead. However the consultant arrived before cardiac arrest occurred.

This case is one of substandard care because antibiotics were given too late and even if Caesarean section was indicated the patient was probably inadequately resuscitated.

Right heart failure and pulmonary hypertension

The case of a patient who was known to have cardiomegaly and whose father died young from pulmonary hypertension, is counted and discussed in Chapter 11.

The patient was admitted in labour, shocked, and Caesarean section was indicated for fetal distress. There had been some antepartum haemorrhage. The anaesthetist was an SHO, most of his experience having been obtained overseas. Fluid resuscitation led to a rise in blood pressure but tachycardia persisted. A routine general anaesthetic was given but she became very hypotensive. Cardiac arrest occurred after delivery of the baby and the consultant anaesthetist was called for the first time. The patient was resuscitated but died in ICU less than two hours later. The cause of death was acute right heart failure due to pulmonary hypertension. Redistribution of blood after delivery may have precipitated the arrest.

The anaesthetist failed to recognise the patient's shocked state and particularly to obtain consultant help. Primary pulmonary hypertension was not known until autopsy. Had it been, use of a PA catheter or CVP line may have guided fluid therapy.

Substandard care occurred because of inadequate investigation and diagnosis in the ante-natal period and failure of the anaesthetist to obtain consultant help initially.

Comments

Although the number of anaesthetic deaths is small it is very disappointing to find avoidable factors and substandard care occurring despite drawing attention to these problems in previous Reports. Problems with the airway, aspiration of stomach contents and hypovolaemic shock are all well recognised potentially avoidable complications of anaesthesia for Caesarean section. All the *Direct* deaths associated with Caesarean section involved the use of general anaesthesia. All obstetric patients requiring anaesthesia should be considered as high risk. Staffing and management procedures should reflect this.

Failure to institute appropriate monitoring, particularly pulse oximetry, in the operating theatre, and particularly in patients whose skin colour may mask post-operative cyanosis constitutes substandard care.

Lack of consultant involvement is a recurring problem which must be solved. It is a feature of several deaths that a trainee or locum anaesthetist failed to appreciate the severity of the patient's condition and refer her to an ICU or request senior assistance.

Better training in diagnosis may prevent mortality in some conditions such as ruptured uterus.

Recognition of the need for intensive care for any serious complication is essential. Any patient requiring mechanical ventilation should be transferred to an intensive care unit. High dependency care may be appropriate for patients who are at risk of developing organ failure and therefore require close monitoring or those who have single (non-pulmonary) organ failure. It is not sufficient to provide an area designated as an HDU without adequate monitoring equipment, training in its use and fully trained nursing staff to undertake the care.

Patients with haemolysis, elevated liver enzymes and low platelets (HELLP) syndrome should be expected to show serious morbidity particularly renal failure, disseminated intravascular coagulopathy and pulmonary oedema. Early recognition and referral to at least high dependency care may improve outcome.

The National Confidential Enquiry into Perioperative Deaths (NCEPOD) 1992-3 Report draws attention to the frequency of lost notes and the quality of medical record keeping within the NHS. The problems encountered in obtaining notes for completion of these maternal mortality reports reflects these difficulties.

One of the NCEPOD recommendations encourages co-operation between specialties to produce a good outcome. This is particularly the case in the patients discussed here. Anaesthetists responsible for obstetric services should liaise with midwives, obstetricians and physicians to agree management for successful delivery. The anaesthetist must become involved in the management of the "at risk" patient at an early stage and can provide the liaison with high dependency and intensive care on behalf of the clinical management team.

Development of clinical guidelines and local protocols should be encouraged. The Royal College of Anaesthetists (1994) has published guidelines for the purchasers of obstetric services and the Obstetric Anaesthetists Association (1995) made recommendations for obstetric anaesthetic services. The latter includes guidance on assistance for the anaesthetists which is reproduced in the Annexe to this Chapter and has the approval of the Association of Anaesthetists of Great Britain and Ireland. These guidelines can be developed as local protocols.

References

The Report of The National Confidential Enquiry into Perioperative Deaths-1992-93. London; 1995.

Royal College of Anaesthetists. *Guidance for Purchasers of Obstetric Anaesthesia.* Royal College of Anaesthetists; July 1994.

Obstetric Anaesthetists Association. *Recommended minimum standards for obstetric anaesthesia services.* Obstetric Anaesthetists Association; Jan 1995.

ANNEXE TO CHAPTER 9

Guidance for assistance for the anaesthetist in obstetric anaesthetic practice

The ideal person to assist the anaesthetist in obstetric practice is an appropriately trained operating department practitioner, operating department assistant or a specifically trained anaesthetic nurse.

If such a person is not available for any reason, then a registered nurse or midwife with current and effective registration who has received an equivalent anaesthetic training to a nationally or regionally recognised standard (though not a local standard) should be employed to perform such duties. National Vocational Qualifications (NVQ) level 3 in Operating Department Practice is the accepted national standard.

To ensure maintenance of competence a person trained to a recognised standard should assist the anaesthetist in obstetric units on a regular basis and not only on an occasional basis.

There should be a plan for all obstetric units to achieve this standard if not already in place with progression to full implementation by the end of 1996.

Consultant anaesthetists in charge of obstetric services will need to monitor the quality and quantity of assistance available during any period in which the full standard cannot be met and take appropriate steps, as outlined in the Association of Anaesthetists document 'Assistance for the Anaesthetist' to protect patients and trainee anaesthetic staff.

CHAPTER 10

Other *Direct* deaths

Summary

Other *Direct* deaths comprise those due to a variety of causes not dealt with in other Chapters. There were nine such deaths in this triennium. In eight cases autopsies confirmed or established the cause of death, whilst in one case no autopsy was requested.

Liver disease

Liver abnormalities associated with hypertensive disorders of pregnancy are discussed and counted in Chapter 2. There were two other *Direct* deaths associated with acute fatty liver which are counted in this chapter.

> A multiparous patient was admitted with a five day history of fever, rigors and then jaundice at 33 weeks gestation. On admission she had evidence of a disseminated intravascular coagulopathy (DIC). Caesarean section was undertaken, but the patient's condition continued to deteriorate and she eventually died from acute hepato-renal failure. Autopsy confirmed changes of acute fatty liver.

> A parous woman was admitted at 36 weeks gestation with jaundice. Intrauterine death was confirmed. Labour was induced and she was delivered of a fresh stillbirth. Post delivery a clotting defect developed, the patient's condition gradually deteriorated and she died twelve days later. Autopsy confirmed acute fatty liver.

In both these cases there was a history preceding admission of vague symptoms and fever, the development of jaundice signifying the sinister pathology in these cases. The development of DIC further complicated their management, all of which was deemed satisfactory. Only the possibility of liver transplantation may have influenced the outcome in these unfortunate cases, who succumbed to a still unknown aetiological cause of liver failure peculiar to pregnancy.

Hyperemesis gravidarum

There were three deaths in this triennium in women being treated for hyperemesis gravidarum, two of whom were in-patients at the time.

> A woman was admitted at about 11 weeks gestation with hyperemesis gravidarum. She had intravenous infusions intermittently over the next several weeks. She failed to respond to usual approaches and because of development of bizarre behaviour was transferred to psy-

chiatric care. Her condition deteriorated rapidly over the next few days and she became comatose and died. Autopsy revealed typical features of Wernike's encephalopathy.

Care was deemed substandard in this case where more attention to fluid and nutritional input could have prevented her death.

> A young woman was admitted at 12 weeks gestation with a history of hyperemesis over several weeks. She exhibited unusual behaviour, was reviewed by the psychiatrists and diagnosed as having an acute psychosis. She was found dead on the ward shortly afterwards. Autopsy examination revealed aspiration of vomitus but the autopsy was deemed an inadequate examination with poor detailed assessment. Wernicke's encephalopathy may have been a potential component in this case.

> An older, obese grand multipara was experiencing problems with hyperemesis. She had been reviewed by physicians for persistent symptoms of vomiting and retrosternal pain, and diagnosed and treated for oesphagitis. She was found dead at home during the seventeenth week of pregnancy. Autopsy revealed aspiration of vomit as the only finding.

Symptoms of nausea and vomiting in pregnancy are relatively common and for the most part resolve spontaneously with time. Persistent vomiting can result in electrolyte and nutritional disturbances which may result in disturbed behaviour. There has been a move away from the use of antiemetics, particularly in early pregnancy, in recent years. There is always a need to try to maintain a balance between drug use and over usage. Anti-emetic drug therapy has brought it's own problems peculiar to pregnancy in the past. However, use of anti-emetrics may be helpful in controlling symptoms at an early stage and thus prevent aspiration syndromes and prolonged nutritional deficiencies. Intravenous thiamine should be administered to all patients receiving an intravenous infusion for this condition.

Deaths associated with the use of ritodrine

Beta-agonists such as ritodrine may have a limited role to play in selected patients in suppressing preterm labour, but their use requires careful monitoring as two maternal deaths illustrate.

> A young woman was admitted at 33 weeks gestation in premature labour. Intravenous ritodrine was commenced and given over a course of three days before being converted to oral administration. Soon after commencing oral ritodrine she developed persistent tachycardia and fetal distress. Caesarean section was performed, following which she developed acute pulmonary oedema. The patient died three weeks later from acute respiratory distress syndrome and pulmonary fibrosis. The only initiating cause for the pulmonary oedema appeared to be the ritodrine.

Another young patient was admitted with premature labour, also at 33 weeks. She was commenced on intravenous ritodrine diluted in normal saline. After 36 hours the infusion rate was gradually reduced because of tachycardia and patient anxiety. She was transferred to the ward, where she soon began to experience dyspnoea. This was initially treated as bronchospasm but continued to worsen. The patient was transferred to another hospital's intensive care unit (ICU) and then underwent Caesarean section for fetal reasons. She failed to recover, developed acute respiratory distress syndrome and died eleven days later of myocardial infarction.

In this case ritodrine had been given via an intravenous infusion, not a controlled infusion pump, and diluted in normal saline. No accurate input output charts had been kept and the unit did not have a written protocol for ritodrine administration.

Cases such as these prompted review by the Royal College of Obstetricians and Gynaecologists Scientific Advisory Committee who issued guidelines for use and indications for administration of ritodrine in April 1994, highlighting the need for careful fluid input/output monitoring during ritodrine administration. Readers are referred to the Guidelines for full details but the main precautions and recommendations relating to maternal safety are reproduced below.

Guidance for infusion rates for ritodrine

Appropriate infusion regimens are as follows:			
Syringe pump Add 3x5 ml ampoules of ritodrine to 35 ml of 5% w/v dextrose		**Controlled infusion device** Add 3x5 ml ampoules of ritodrine to 500 ml of 5% w/v dextrose	
Dose	Rate	Dose	Rate
50 micrograms/min	1 ml/hour	50 micrograms/min	10 ml/hour
100 micrograms/min	2 ml/hour	100 micrograms/min	20 ml/hour
150 micrograms/min	3 ml/hour	150 micrograms/min	30 ml/hour
200 micrograms/min	4 ml/hour	200 micrograms/min	40 ml/hour
250 micrograms/min	5 ml/hour	250 micrograms/min	50 ml/hour
300 micrograms/min	6 ml/hour	300 micrograms/min	60 ml/hour
350*micrograms/min	7 ml/hour	350*micrograms/min	70 ml/hour

* maximum recommended dose.

Other key recommendations for the administration of ritodrine

A controlled infusion device is preferable, either a syringe pump or, if unavailable, an Ivac pump or a volumetric giving set. The infusion rate should be increased every 15 minutes to a maximum concentration of 350 micrograms/min until the contractions have ceased or the maternal pulse is greater than 140/minute. The total daily intravenous dose should not exceed 120 mg.

Whilst the drug is administered intravenously the following observations should be performed:

- maternal pulse, at least every 15 minutes

- blood pressure, every 15 minutes

- 4 hourly blood glucose (eg by "BM stix")

- strict record of fluid balance (input/output chart)

- urea and electrolytes should be checked 24 hourly or more often if indicated, together with ECG (to avoid hypokalaemia)

- auscultation of lung fields.

Chest pain, dyspnoea or dry cough, should lead to immediate cessation of the infusion.

Particular caution should be observed in the following conditions: pre-existing cardiac disease, antepartum haemorrhage, diabetes, chorioamnionitis, severe hypertension, multiple pregnancy, intrauterine growth retardation, cord compression.

Bowel injury at Caesarean section

Caesarean section, as with any laparotomy, can result in injuries to abdominal contents which may initially go unnoticed but result in severe post operative complications, which, if not corrected promptly, can lead to in death.

> An older woman with a history of ulcerative colitis was admitted at term with ruptured membranes. She had some vaginal bleeding and it was thought she may have experienced an abruption. A junior trainee performed a Caesarean section and noted that a portion of the 'colon' was adherent to the peritoneum of the abdominal wall and dissected this free. During the first few post operative days the patient became increasingly unwell with abdominal distention, absent bowel sounds and pyrexia. A laparotomy was performed by the consultant obstetrician who found large amounts of purulent fluid and a perforation in the small bowel, which was oversewn. The patient's condition failed to improve and she required a further laparotomy two days later when extensive intra-abdominal abscess formation and sub-phrenic abscess were found. Her condition continued to deteriorate and she died from septicaemia.

In this case injury to the bowel occurred at the time of the Caesarean section whilst dividing adhesions. Signs of peritonitis developed post operatively and delay occurred in re-opening the patient and seeking a surgical colleague's advice.

Most patients make a rapid recovery after Caesarean section. Failure to do so should alert the clinician to potential complications. Peritonitis due to bowel perforation can rapidly result in large fluid imbalances associated with the accompanying ileus. Care in this case was considered substandard by not involving a general surgeon at the time of the original laparotomy and with regard to the post operative care. By the time of the second laparotomy the patient's condition was already severely compromised and despite extensive antibiotic treatment, septicaemia intervened and death occurred.

Choriocarcinoma

One patient died following an unusual presentation of choriocarcinoma.

> This older woman had a spontaneous vaginal delivery and was discharged home on the second day. She was seen by her GP within the next few days complaining of breathlessness and was treated with antibiotics. The next day she collapsed and was admitted to hospital where a pulmonary embolism was diagnosed and she was treated with heparin. Her condition continued to deteriorate and, despite intensive care, she died five weeks later. At autopsy multiple tumour emboli were found in the lungs. These were shown to be choriocarcinoma. A small nodule found at the fundus of the uterus was confirmed to be the primary choriocarcinoma.

This patient did indeed have embolism to the lung but of tumour not thrombi. It is unusual for such cases to present with acute chest symptoms. There were no other symptoms (persistent vaginal bleeding etc.) to suggest that a choriocarcinoma may have been present and thus appropriate therapy was not instigated at a time when cure might have been expected.

Comments

The cases in this chapter have resulted from a miscellaneous group of causes. However lessons are to be learnt from those associated with hyperemesis and intravenous administration of ritodrine which point to the need for increased vigilance.

Reference

The Royal College of Obstetricians and Gynaecologists. *Guidelines No 1-for the use of ritodrine.* April 1994.

CHAPTER 11

Cardiac disease

Summary

There were 41 deaths associated with cardiac disease. Thirty seven were classified as *Indirect* and are counted in this chapter. Four *Late* deaths are counted in Chapter 15. In one additional case, counted in Chapter 9, cardiac disease contributed to death from suxamethonium anaphylaxis.

Substandard care was considered to be present in ten of the thirty seven cases.

Nine of the deaths were due to complications of congenital heart disease and 27 to acquired heart disease, as shown in Table 11.1. The number of deaths associated with acquired heart disease has increased markedly compared with the years 1985 - 1990. A notable feature was that nine deaths resulted from ruptured aneurysm of the aorta (and its branches) above the diaphragm compared with three in 1985-87, and one in 1988-90 as shown in Table 11.2.

Table 11.1

		Acquired		
	Congenital	Ischaemic	Other	Total
Number of maternal deaths from congenital and acquired cardiac disease; United Kingdom 1985-93				
1985-87	10(44%)	9(39%)	4(17%)	**23**
1988-90	9(50%)	5(25%)	4(25%)	**18**
1991-93	9(24%)	8(22%)	19(52%)	37

Table 11.2

Maternal deaths due to cardiac diseases; United Kingdom 1991-93	
Congenital	
Ventricular septal defect	3
Atrial septal defect	2
Pulmonary hypertension	2
Hypertrophic obstructive cardiomyopathy	1
Chromosome 3 abnormality	1
Total	**9**
Acquired	
Aneurysm of thoracic aorta and its branches	9
Aneurysm of coronary vein	1
Ischaemic heart disease	8
Mitral valve disease	2
Cardiomyopathy	2
Myocardial fibrosis	1
Viral myocarditis	2
Secondary pulmonary hypertension	1
Non bacterial endocarditis	1
Total	**27**
Unexplained	1
Overall total	**37**

Congenital heart disease

Cases of primary pulmonary hypertension, hypertrophic cardiomyopathy (HOCM) and chromosome 3 abnormality have been included in the nine cases of congenital heart disease for consistency with earlier reports.

Substandard care was considered to be a feature in three of the nine cases of congenital heart disease. Two had a ventricular septal defect (VSD) and one primary pulmonary hypertension.

Ventricular septal defect (VSD)

A woman with a VSD proven by angiography was booked for delivery at a consultant maternity unit in a peripheral hospital. There is no record of her seeing a cardiologist until she was admitted at 36 weeks gestation in heart failure. Her condition deteriorated and she was transferred to the local University teaching hospital. The fetus died. She was subsequently delivered by Caesarean section in the hope that delivery of the dead fetus and placenta would reduce her oxygen demand. Nevertheless she died of progressive heart failure following a second operation for a burst abdomen. Death was certified as due to cardiac failure, cardiomyopathy and septicaemia. Most regrettably no autopsy was performed so the latter causes could not be confirmed. It was possible that the patient could have had endocarditis.

A recent immigrant booked with her general practitioner at 14 weeks gestation. She had a history of unspecified congenital heart disease diagnosed in her country of birth. The GP failed to notice finger clubbing and did not appreciate the significance of her very high haemoglobin concentration (17.5 gm/dl). At 21 weeks gestation she presented to the Accident and Emergency Department at a teaching hospital with abdominal pain. Because of cyanosis and the above features Eisenmenger's syndrome with a VSD was diagnosed by echocardiography. By that stage of pregnancy termination was considered too dangerous. Because echocardiography suggested rising pulmonary artery pressure elective delivery by Caesarean section under general anaesthesia was performed at 32 weeks gestation. She died three days later because of an inability to maintain systemic oxygenation, probably because of lack of pulmonary blood flow.

In both these cases care was substandard. They illustrate the importance of referring all known or suspected cases of heart disease for expert evaluation in pregnancy.

A 28 year old primigravida had an uncomplicated pregnancy and delivery. She subsequently developed bacterial endocarditis and died two weeks after a normal delivery. At autopsy a previously undetected ventricular septal defect was demonstrated. No further details are available, but care was not judged to have been substandard.

Atrial Septal Defect (ASD)

Atrial septal defect was implicated in two deaths.

The first woman was found dead in bed at home at 24 weeks gestation. Autopsy showed a large, hitherto undiagnosed ASD. No other abnormality was found and a dysrhythmia was implicated.

The other woman was admitted with hemiplegia and dysphasia at three months gestation. Investigation showed occlusion of the right anterior and middle cerebral arteries and she subsequently succumbed to brain stem coning. At autopsy there was an ASD and thrombi in the pelvic veins with cerebral and pulmonary emboli. Death was certified as due to paradoxical cerebral embolus.

Care was not considered to have been substandard in either of these two cases.

Primary pulmonary hypertension

Four of the 37 cardiac deaths were due to pulmonary hypertension. One of these was associated with Eisenmenger's syndrome and has been discussed under ventricular septal defect and another, associated with acquired heart disease, is described later in this chapter. An additional patient described in Chapter 12 died because of pulmonary hypertension due to systemic lupus erythematosus.

> A young multigravid woman with known cardiomegaly became breathless in pregnancy. She was treated for asthma by her GP. She was later admitted in hypovolaemic shock presumed to be due to abruptio placentae at 36 weeks gestation. She initially improved with intravenous fluids but because of concern about the fetal condition, the obstetric registrar informed his consultant who advised immediate Caesarean section. The general anaesthetic was given by a Senior House Officer (SHO) acting up as registrar who did not inform his consultant even though the blood pressure was only 50/30 mm Hg shortly before delivery. The patient had a cardiac arrest soon after delivery and died in the intensive care unit (ICU) less than two hours later. Subsequently it was discovered that the patient's father had died from primary pulmonary hypertension and this was also the cause of her death.

In this case care was substandard because of lack of involvement of a cardiologist or a senior anaesthetist. A cardiologist should have been consulted in the antenatal period because of cardiomegaly and breathlessness. The SHO in anaesthesia should have requested more experienced help when dealing with such a sick patient. More judicious use of fluids and central venous pressure monitoring might have saved the patient's life. This case emphasizes the significance of pulmonary hypertension due to increased pulmonary vascular resistance in pregnancy.

> Primary pulmonary hypertension with pneumonia was also the cause of death in a woman who died 41 days following Caesarean section for pre-eclampsia. However the patient also had aortic valve disease so it is possible that pulmonary hypertension was secondary to this abnormality.

One patient died suddenly in left ventricular failure four weeks after delivery. She had never had any symptoms referable to the heart but at autopsy was found to have hypertrophic obstructive cardiomyopathy (HOCM).

A multiparous woman was found dead on the toilet 16 hours after the onset of labour. Resuscitation was unsuccessful and both she and the unborn baby were pronounced dead. At autopsy the only abnormality was a mild degree of pulmonary oedema. The patient had duplication of part of chromosome 3, an abnormality shared by some of her relatives. These relatives have congenital cardiac abnormalities so it is possible that her death was caused by a cardiac dysrhythmia.

There was one *Late death* due to left ventricular failure counted in Chapter 15. She was also known to have mitral valve prolapse but it is unlikely that this contributed significantly to her death.

Acquired heart disease

Twenty seven deaths associated with acquired heart disease are counted in this chapter and the diagnoses shown in Table 11.2. Four *Late* deaths, two from ischaemic heart disease and two with cardiomyopathy are counted in Chapter 15.

Seven of the 27 cases of acquired heart disease were considered to have received substandard care.

Rheumatic heart disease

For many years rheumatic heart disease was the major medical cause of maternal mortality in the United Kingdom and it still is in many developing countries. There were only two deaths attributed to rheumatic heart disease in this report.

In one case substandard care was implicated because the patient, a recent immigrant, refused to allow examination on religious grounds even by a female doctor. She was admitted at 25 weeks gestation with weakness and found to have haemophilus septicaemia and mitral valve disease with presumed endocarditis. The source of infection was unknown. A few days after admission the fetus died and the uterus was evacuated following administration of gemeprost pessaries. Despite full antibiotic therapy the patient died two weeks after admission from a stroke thought to be due to an embolus from bacterial endocarditis. No autopsy was performed.

The second patient died from an obstructed mitral valve replacement at 24 weeks gestation. The mitral valve had been replaced four years previously. She saw a consultant obstetrician very frequently between five and 21 weeks gestation. Anticoagulation was changed from warfarin to subcutaneous heparin, 10,000 units twice a day from five to 12 weeks gestation, when warfarin was recommenced. The level of anti-coagulation achieved is not reported. The patient collapsed at home and was dead on arrival in hospital.

This case illustrates the continuing difficulty of anticoagulant management in patients with artificial heart valves.

Ruptured aneurysm of the thoracic aorta and its branches

Aneurysms of the thoracic aorta are included in this chapter, because the patients are usually managed by cardio-thoracic surgeons and cardiologists; whereas aneurysms of the abdominal aorta and its branches are treated by vascular surgeons and are considered in Chapter 12. There were nine deaths from thoracic aneurysms which is part of the reason why there has been a marked increase in deaths from acquired heart disease as shown in Table 11.1. However, there was only one death from aortic aneurysm recorded in the 1988 - 1990 series so it appears that there has been an absolute increase in the number of deaths from ruptured aortic aneurysm. It is tempting to ascribe this to the increasing age at which women are bearing children but the average age of death of the nine women was only 29 years (range 20 to 43) and little different from the average age of all women during pregnancy between 1991 and 1993.

There were three cases in which care was judged to be substandard:

> One young patient weighing 102 kg was admitted under the obstetri-cians in a district hospital at 38 weeks gestation. Because she had dis-orientation, vomiting, teichopsia and proteinuria, pre-eclampsia was the only diagnosis considered but she had chest pain and was also hypertensive, with atrial fibrillation and absent pulses in a cyanosed right arm. A chest X-ray was ordered but never taken. She was even-tually seen by an SHO in medicine three hours after admission. He could not account for the findings and suggested a fluid challenge and transfer to a medical ward. The patient died following a cardiac arrest two hours later. Autopsy showed cystic medial necrosis of the aorta with dissection of the ascending thoracic aorta tracking into at least two coronary arteries. The coronary arteries were atheromatous and the cause of death was tamponade due to the dissection rupturing into the pericardium.

Seriously ill patients should be seen quickly by senior doctors and these should include physicians and/or surgeons if the illness is not obviously of an obstetric nature. The absence of a chest X-ray (possibly because of mis-placed fears of radiating the fetus) is unacceptable in such a sick patient. It might well have revealed the diagnosis.

> An older grande multiparous woman, known to be hypertensive before pregnancy, was admitted as an emergency because of chest pain at 38 weeks gestation. She was vomiting and hypertensive. She was seen by a medical registrar; the ECG was normal and "oesophageal

spasm" was diagnosed. Three and a half hours later a Caesarean section was performed for fetal distress. After the procedure she was initially well but 16 hours later she became hypotensive and confused. A further 10 hours later she had a cardiac arrest from which she could not be resuscitated. Autopsy showed a dissecting aortic aneurysm extending from the aortic valve ring to the abdominal aorta and into other major vessels, the coronary arteries and rupturing into the pericardium.

No chest X-ray was ever taken, which is unacceptable in a hypertensive patient admitted because of chest pain; and no consultant of any discipline saw the patient at any time during her illness, including the ten hours before she died when, by any criterion, she was seriously ill.

A multiparous woman in her twenties was admitted to hospital at term because of chest pain. She was known to be hypertensive before pregnancy and was taking atenolol. The pain settled spontaneously. No chest X-ray or ECG was performed and she was discharged after two days. Three days later she experienced numbness and tingling in her left hand. Four days later she collapsed and diedat home. Autopsy showed a dissecting aneurysm arising in the ascending arch of the aorta and extending into the pericardium which was filled with blood.

It is likely that the dissection started at the time of the patient's admission six days before she died. Again no chest X-ray was taken in a hypertensive woman admitted with chest pain.

Another primigravida was known to have aortic valve disease. She had regular follow up and was seen early in her pregnancy by her cardiologist. The gradient across the aortic valve was estimated to be 50 mm Hg and no problems were expected. There were no features of Marfan's syndrome. At 38 weeks gestation she was admitted to hospital with chest pain. The ECG was normal and chest X-ray was reported as "clear" in the clinical notes. Six hours after admission she collapsed. Echocardiography during cardiopulmonary resuscitation suggested tamponade but pericardiocentesis and subsequent open chest surgery by the cardiothoracic surgery registrar were unsuccessful. The fetus did not survive post-mortem Caesarean section. Autopsy confirmed death from haemopericardium due to dissecting aneurysm arising in the ascending aorta. It was postulated that turbulent blood flow due to confirmed aortic valve disease may have made the aorta even more likely to rupture in pregnancy.

By contrast another patient was admitted at 25 weeks gestation with chest pain and had immediate echocardiography and CT scanning. The aorta was dilated and dissection confirmed at the regional cardiothoracic centre. Following Caesarean section the aortic root was replaced successfully but in the immediate post operative period she suffered an occlusion of the right coronary artery leading to myocardial infarction. She died two days later while still on cardiopulmonary bypass and while awaiting a cardiac transplant.

The above two cases emphasise how despite heroic efforts dissecting aneurysm still has a high fatality rate.

> A further multigravid patient was found dead three days after Caesarean section. Autopsy showed haemopericardium due to dissecting aneurysm of the aorta.

> An older patient first presented at 20 weeks gestation with an epileptic fit. She was admitted to hospital where she developed focal neurological signs but these were thought to be due to intracranial thrombosis. She died two days later following further seizures. Autopsy showed dissection of the ascending thoracic aorta with occlusion of both carotid arteries.

> Another patient was admitted in cardiogenic shock with intractable pulmonary oedema at 34 weeks gestation. Autopsy revealed a dissecting aneurysm which extended from the root of the aorta to beyond the origin of the renal arteries.

> One patient died 11 days after delivery. Clinical details are sparse but the autopsy showed dissection of the left coronary artery and the immediate cause of death appears to be pulmonary oedema.

Coronary artery dissection is rare but 70% of cases appear in women and 25% of these cases occur peripartum.

Ruptured aneurysm of coronary vein

> Four days after normal delivery, a young woman complained of severe chest pain at home. She died in the ambulance on the way to hospital. Autopsy showed the immediate cause of death to be a severe pulmonary haemorrhage subsequent to inhalation of gastric contents which seems to have been caused by a dissecting aneurysm of one of the coronary veins which occluded the vessel. The autopsy findings excluded trauma due to resuscitation and the myocardium and other coronary veins were also normal. This exceptionally rare event does not appear to have been recorded before.

Ischaemic heart disease

There were eight deaths from ischaemic heart disease, five more than in 1988 - 1990. The patients were in general older than the normal obstetric population, the age range being between 26 to 41 years, and the mean age of death was 34 years. Six were noted to be smokers, one smoking more than 40 cigarettes per day. One was a non-smoker and in two the smoking history was not recorded. Other risk factors were family history of myocardial infarction (2 patients), obesity (2 patients) and hypertension (1 patient).

Time of death was distributed evenly throughout pregnancy. One patient had a myocardial infarction during evacuation of retained products of conception for an incomplete abortion at 10 weeks. Four patients were found dead whilst still pregnant: two at 20 weeks, one at 26 weeks and one at 32 weeks gestation. One patient collapsed following Caesarean section at 36 weeks for breech presentation. Autopsy showed gross coronary artery atheroma. One patient died two weeks after delivery from a massive stroke due to mural thrombosis from a myocardial infarction. She had been admitted to hospital at the time of myocardial infarction and died despite strenuous efforts. Another patient in her twenties was obese and a heavy smoker. She was found dead of a myocardial infarction at home 26 days after delivery.

None of these cases were judged to have received substandard care.

Endocarditis

A multigravid woman in her twenties was admitted to hospital with a severe asthma attack in the second trimester. She required ventilation and showed some improvement but eight days after admission her pupils became dilated. Computed tomography showed massive brain damage and ventilatory support was withdrawn 36 hours later. Autopsy showed embolic occlusion of the left middle cerebral artery which had caused cerebral infarction. There were also emboli in the heart, spleen and kidneys and their source was non-bacterial vegetations on a normal mitral valve. Antemortem and postmortem blood and tissue culture and histology showed no evidence of bacterial, viral or fungal infection.

This is a most unusual case. This form of endocarditis is usually seen in elderly patients or those suffering from systemic lupus erythematosis or cancer. It may however be associated with a generalised thrombotic state and it is relevant that venous thromboses were found in the uterine vessels. Perhaps pregnancy and dehydration in association with the severe asthma attack increased the thrombotic risk in this patient. There was no element of sub-standard care.

Two other cases of bacterial endocarditis arising after delivery are described earlier, one in a patient with undiagnosed VSD and the other with undiagnosed mitral valve disease.

Myocarditis

There were two cases of presumed viral myocarditis.

One multigravid woman was admitted having collapsed at 10 weeks gestation. She died later the same day from low output heart failure having had multiple cardiac arrests. These precipitated both laparotomy because of concern about intra-abdominal bleeding and thoracotomy because of possible haemopericardium. After death she was found to have elevated IgG and IgM titres to cytomegalovirus; the histology of the myocardium was in keeping with viral myocarditis.

The other patient was 25 weeks pregnant and expecting a multiple birth. She was found dead in bed after a vague illness lasting for one week. At autopsy there was a lymphocytic infiltrate in the myocardium highly suggestive of myocarditis. The lungs also had a lymphocytic infiltrate suggestive of viral pneumonia.

Cardiomyopathy

There were four deaths from cardiomyopathy, two of which are counted in Chapter 15. One was due to dilated cardiomyopathy, thought not to be peri-partum in origin and one was in association with myotonic dystrophy. One additional patient with hypertrophic cardiomyopathy who died for pulmonary embolus is described in Chapter 3.

One patient with a possible history of alcohol abuse concealed her pregnancy and was admitted unbooked with fulminating pre-eclampsia and intra-uterine death. The gestation was unknown but the fetus weighed 3.05 kg, suggesting that she was near term. After the uterus was evacuated she developed pulmonary oedema but required increasing doses of chlormethiazole to control her aggression. She eventually had a respiratory arrest and never recovered neurologically. The autopsy was unsatisfactory since no histology was performed; but the naked eye features of cerebral anoxia (with no focal lesion) and a grossly dilated heart with soft myocardium were considered by the pathologist to be pathognomic of cerebral anoxia caused by cardiac arrest due to cardiomyopathy. However in the absence of histology the diagnosis of alcoholic cardiomyopathy must be considered unproven. Care was judged to be substandard: the patient had no ante-natal care because she concealed her pregnancy.

Another patient, a known asthmatic, developed tachycardia and severe acute hypertension, with visual disturbances, during labour. An attempted forceps delivery was unsuccessful and a Caesarean section was performed. There was moderate bleeding from uterine trauma and blood was transfused. the lowest haemoglobin concentration recorded was 10.0g/dl. Postoperatively she complained of headaches and had a persistent tachycardia of 140bpm. An electrocardiogram was not performed. On the fourth postoperative day she suddenly collapsed and resuscitative measures failed. An autopsy showed no evidence of eclampsia but the cardiac changes were suggestive of early phase cardiomyopathy.

Care was considered to be substandard because of failure to investigate adequately persistent tachycardia and headaches.

Myocardial fibrosis

A multigravid patient had previously been treated for Hodgkin's disease with adriamycin and radiotherapy, subsequently developing radiation pneumonitis. She had an uneventful pregnancy and puerperium. Four weeks after delivery she collapsed with chest pain and could not be resuscitated. Autopsy confirmed radiation pneumonitis and there was severe fibrous scarring of the left ventricle with normal coronary arteries. These findings were compatible with adriamycin myocarditis enhanced by radiotherapy.

Acquired pulmonary hypertension

Three women who died from primary pulmonary hypertension, one associated with Eisenmenger's syndrome, have already been mentioned in the congenital heart disease section of this Chapter.

> One further woman acquired pulmonary hypertension because of systemic sclerosis including oesophageal involvement. She also had thrombocytopenia. Her condition was diagnosed six years previously following the birth of her first child. In this pregnancy she was breathless from 14 weeks gestation. There was no communication between the physician and obstetrician caring for the patient. At 27 weeks gestation she developed severe systemic hypertension which was not controlled satisfactorily by a wide range of agents including angiotensin converting enzyme inhibitors. She remained breathless and was therefore transferred to a teaching hospital. Subsequent echocardiography indicated severe pulmonary hypertension with estimated pulmonary artery pressure 50 - 60 mm Hg. She went into spontaneous labour at 27 weeks gestation and was delivered by elective Caesarean section under general anaesthesia. She was found to have had an abruption with a 500 ml retroplacental blood clot. Immediately following delivery she collapsed and could not be resuscitated. Autopsy indicated that death was due to acute on chronic right ventricular failure due to pulmonary hypertension secondary to systemic sclerosis.

Care was judged to be substandard. There was no communication between obstetrician and physician and neither seemed aware of the severity of the patient's condition. Perhaps because of this there was also no consultation with anaesthetists before labour. Echocardiography at 14 weeks gestation, when the patient first became breathless, would probably have indicated pulmonary hypertension. At that gestation termination of pregnancy would have been feasible.

Unexplained cardiac death

One patient was found at home two weeks after delivery suffering from epileptic fits and unconscious. Autopsy showed that death was due to pulmonary oedema. The coronary arteries were widely patent so the pulmonary oedema was most likely due to arrythmia.

Comments

In recent years there has been a marked shift in the pattern of cardiac deaths in pregnancy in the UK. Structural heart disease such as mitral valve disease or septal defects is relatively less common now in comparison with ischaemic heart disease, cardiomyopathy and aneurysm of the aorta.

Substandard care was present in 10 of the 37 cases described in this chapter. In three cases the actions of the patient were responsible or contributed significantly to her death. In six cases senior and specialist help was not sought in patients with a known history of heart disease or who were acutely ill. This is an obvious failing of the delivery of health care which must be rectified. In one further case there was inadequate co-operation in different specialities looking after a patient in pregnancy.

There were striking differences in substandard care between ischaemic heart disease, (seven deaths and no substandard care) and aneurysm (nine deaths with three cases of substandard care). In each of these three cases no chest X-ray was performed despite the patient complaining of chest pain and despite there being obvious risk factors from the history or in examination to suggest vascular disease. There should be no hesitation in performing chest X-rays in pregnancy. With modern apparatus the radiation risk to the fetus is negligible.

Pulmonary hypertension whatever its origin remains a major cause of maternal mortality. Although cardiologists are aware of this risk, other physicians and obstetricians may not be.

CHAPTER 12

Other *Indirect* causes of maternal deaths

Summary

63 other *Indirect* deaths were recorded in this triennium, representing 28% of all *Direct* and *Indirect* deaths. The total number of *Indirect* deaths, which includes those counted in Chapter 11, is 100, 43% of all *Direct* and *Indirect* deaths in comparison with 34% for the previous triennium.

There were 23 reported *Late Indirect* deaths which are counted in Chapter 15.

Definition

Indirect maternal deaths are defined as those resulting from a previously existing disease or disease that developed during pregnancy which did not have a direct obstetric cause but which was aggravated by the physiological effects of pregnancy. Also included are deaths in which the pregnancy significantly affected the diagnosis, treatment or management of the associated disease (eg diabetes, epilepsy, appendicitis).

Causes of death

The causes of death are summarized in Table 12.1. By comparison with earlier reports striking increases are noted in deaths from ruptured aneurysms (see also Chapter 11) and from streptococcal sepsis.

Table 12.1

Causes of Indirect deaths ; United Kingdom 1991-93		
Diseases	**Number**	**Total**
Infectious diseases		
Streptococcus	5	
E Coli	1	
Enterococcus	1	
Pseudomonas	1	8
Neoplastic diseases		
Breast	1	1
Endocrine, metabolic and immunity disorders		
Diabetes mellitus	3	
Congenital adrenal hyperplasia	1	
Phaeochromocytoma	1	
Systemic lupus erythematosus / scleroderma	4	9
Diseases of the blood		
Sickle cell disease	3	3
Diseases of the central nervous system		
Subarachnoid haemorrhage	9	
Intracerebral haemorrhage	9	
Epilepsy	6	
Bulbar palsy	1	25
Diseases of the circulatory system		
Splenic artery aneurysm	2	
Air embolism	1	3
Diseases of the respiratory system		
Pneumonia	1	
Asthma	1	2
Diseases of the digestive system		
Bowel obstruction	2	
Biliary cirrhosis	1	
Liver failure	3	6
Sudden unnatural deaths		
Possible transfusion reaction	1	
Suicide	5	6
Total		63

Infectious diseases

Eight deaths related to infectious diseases are counted in this chapter.

Substandard care was judged to be present in a case where the initial problem was probably *E.coli* septicaemia.

> The patient was a young multigravid woman who, throughout her pregnancy, had intermittent anorexia, weight loss, abdominal pain and depression. She was admitted at 27 weeks gestation with right iliac fossa pain and after a surgical consultation an appendicectomy was performed at which a normal appendix was removed. Urine culture taken at approximately the same time grew *E.coli*. Post-operatively she remained pyrexial and received intravenous cefuroxime, following which she became markedly hypotensive and the heart rate increased to 140 beats per minute. This was thought to be an anaphylactic reaction to cefuroxime but in retrospect it is more likely that it was due to endotoxic shock. Following treatment for the presumed anaphylactic reaction the blood pressure continued to fall and her haemoglobin had fallen to 6.8 gm/dl. Because of the possibility of intra-abdominal haemorrhage, a second laparotomy was performed which was also normal. By the end of the second laparotomy she was grossly fluid overloaded having received 5.5 litres of fluid, only passed 200 ml urine and with a central venous pressure of 30 cm water. From this time her condition relentlessly deteriorated with pulmonary oedema and inability to maintain adequate oxygenation. The fetus was delivered by Caesarean section and did well. Following delivery she was referred to a specialist unit for "jet" ventilation because of acute respiratory distress syndrome but she died one month after delivery. At autopsy death was found to be due to broncho-pneumonia associated with acute respiratory distress syndrome.

Although the initial presentation was confusing and the results of urine culture were not available when the patient had her first laparotomy, the gross fluid overload in the absence of earlier central venous pressure monitoring represents substandard care.

> A multiparous woman with a twin pregnancy presented in labour at 38 weeks gestation. She was febrile and thought by her GP to have a viral illness. The first twin was delivered by ventouse, the second by Caesarean section because of cord prolapse. The procedures were covered with intravenous cefuroxime. Her condition steadily deteriorated, with the development of pneumonia and acute respiratory distress syndrome (ARDS) requiring tracheostomy. Five weeks after delivery she died from a massive intra-abdominal haemorrhage and disseminated intravascular coagulation (DIC). Just before she died, blood cultures eventually grew an enterococcus sensitive to the vancomycin that she was receiving.

Another patient had been admitted with severe pre-eclampsia at 25 weeks. Her condition deteriorated at 30 weeks and a Caesarean section was planned. However about 18 hours before the planned operation she developed septicaemia possibly because she also had Gaucher's disease. Despite immediate delivery and exemplary intensive care she died of overwhelming *pseudomonas* infection.

Streptococcal septicaemia

There were five deaths all due to proven or assumed streptococcal septicaemia.

Because the streptococcal infection was so fulminant, with all patients dying within 24 hours of becoming ill, it is difficult to be certain that earlier or more appropriate therapy would have made any difference to the outcome but substandard care was judged to be present in two cases.

> A multigravid woman was admitted to the labour ward because of diminished fetal movements, severe diarrhoea and sickness. Three hours later she was cyanosed, tachychardic and hypotensive, with an erythematous rash and having bouts of profuse watery diarrhoea. Treatment with flucloxacycllin, gentamicin and metronidazole was commenced. Two hours following this she was in extreme respiratory distress and because of lack of ICU beds, had to be transferred 20 miles to another town where she died later the same evening. *Streptococcus pyogenes Group A* was identified postmortem in all tissues of the body. She had a sore throat two weeks before her illness but the tonsils appeared normal at autopsy.

Care was considered substandard because of lack of resources; no ICU bed for 20 miles in an urban area, but this probably would not have affected the outcome.

> Another patient was admitted in the late afternoon feeling cold and shivery with backache. She developed fever (39° C) and severe vomiting and diarrhoea during the night. Intrauterine fetal death occurred. Later that morning antibiotics were started but she rapidly developed DIC and could not be resuscitated following a cardiac arrest two hours later. Blood culture yielded pure profuse growth of haemolytic *Streptococcus pyogenes Group A*.

Care was considered to be substandard because of the delay in starting antibiotic treatment and because of difficulty in obtaining consultation from a physician.

> A further patient when 34 weeks pregnant suddenly developed vomiting and abdominal pain one night. Over the past week other members of the family had suffered symptoms of upper respiratory tract infection. By early in the morning she was complaining of shortness of breath and the pain was more severe. Whilst arrangements were made for her admission to the maternity unit she had a respiratory arrest from which she could not be resuscitated. At autopsy she was found to have disseminated intravascular coagulation; gram positive organisms were seen on histology and ß *haemolytic streptococcus Group A* was isolated from all swabs taken postmortem including the vagina. The portal of entry could have been the nasopharynx or possibly the genital tract.

Cellulitis of the leg developed in one patient during labour. Clinically this was thought to be streptococcal and she was treated with parenteral erythromycin because of penicillin sensitivity. Fetal distress developed and she was delivered by Caesarean section, by which time the baby had died. The patient's condition deteriorated markedly and she died on the intensive care unit of multi-organ failure three days later. No significant growth was obtained from any maternal tissues but histology of the affected skin showed numerous streptococci.

Streptococcus Pyogenes Group A was also isolated postmortem from another woman who died within 24 hours of delivery by Caesarean section for abruptio placentae.

These cases illustrate the extreme virulence of *Streptococcus Pyogenes Group A* even in the modern antibiotic era.

In addition, one patient, counted in Chapter 7, died from herpes simplex infection following primary herpes infection of the genital tract.

Neoplastic disease

Only one case of neoplastic disease is counted in this chapter. *Fortuitous* deaths from malignant disease are counted in Chapter 14. These are deaths in which the malignancy did not affect the outcome or course of the woman's pregnancy or conversely where pregnancy did not affect the outcome of the disease.

This patient had carcinoma of the breast and developed a painful breast in the second trimester. She eventually had a needle biopsy which was negative. However the condition progressed to obvious cancer and she had a mastectomy at 29 weeks gestation. At the time of Caesarean section she had bilateral oophorectomy and histology showed deposits within the ovarian tissue. She subsequently became breathless and was admitted to hospital again four days before she died and two weeks after delivery. Autopsy was refused but on admission she was investigated extensively for pulmonary oedema and was thought to have lymphangitis carcinomatosa or acute respiratory distress syndrome caused by the extensive tumour.

Endocrine, metabolic and immunity disorders

Diabetes mellitus

There were three deaths from diabetes mellitus.

In one case care was clearly substandard since this multigravid patient did not co-operate in attending clinics: she was a known "brittle" diabetic and, prior to her pregnancy, had often been admitted with ketoacidosis. Her pregnancy was uneventful but ten days after delivery by Caesarean section she was admitted for nine days because of ketoacidosis and a urinary tract infection. She also had chest pain and was anti-coagulated with warfarin in case she had a pulmonary embolus. She was readmitted the day after discharge with severe ketoacidosis and a very high International Normalised Ratio (INR) level (8.1) suggesting overdose of warfarin. She was discharged three days later. She was readmitted for the third time after delivery two weeks later in severe ketoacidosis from which she did not recover. The community midwives and the diabetic support team were never able to find the patient at home at any time after her delivery.

Substandard care was present because of lack of patient cooperation.

A multigravid insulin dependent diabetic was found dead at home at 14 weeks gestation. Her diabetic control with human actrapid and ultratard insulins was considered satisfactory though there was a tendency to hypoglycaemia. Autopsy revealed no serious abnormality but analysis of a sample of vitreous fluid revealed a low glucose concentration of 0.3 mmol/l. A postmortem blood sample contained 27.6 miu insulin/l which is within the normal therapeutic range. Death was therefore considered to be due to hypoglycaemia, which is an exceedingly uncommon cause of death in pregnancy.

Another patient died in part because of hypoglycaemia. She was a known diabetic, under the care of a consultant obstetrician and consultant endocrinologist, who aspirated regurgitated stomach contents while in a hypoglycaemic coma. She had had a stillbirth at 36 weeks gestation in her first pregnancy and attempts to achieve rigorous diabetic control to ensure fetal wellbeing may have accounted for hypoglycaemia on this occasion.

There was one *Late* death from diabetic ketoacidosis counted in Chapter 15.

This patient was considered to have "impaired glucose metabolism" on the basis of a glucose tolerance test at 36 weeks gestation. She had polyhydramnios and delivered a 4.1 kg infant with shoulder dystocia. She was not followed up and died three months later with severe diabetic ketoacidosis and aspiration pneumonia.

Congenital adrenal hyperplasia

Substandard care was present in the case of a patient with congenital adrenal hyperplasia who died three weeks after delivery.

The patient had an adrenalectomy because of difficulty controlling 21-hydroxylase deficiency. However clinically and biochemically some adrenal tissue was thought to have remained post-operatively since she had a normal resting cortisol and normal short Synacthen test. She became pregnant with Pergonal stimulation. No exogenous steroids were given in pregnancy even though the serum sodium was as low as 128 mmol/l and a random cortisol was 340 nmol/l (probably low for pregnancy); however, the patient remained asymptomatic during pregnancy. She had a long and difficult labour. On the postnatal ward her blood pressure was 100/60 mm Hg and she was discharged with a haemoglobin concentration of 7 g/dl, serum sodium 131 mmol/l and serum cortisol that was eventually recorded as 97 nmol/l. An endocrinologist had been asked to see her in the puerperium but she was discharged before he arrived on the ward. Twelve days after delivery she was seen by her general practitioner complaining of abdominal pain and antibiotics were given. Three days later she was found dead. At autopsy there was pulmonary oedema but the heart and lungs were otherwise normal. The adrenal glands were absent.

Although the mechanism of death was pulmonary oedema it is most likely, given the clinical context, that this was due to acute adrenal insufficiency. The health team was misled by the evidence of adrenal sufficiency present before pregnancy and did not pay sufficient attention to the clinical and biochemical features developing during pregnancy and the puerperium. Steroid replacement therapy should of course have been given through pregnancy, should have been given parenterally over the time of labour and should have been continued in the puerperium. The patient contributed to substandard care by her reluctance to stay in hospital. It is however quite common for patients with congenital adrenal hyperplasia to be ambivalent about medical care. The general practitioner contributed to substandard care by failing to appreciate the significance of abdominal pain in a patient at risk for adrenal insufficiency.

Phaeochromocytoma

A woman who had been investigated in the past for palpitations and syncope presented to the Accident and Emergency Department with vomiting, dizziness and headache. Previous urinary catecholamine levels had been normal. She was about six weeks pregnant. On examination she was shocked and had an unrecordable blood pressure. Aggressive attempts at resuscitation in ICU were unsuccessful and she died because of pulmonary oedema later the same day. Autopsy confirmed pulmonary oedema. There was a 4 cm phaeochromocytoma in the left adrenal gland confirmed by histology. The patient may have had a catecholamine induced cardiomyopathy but gross examination of the heart was normal and no histology was performed on the heart.

This case illustrates the high mortality from undiagnosed phaeochromocytoma in pregnancy, usually quoted as 50%.

Systemic lupus erythematosus and scleroderma

There were three deaths due to systemic lupus erythematosus (SLE) and one in which SLE or scleroderma may have been involved. In one the care was judged to be substandard:

The patient was known to have had lupus for two years and was being treated with azathioprine and glucocorticoids. During the first part of her pregnancy she was managed in a peripheral hospital by consultants in obstetrics and nephrology and was breathless from 14 weeks gestation. She was eventually admitted to the local hospital at about 32 weeks and was transferred to a University teaching hospital in early labour. Examination in the University hospital indicated pulmonary hypertension and this was subsequently confirmed by Swan-Ganz catheterization, when the pulmonary artery pressure was 90 mm Hg systolic. Because of the known risks of general anaesthesia in the presence of pulmonary hypertension the patient was delivered by Caesarean section under local infiltration but she collapsed shortly after delivery and could not be resuscitated because of inadequate pulmonary blood flow.

Care at the University hospital was exemplary but overall was considered substandard since her attendants in early pregnancy had not appreciated the severity of her illness and the significance of her breathlessness. Note the similar patient described in Chapter 11 who died soon after delivery because of pulmonary hypertension in association with scleroderma. Again the attending doctors had not appreciated the significance of breathlessness and the possibility of pulmonary hypertension.

Another patient in her mid twenties had had a very aggressive form of systemic lupus for about one year when she developed acute pancreatitis at 14 weeks gestation. She was already being treated with glucocorticoids and the disease progressed rapidly, with renal failure and disseminated intravascular coagulation causing uncontrollable bleeding from which she eventually died. In addition the autopsy showed disseminated invasive aspergillosis.

A third patient with systemic lupus and known lupus nephritis had been advised against pregnancy because of her severe renal involvement and had been advised to have a termination when she did conceive. At about 12 weeks gestation she died on the way to work. The autopsy showed acute congestive cardiac failure and confirmed the renal findings. Her clinical care was not considered substandard.

One multiparous patient was known to have an autoimmune disease, variously described as SLE or scleroderma. She was delivered by Caesarean section at 34 weeks gestation because of abdominal pain in association with pre-term rupture of membranes. The delivery was uneventful and she was discharged home, only to be readmitted three weeks later with headache and teichopsia. Epileptic seizures heralded a steady deterioration in her level of consciousness and she died three days later. Autopsy showed cerebral vasculitis with pulmonary interstitial fibrosis. These was no evidence of cerebral vein thrombosis which was one of the diagnoses that had been considered. The autopsy findings are more in keeping with SLE than scleroderma.

Diseases of the blood

Two patients counted in this chapter died from sickle cell crisis and another died from hepatic sickle cell sequestration syndrome. A further patient counted in Chapter 6 died from septic abortion but also had Von Willebrand's disease. Von Willebrand's disease probably contributed to this patient's death from disseminated intravascular coagulation.

Sickle cell diseases

Care was judged to be substandard in a patient with haemoglobin SC disease, the combination haemoglobinopathy of haemoglobins S and C.

> The patient had been in contact with a haemoglobinopathy nursing counsellor throughout the antenatal period. She saw the counsellor at 36 weeks gestation when she was complaining of breathlessness. The counsellor was concerned and took her to the antenatal clinic where she only saw a midwife and was then sent home. Three days later she reappeared in the labour ward much more breathless and with abdominal pain. Her peripheral circulation was shut down and she had anuria. Although a diagnosis of abruption was made on admission, she was not delivered by Caesarean section until 12 hours later, by which time the baby was dead. Post operatively she required ventilation in the intensive care unit. She died from renal hepatic and cardiac failure eight days later. Autopsy confirmed sickle cell crisis.

Care was substandard because insufficient attention was paid to her initial presentation with breathlessness; because sickle cell crisis was not considered, even when she presented to the labour ward three days later, and because there was an unacceptable delay between presentation and delivery for abruption. Clinicians frequently underestimate the severity of haemoglobin SC disease since patients are not so anaemic as with homozygous haemoglobin SS disease. The possibility of sickle cell crisis should always be considered in such patients presenting with pain or breathlessness.

> Another patient with sickle cell disease was managed in pregnancy by a consultant haematologist and consultant obstetrician. The precise nature of the sickling condition is not stated but since the haemoglobin concentration was 6.8 g/dl in early pregnancy it is likely that she had homozygous haemoglobin SS disease. Transfusion was avoided in pregnancy. After delivery she developed a cough and became severely breathless. She was treated initially in the ICU for pneumonia by consultants in obstetrics, haematology, microbiology and intensive care. No pathogens were ever grown. Two days later she was transfused. She required ventilation and, subsequently, extra corporeal membrane oxygenation for poor oxygen saturation. She died from brain stem haemorrhage.

Autopsy was refused but in retrospect it seems more likely that she had sickle lung crisis rather than pneumonia. Earlier exchange transfusion might have saved her but care was not considered substandard.

Substandard care in terms of the patient's responsibility was, however, present in a woman with hepatic sickle cell sequestration syndrome.

> She had the sickle ß thalassaemia combination and had recurrent crises. She had been advised against pregnancy and had refused termination when seen in early pregnancy. She then had *pseudomonas* septicaemia, gallstone obstruction of the common bile duct requiring

surgery and was put on total parenteral nutrition. One day after spontaneous pre-term delivery at 29 weeks gestation she became grossly distended and died of liver failure in association with thrombocytopenia. Autopsy was refused but post mortem liver biopsy was characteristic of acute hepatic sequestration syndrome.

Disorders of the central nervous system

Intracranial haemorrhage

There were 18 deaths from intracranial haemorrhage which are included in this section. In addition there were 5 deaths from cerebral haemorrhage in association with eclampsia or severe pre-eclampsia which are included in Chapter 2 and one death from cerebral haemorrhage due to heparin induced thrombocytopenia, the heparin having been given for the treatment of deep vein thrombosis. This death is included in Chapter 4. There were no cases of substandard care.

Subarachnoid haemorrhage

There were nine deaths from primary subarachnoid haemorrhage. Berry aneurysm was identified in six cases at autopsy and considered likely on the basis of histology in a seventh case. No autopsy was performed in two cases; in one a berry aneurysm was thought likely to be present from the CT scan appearance whilst in the other no cause was found for the subarachnoid haemorrhage which was diagnosed clinically. Berry aneurysm was therefore confirmed, or likely, in eight of the nine cases dying from subarachnoid haemorrhage. Seven of these cases presented in the second and third trimesters, before delivery, at gestations varying from 18 to 41 weeks. Two cases presented after delivery, one at seven days and one in a case complicated by eclampsia.

> A multigravida was found having an epileptic fit at 30 weeks gestation following two previous admissions for hypertension. She was delivered and recovered, apart from a continuing headache. Four days later, following a fall, her level of consciousness deteriorated and, despite treatment, she died of a ruptured berry aneurysm. Both eclampsia and the fall may have been contributing factors.

Intracerebral haemorrhage

There were nine cases where intracerebral haemorrhage was the primary presenting feature. In contrast to the patients with subarachnoid haemorrhage where seven out of eight presented before delivery, four of the nine cases of intracerebral haemorrhage presented between one and ten days after delivery; five cases presented before delivery (at 24, 26, 27, 28 and 33 weeks gestation).

> The first patient, a previously well controlled epileptic, had multiple fits on one day and was admitted to hospital unresponsive. Imaging showed a massive intracerebral haemorrhage due to AV malformation. Evacuation of the haematoma was unsuccessful.

A woman in her twenties with hypertension and renal failure collapsed at 26 weeks gestation. A Caesarean section was performed but she was found to be brain dead.

Another patient collapsed at 27 weeks gestation. She had received no antenatal care. On arrival at hospital, CT scans showed intracerebellar haemorrhage. Perimortem Caesarean section was performed, with a resulting live birth. Autopsy showed no cause for the haemorrhage. The consensus of opinion was that the clinical and pathological picture was consistent with cocaine abuse although this was not proven.

A young patient in her first pregnancy was admitted at 28 weeks gestation with a severe frontal headache. CT scan showed a posterior fossa arterio-venous malformation. After failed embolisation, neurosurgical ligation was performed but the patient died from further brain stem haemorrhage in the recovery period.

Another patient was admitted at 33 weeks gestation because of abdominal pain. The platelet count was 48×10^9 /litre. There was blood in the urine. She was normotensive and there were no other features of pre-eclampsia. Later that evening she developed a severe headache, had a seizure and became obtunded. The fetus was delivered by Caesarean section. CT scan showed a massive intracerebral haemorrhage. After protracted negotiations arrangements were made for transfer to a neurosurgical unit, only to be cancelled because the ICU bed was no longer available. After further negotiations another surgical unit agreed to take the patient about five hours after the CT scan. The patient died following a burr hole procedure at the second neurosurgical centre. Autopsy showed no source for the intracerebral haemorrhage and no evidence of pre-eclampsia. In view of the initial clinical presentation, there may have been a bleeding diathesis.

Care was considered sub-standard because of the delays in obtaining specialised neurosurgical treatment.

One patient with a known arterio-venous malformation died ten days after delivery. Arterio-venous malformation was thought to be the cause of death on clinical grounds in one patient who died one day after delivery where no autopsy was performed. In another case dying eight days after delivery no cause for intracerebral haemorrhage was found at autopsy. In the remaining case who died seven days after delivery, no autopsy was performed. This patient had hypertension in pregnancy and was taking atenolol after delivery but her last recorded blood pressure was 85mm Hg diastolic, making it unlikely that hypertension was the immediate cause of her intracerebral haemorrhage.

Epilepsy

Six maternal deaths from epilepsy are counted in this chapter. The deaths from epilepsy are difficult to categorize because there are several elements of uncertainty: usually the patient is found dead and the pathological changes are subtle, ie no other cause of death, congestion of the meningeal vessels and congestion and oedema of the lungs. In the presence of a history of epilepsy and the absence of other causes of death, death was ascribed to epilepsy. In addition, and in particular with relation to substandard care, it is difficult to know just how non-compliant the patients were, or indeed whether they were capable of taking prescribed drug treatment regularly. However in two cases non-compliance certainly does not seem to have been relevant.

> A woman was taking anti-convulsant drugs for epilepsy but had no fits for five years. At 28 weeks gestation she developed a rash thought to be due to varicella; four days later she was found dead at home. At autopsy the above findings were noted and there was no evidence of varicella in the lungs, brain or placenta. Death was ascribed to epilepsy possibly precipitated by acute infection.

> Another patient was taking carbamazepine for epilepsy but she had no seizures for many years and a carbamazepine level taken in early pregnancy was sub-therapeutic. The drug was therefore stopped. At 33 weeks gestation she was found dead at home by her husband. Autopsy showed evidence of asphyxial haemorrhages in the pericardium and massive haemorrhagic oedema of the lungs with aspiration of gastric contents. The cause of death was therefore given as an epileptic fit, most likely to be due to the patient's epileptic history since there were no other features to indicate complications of pregnancy such as eclampsia.

In the three other cases non-compliance was raised as a possibility.

> One patient was found slumped over the bath at home. She was resuscitated and admitted by the ambulance service to an intensive care unit where she was given assisted ventilation but 17 hours after admission she had a cardiac arrest from which she could not be resuscitated. She was a known epileptic with previous suicide attempts, a poor memory and the possibility that some of her seizures may have been artefactual (pseudo-seizures). Paradoxically her epilepsy control had improved before her final seizure so that she was only having fits about once per month; but her general practitioner suspected that she was not taking all the anti-convulsant drugs that she was given. Anti-convulsant levels were checked but there are no records available of the results.

> Another patient, known to have epilepsy since childhood, had never achieved good control of her condition and was also thought to have pseudo-seizures. However, at 32 weeks gestation she started having uncontrollable seizures which continued in the ambulance on the way to hospital. She suffered a cardio-pulmonary arrest in the ambulance, from which she could not be resuscitated. Two weeks before her death the carbamezapine blood level was therapeutic but the valproate level was 2.54 mg/dl, less than the therapeutic range of 4-10 mg/dl. Again, non-compliance was suspected, though it is acknowledged that valproate levels are very poor indicators of therapeutic efficacy.

The third patient in whom non-compliance was suspected was found dead by her husband nine days after delivery. She had marked social difficulties and had taken an overdose in the past. Non-compliance was suggested because of low valproate levels recorded antenatally.

In none of these three patients was non-compliance sufficiently proven to justify categorizing care as substandard and there were no other features of the deaths from epilepsy that indicated substandard care.

One patient, a known epileptic, was found dead in the bath four weeks after delivery. Death was certified as due to drowning due to epilepsy. It might be considered that her recent pregnancy was unconnected. However previous reports have commented on an increased susceptibility to seizures while taking baths in the post-natal period.

Patients who only have infrequent attacks usually have no problems with epilepsy in pregnancy. But those patients whose epilepsy is difficult to control when not pregnant are even more to difficult to control during pregnancy. This is partly because of non-specific features such as stress and fatigue but also because of changes in anti-convulsant drug metabolism. On balance there is a tendency to need more anti-convulsant drug to achieve the same levels of free (unbound) drug in pregnancy as have been achieved in the non-pregnant state. This adjustment can only be made by frequent contact with doctors who are measuring blood levels.

Bulbar palsy

This patient was first admitted to hospital as a child with brain stem encephalitis of unknown cause which left her with a residual bulbar palsy. She eventually had a tracheostomy and by puberty had put on a lot of weight but was able to lead a reasonably normal life. On booking at 16 weeks gestation she was grossly obese. At 29 weeks gestation she presented to the labour ward in respiratory distress, probably due to aspiration of secretions. She collapsed and was delivered by Caesarean section. Postoperatively she never recovered and autopsy showed that death was due to broncho-pneumonia, hypoxic encephalopathy following cardiac arrest and brain stem rarefaction, possibly post encephalitic.

There was no element of substandard care in this patient. Pregnancy and her extreme obesity probably exacerbated her respiratory insufficiency to cause the acute attack that precipitated her collapse.

Diseases of the circulatory system

Aneurysms

Two cases of ruptured aneurysm or arterio-venous (AV) malformation of the aorta and its vessels below the diaphragm, which are usually managed by vascular surgeons, are counted in this chapter. A further nine cases of rupture of aneurysm of the aorta above the diaphragm are counted in Chapter 11 as rupture of the thoracic aorta is usually managed by cardio-thoracic surgeons.

A woman in her thirties had nephrotic syndrome and chronic biliary cirrhosis for which she received a liver transplant three years before her pregnancy. She was taking azathioprine and prednisolone because of her liver transplant. Her pregnancy was relatively uneventful. At 37 weeks gestation she presented with spontaneous rupture of membranes and was delivered by Caesarean section. No problems were encountered at the operation. Eight hours after delivery she started having syncopal episodes which were thought to be related to hypovolaemia. There were no signs in the abdomen and she responded to fluid replacement; however 20 hours after delivery she collapsed with marked abdominal distension. At laparotomy, performed by a consultant surgeon and consultant obstetrician, six litres of blood were removed from the abdominal cavity. It was obvious that blood was coming from the upper abdomen, the aorta was compressed and bleeding ceased but she died despite extensive and continuing resuscitative measures in theatre. Autopsy showed aneurysm or dilatation of the splenic artery and vein with a rupture in the splenic vein. The precise nature of the anomaly was not determined. It was considered to be either a congenital abnormality of the splenic artery and vein or possibly a consequence of previous hepatic transplant surgery.

A patient was booked for consultant care with a history that six years previously she had a carotico-cavernous fistula which caused cavernous sinus thrombosis and sixth nerve palsy. Since the fistula was thrombosing spontaneously no further treatment had been advised at the neurosurgical centre. Her pregnancy was uneventful. Because of her past history she had an elective forceps delivery and this caused extensive vaginal tears, including a third degree tear. The tears were sutured and the vagina packed by a consultant. Twenty four hours after delivery the patient collapsed with a distended abdomen and a laparotomy was performed. A consultant vascular surgeon attended and found that the majority of the blood was arising from below the diaphragm. At this stage cardiac output could only be maintained by external cardiac massage and the surgeon opened the pericardium to allow internal cardiac massage, only to find the pericardium filled with blood, indicating tamponade. However by this stage the patient's pupils were fixed and dilated and further attempts at resuscitation were abandoned. Two autopsies were performed. The first autopsy could not be attended by any of the clinicians and death was ascribed to haemorrhage from the uterus. At the second autopsy the true cause of death was found: bleeding from aneurysms of the splenic artery and the left main coronary artery. Histology showed severe cystic medial necrosis of the aorta.

It is argued whether cystic medial necrosis is a specific abnormality indicating arterial disease with a subsequent tendency to dissection. However this patient was clearly at risk for arterial disease in view of her past medical history. These and the other nine cases of ruptured aortic aneurysm counted in Chapter 11 emphasize the risk of vascular rupture in pregnancy.

> A young multiparous woman was delivered ten days prior to her death. Pregnancy, delivery and the puerperium were all normal. Sexual intercourse had been resumed five days after delivery. On the tenth day, after she had been engaged in sexual intercourse, for approximately an hour and while in a rear entry position, the patient jerked, collapsed, groaned and died. A quantity of blood was passed per vaginam. Autopsy showed that death was due to air embolus. The air bubbles largely filled the coronary arteries which were devoid of blood, as were the atria and ventricles. Bubbles were detected in numerous other major blood vessels. The patient also had a blood amphetamine level of 175 ng/ml.

Amphetamines decrease tiredness and may increase libido while at the same time delaying orgasm. They also have a variable affect on blood pressure and heart rate. This could have affected uterine involution and predisposed to the possibility of embolism. The knee chest position which elevates the uterus above the level of the heart may produce a pressure gradient which "sucks" air into the venous circulation. Air embolism during pregnancy and the puerperium has been described (Lifschultz and Donoghue 1983). However the amount of air in the circulation was more than could reasonably be expected from normal intercourse even after an hour and there may have been some unusual practice involved.

Diseases of the respiratory system

There were two deaths from primary respiratory disease. Note also the patient described in Chapter 11 who died from non-bacterial endocarditis, possibly due to dehydration in association with a severe asthma attack. In one case described below substandard care was present:

> The patient was a 26 year old multiparous woman who had been admitted on two occasions because of intra-uterine growth retardation and abdominal pain. She was admitted on a third occasion at 33 weeks gestation complaining of supra-pubic pain for which no cause could be found. However 12 hours after admission she developed respiratory symptoms and vomited blood stained mucus. Later on in the morning she developed chest signs and X-ray showed extensive abnormal shadowing in both bases and in the left mid zone. She was considered to have extensive pneumonia and was given ampicillin. She refused intravenous antibiotics initially. She was seen by a medical registrar later that day. No additional treatment was ordered. On the next day the patient was intermittently cyanosed and was given cefuroxime. On the following day, two days after the onset of pneumonia, she was given intermittent positive pressure respiration and she was seen by a consultant physician. He considered that she had an atypical pneumonia and advised that ampicillin should be discontinued and erythromycin commenced. Also during the three days of the patient's admission, she had been developing hypertension and proteinuria and for this reason she was delivered by Caesarean section under gen-

eral anaesthesia. It was considered that she was too breathless to tolerate a local anaesthetic. Following the general anaesthetic she was transferred to the intensive care unit but she could never be oxygenated satisfactorily and she died 15 days later with multiple organ failure. One week before she died serological results confirmed elevating antibody titres to mycoplasma.

The widespread X-ray abnormalities should have alerted the clinicians to the possibility of atypical pneumonia and in any case ampicillin alone was inappropriate treatment for a patient developing pneumonia in hospital. An expert medical opinion should have been obtained earlier. The patient also contributed to substandard care by refusing parental therapy and by refusing physiotherapy.

An atopic patient who had been known to have asthma for ten years presented in labour at term. Her last severe attack of asthma had been three months previously when she was treated with a salbutamol nebulizer and oral prednisolone. However her asthma was considered to be well controlled for the remainder of her pregnancy. While in the second stage of labour she suddenly complained of shortness of breath and became increasingly cyanosed. She had a cardio-pulmonary arrest. The fetus was delivered by Kielland's forceps and did well. Cardio-pulmonary resuscitation was performed promptly but she had very stiff lungs which were difficult to inflate. The chest was needled on both sides in case she had a pneumothorax but without any benefit. Amniotic fluid embolism was also considered but she could not be resuscitated and the autopsy showed extensive mucus plugging, indicating severe acute asthma.

This is a most unusual case and quite inexplicable. It is exceptionally uncommon for patients to have acute attacks of asthma in labour and death from an acute attack of asthma in labour is even less common.

Diseases of the digestive system

Bowel obstruction

Six deaths due to diseases of the digestive system are counted in this chapter.

A primigravida was admitted with abdominal pain when she was 33 weeks pregnant. In the past she had an appendicectomy. Ultrasound examination showed a trace of free fluid and some distended loops of bowel but no action was taken as her clinical condition was improving. Four days later she had a further episode of severe pain and vomiting; naso-gastric aspirates were obtained and a Professor of surgery was consulted. He felt that she was experiencing intermittent intestinal obstruction but since she was again improving he advised conservative treatment and she was allowed free fluid intake. Three days later she started in labour which was uncomplicated. Immediately after she was delivered a laparotomy was performed; there was a segment of ileum obstructed by an adhesion from the previous appendicectomy.

The affected bowel was resected but there was faecal soiling of the peritoneal cavity. She was transferred to intensive care but sepsis continued and a further laparotomy was performed with peritoneal toilet and further drainage. Nine days after delivery the anastomosis broke down and ileostomy was performed. Nevertheless she died of intra-abdominal sepsis and peritonitis 32 days after delivery. The above findings were confirmed at autopsy, when she was also found to have superior vena cava thrombosis. Since she had a deep vein thrombosis in the past it is possible that she also had thrombophilia.

This patient received high quality care and the timing of surgery in relation to her pregnancy and delivery was appropriate.

Substandard care was involved in one case of bowel obstruction.

A multiparous patient was admitted at 33 weeks gestation with abdominal pain. Because the cervix was dilated pre-term labour was diagnosed and ritodrine was started intravenously. However this was discontinued when the patient became pyrexial and started vomiting. She was delivered by Caesarean section for fetal distress and free fluid was noted in the abdomen but the abdomen was not explored. The fetus was delivered in poor condition and did not survive. The patient continued to complain of abdominal pain post-operatively and was taken back to theatre for laparotomy six hours after delivery. Gangrenous bowel was found and was resected. She then had four further laparotomies for congenital malrotation of the gut and died four weeks after delivery.

In the presence of free fluid at Caesarean section and because of the patient's history, the registrar was at fault in not exploring the abdomen at the time of Caesarean section. However it is doubtful whether a bowel resection performed six hours earlier would have made much difference to the final outcome.

Liver Diseases

Biliary cirrhosis

Substandard care was also present in a patient who died from alcoholic liver disease. She had been known to have cirrhosis for ten years, refused advice and offers to undergo detoxification. She was also epileptic, a heavy smoker and an amphetamine user. She died undelivered at 34 weeks, having been found dead at home with a massive haematemesis. Substandard care was present because she refused medical treatment.

Liver failure

A patient with known auto-immune liver disease taking azathioprine was admitted at 28 weeks gestation complaining of abdominal pain. She had been vaguely unwell for several weeks beforehand. Liver function at the time of admission was normal. One day after admission she suddenly collapsed and could not be resuscitated. At autopsy there were disseminated platelet microthrombi present throughout the lungs and there was pulmonary oedema. No cause was found for the platelet microthrombi.

Another patient with insulin dependent diabetes and Marfan's syndrome had an abruptio placenta at 38 weeks gestation. She was delivered by Caesarean section under isoflurane anaesthesia. On the day after delivery she developed acute liver failure which led to fatal multi-organ disease. Autopsy showed centrilobular necrosis without fat infiltration. The cause of this hepatic necrosis was not established. The histology and clinical findings were not compatible with HELLP syndrome, acute fatty liver disease of pregnancy or a reaction to isoflurane.

Viral Hepatitis

A further woman died of viral hepatitis.

This patient underwent emergency Caesarean section at 37 weeks gestation for severe pre-eclampsia. She recovered well and was discharged home after seven days. She was readmitted some four weeks later with chest symptoms and yellow sputum. Jaundice was noted. Despite intensive care she deteriorated and died four days later of multiple organ failure and bronchopneumonia secondary to viral hepatitis.

Sudden unnatural deaths

Possible transfusion reaction

A patient was perfectly well until she was delivered at 37 weeks gestation by forceps with manual removal of placenta. Following this she had a postpartum haemorrhage recorded as one litre. Initially her blood pressure was normal; one hour after delivery the blood pressure had fallen to 110/60 mm Hg and she was given oxygen. Two hours after delivery she was transfused, her blood pressure was normal and she was well. Thirteen hours after delivery she was acutely ill, yellow, with blue lips. She was oliguric, having only passed 15 ml urine since delivery and the urine showed massive proteinuria and haematuria. She had grossly abnormal liver function with AST 3340 u/l and was transferred to a liver unit with additional renal failure, haemolysis, disseminated intravascular coagulation and pancreatitis. She died eight days later.

It is difficult to believe that haemorrhage at the time of delivery was the cause of this patients's subsequent severe disseminated intravascular coagulation and acute illness. Although haemorrhage is often underestimated it would have had to be very gross to account for such a catastrophic illness. The timing and nature of her sudden deterioration after transfusion suggests a blood transfusion reaction; it is not clear whether this was considered at the time.

Suicide

There were five cases of suicide counted in this chapter; two after termination of pregnancy, one before delivery and two after delivery. In all cases except the first, the patients had been known to the psychiatric services beforehand. These are discussed more fully in the Annexe to Chapter 15 relating to deaths from suicide.

Comments

In this series there were nine deaths from ruptured aortic aneurysm counted in Chapter 11 and two deaths from splenicAV malformation counted in this chapter. In the 21 years between 1970 and 1990 there were a total of 24 deaths from ruptured aortic aneurysm and 16 deaths from ruptured splenic artery aneurysm, ie an average of 3.4 and 2.2 per triennium respectively. It would appear that in this triennium there has been a marked increase in deaths from aortic aneurysm though there has been no change in the death rate from splenic artery aneurysm. Whether this is a chance phenomenon is unclear but if it is not, the mechanism is uncertain. At least clinicians should be aware of this potential problem so that they are prepared to investigate and call in medical and/or surgical help for those with unexplained chest pain or collapse.

In addition there were nine deaths from ruptured berry aneurysm. A total of 20 deaths, 20% of all *Indirect* maternal deaths, were therefore due to rupture of aneurysms in pregnancy.

There has also been a marked increase in deaths from streptococcal sepsis, five cases in this triennium, compared with only one in the UK in the six years from 1985 to 1990. There has been a worldwide increase in the virulence of the streptococcus and pregnant women may be at increased risk, possibly because of immune suppression. The presentation was almost always acute and non-specific with shakes, fever, vomiting and diarrhoea. There may be no obvious portal of entry and in particular no evidence of genital tract sepsis. If antibiotic treatment is to be of any use, it must be given on clinical suspicion before the results of microbial culture are available. Under these circumstances blind treatment with high dose parenteral penicillin is indicated and it is unlikely to do any harm to further management once appropriate cultures have been taken. If the patient is sensitive to penicillin she should be given erythromycin.

Indirect deaths comprise 43% of all Direct and Indirect maternal deaths. The importance of co-ordinated care for women with medical problems in pregnancy has been emphasized in previous reports but needs re-emphasizing particularly with changing patterns of maternity care. Obstetric teams must have good communications with senior experienced physicians and surgeons who are prepared to come and advise with regard to intercurrent problems in pregnancy. Physicians, in particular, need to be appointed who have a particular interest in the medical problems of pregnancy. Only then will there be a reduction in the number of Indirect maternal deaths, many of which represent substandard care.

Reference

Lifschultz DB, Donoghue ER. Air embolism during intercourse in pregnancy. *J Forensic Sci* 1983; **28** :1021-22.

CHAPTER 13

Caesarean section

Summary

One hundred and three deaths followed Caesarean section, comprising 63 *Direct* deaths, 35 *Indirect* deaths and five *Fortuitous* deaths. In nine of these cases the mother was receiving cardiopulmonary support, was close to death at the time of operation and did not regain consciousness; these 'perimortem' Caesarean sections are considered separately. In addition there were five cases in which Caesarean section was performed post-mortem.

If the peri- and postmortem sections are excluded there were 59 *Direct*, 32 *Indirect* and three *Fortuitous* deaths in which delivery had been by Caesarean section and these are counted in the appropriate chapters.

Of the *Late* deaths listed in Chapter 15, 13 had been delivered by Caesarean section. In none of these cases was it thought that the Caesarean section contributed to the demise of the patient.

There was a dramatic fall, of nearly 44%, in the number of deaths follow-ing elective sections but a doubling of the number after unplanned emer-gency procedures. In the latter cases a common finding was that junior staff took too much responsibility, or had it devolved to them.

The number of perimortem Caeasarean sections was fewer than in previ-ous Reports, and with improved fetal outcome, only two of eleven babies being lost. One was a neonatal death of a second twin; in the other case the fetus was known to be dead but Caesarean section was performed to facil-itate surgical treatment of the mother. This reflects the fact that these pro-cedures are being carried out in better and more controlled circumstances. However, there continues to be a small number of postmortem Caesarean sections performed in hopeless circumstances and with no fetal survivors, in spite of previous recommendations.

Substandard care relevant to the Caesarean section and perioperative man-agement in *Direct* and *Indirect* deaths was identified in 31 cases (34.1%). Substandard care was as common in consultant and senior registrar cases as it was among the operations performed by registrars. The main defi-ciencies were lack of supporting facilities and staff when dealing with high risk cases; misjudgement of the severity of the patient's condition, and of transfusion requirements and fluid balance; and inappropriate deputising or assumption of responsibility.

During the years 1991-93 there were 103 deaths of women following Caesarean section, including nine 'perimortem' deliveries in women who were on life support systems and had no hope of recovery (Table 13.1). Five of the deaths were *Fortuitous* and are not included in the following analyses. In addition there were five postmortem sections which are discussed separately.

The number of *Direct* deaths following Caesarean section (63) was slightly higher than the 60 deaths recorded in the previous triennium, but there was a rise in *Indirect* deaths from 24 to 35. (Table 13.1).

Table 13.1

Deaths connected with Caesarean section*;United Kingdom 1985-93			
	Total deaths	*Direct* deaths	*Indirect* deaths	*Fortuitous* deaths
1985-87	**76 (11)**	50 (4)	22 (6)	4 (1)
1988-90	**91 (12)**	60 (3)	24 (6)	7 (3)
1991-93	**103 (9)**	63 (4)	35 (3)	5 (2)
1985-93	**270 (32)**	**173 (11)**	**81 (15)**	**16 (6)**

* Postmortem Caesarean sections excluded.
 Perimortem Caesarean sections included and shown in parentheses

In previous Reports the estimated fatality rate per thousand Caesarean sections has been quoted. However, because of known inaccuracies in the available denominator data it is not possible on this occasion to derive valid estimates.

Elective and Emergency operations

Because the risks of emergency surgery increase in cases where the patient has not been adequately prepared emergency Caesarean sections have been subdivided into *'planned emergencies'* in which appropriate assessment and preparation has been made, including an adequate period of fasting and the administration of antacids; and *'unplanned emergencies'* where full preparation was not possible because of overriding urgency in the management of the patient.

Direct and *Indirect* deaths, excluding peri- and postmortem operations, are shown in Table 13.2. There was a dramatic fall in the proportion of deaths following elective operations (16.5% of all Caesarean section deaths compared with 36% in 1988-90) but 57 (62.6%) deaths followed planned emergency procedures, compared with 52% in 1988-90. There was also an increase in the number of deaths (from nine to 19) following unplanned emergency operations. As the appropriate denominators are not available it is not possible to estimate the relative risks but clearly the conditions associated with emergency procedures (which includes most of the deaths occurring in patients who have been in labour) requires further study.

Table 13.2

| | | Deaths | |
	Direct	Indirect	Total
Elective	8	7	15
Planned emergency	38	19	57
Unplanned emergency	13	6	19
Total	59	32	91

Title: Direct and Indirect deaths* related to elective and emergency procedures,;United Kingdom 1991-93

* Peri and Postmortem Caesarean sections excluded

Direct maternal deaths

The estimated numbers and percentages of *Direct* deaths associated with Caesarean section for the last three triennia are shown in Table 13.3 and the principal clinical indications for the operation are detailed in Table 13.4.

Table 13.3

Direct maternal deaths within 42 days of Caesarean section*; United Kingdom 1985-93

	All *Direct* deaths	*Direct* deaths following Caesarean sections #	Percentage of all *Direct* deaths
1985-87	139	50 (4)	36.0
1988-90	147	60 (3)	40.8
1991-93	129	63 (4)	48.8

* Postmortem Caesarean sections excluded
# Perimortem Caesarean sections included and shown in parentheses

142

Tables 13.4

Primary indications for Caesarean section* in Direct maternal deaths; United Kingdom 1991-93			
Indication	Elective CS	Planned Emergency CS	Unplanned Emergency CS	Total
Hypertensive disorders	1	8	5	14
'Fetal distress'		11	1	9
Protracted labour		6		6
Antepartum haemorrhage	1	6	4	11
Previous CS	3	1		4
Other obstetric indications	2	4	1	7
Other maternal indications	1	2	2	5
Total	8	38	13	59

*Four perimortem and one postmortem Caesarean sections excluded

The pattern follows broadly that seen in previous Reports apart from the major reduction in the number of elective operations. Three of the four unplanned emergency operations for antepartum haemorrhage were carried out by junior staff. In two cases the consultant apparently had not been informed and in the third the operation had been inappropriately deputed. In one case the status of the operator was not recorded.

> A woman with placenta praevia had two previous sections. The operation was performed by an acting registrar with the sanction of the consultant. Because of bleeding a hysterectomy was required and over 50 units of blood were transfused. A deep vein thrombosis went undiagnosed and death supervened from a pulmonary embolism.

> An obese woman with multiple life threatening medical problems had an antepartum haemorrhage of 1.5-2 litres. was delivered by a registrar and cardiac arrest occurred during the operation. She died from a pulmonary embolism after two weeks in the intensive care unit.

> A woman who had a previous Caesarean section had a repeat section for abruptio placentae. During the procedure there was unrecognised bowel perforation. In spite of two laparotomies she died in the second week.

Indirect Maternal deaths

There were 35 *Indirect* deaths following Caesarean section, including three perimortem sections. The causes of death are listed in Table 13.5 and individual cases are discussed in the appropriate chapters. The perimortem operations are discussed later in this chapter.

Tables 13.5

Causes of death following Caesarean section, Indirect deaths; United Kingdom 1991-93	
Cause of death	**Number**
Pulmonary hypertension	1
Ventricular septal defect	1
Eisenmenger syndrome	1
Pulmonary hypertension, scleroderma	1
Myocardial infarction	2
Aortic aneurysm	3
Splenic aneurysm	1
?Cardiomyopathy	1
Viraemia	1
Viral hepatitis	1
Endotoxaemia, bronchopneumonia	1
Cellulitis, endotoxin shock	1
Streptococcal septicaemia	2
Pneumonia	2
Carcinoma of breast	1
Diabetes mellitus	1
Diabetes mellitus, Marfan's syndrome	1
Systemic lupus, pulmonary hypertension	1
Systemic lupus, cerebral vasculitis	1
Sickle cell crisis	1
Intracranial haemorrhage	2
Subarachnoid haemorrhage	3
Hypoxic encephalopathy	1
Gangrenous colon, malrotation	1
Perimortem sections	
Chronic renal failure	1
Intracranial haemorrhage	2

Tables 13.6

Causes of death following Caesarean section, Fortuitous deaths; United Kingdom 1991-93	
Cause of death	**Number**
Multiple melanoma	1
Burkitt's lymphoma	1
Leukaemia	1
Perimortem sections	
Pneumococcal meningitis	1
Road traffic accident	1
Postmortem sections	
Multiple injuries	1
Road traffic accident	1
Unexplained sudden death	1

Fortuitous deaths

There were five *Fortuitous* deaths following Caesarean section, including two perimortem operations. In addition there were three postmortem deliveries following fortuitous deaths. The causes of death are listed in Table 13.6. The peri- and postmortem operations are discussed later.

Late deaths

There were 12 *Late* deaths in which delivery had been by Caesarean section. In no case did the Caesarean section in any way contribute to, or hasten, the demise of the patient.

Immediate causes of death in *Direct* and *Indirect* deaths following Caesarean section

The attributed immediate causes of death following Caesarean section for the last three triennia are shown in Table 13.7. Pulmonary embolism and hypertensive disorders remain the major causes of death and the potentials for improvement in the management of these conditions are discussed in the appropriate chapters.

Table 13.7

The numbers and percentages (in parentheses) of all deaths after Caesarean section, including perimortem sections, classified by immediate cause of death; United Kingdom 1985-93

	Haemorrhage	Pulmonary embolism	Sepsis	Hypertensive disorders	Anaesthesia	Other Direct causes	Indirect and Fortuitous	**Total**
1985-87	5 (7)	9 (12)	2 (3)	14 (8)	4 (5)	16 (21)	26 (34)	**76**
1988-90	11 (12)	13 (14)	4 (4)	13 (14)	3 (3)	16 (18)	31 (34)	**91**
1991-93	11 (11)	13 (14)	8 (8)	8 (8)	7 (7)	16 (16)	40 (39)	**103**
Total	27 (10)	35 (13)	14 (5)	35 (13)	14 (5)	48 (18)	97 (36)	270

Peri- and postmortem Caesarean sections

Perimortem

Perimortem Caesarean sections are defined as cases in which the mother was close to death at the time of operation, was unconscious, was receiving cardiopulmonary support (CPR) and failed to regain consciousness after delivery.

There were nine such cases, including two twin pregnancies, and nine of the eleven babies survived. A second twin died from anoxic brain damage and one baby was stillborn.

> A woman receiving treatment for chronic renal failure had a cerebral haemorrhage at 27 weeks gestation and was declared brain dead. CPR was instituted immediately and maintained until a living infant was delivered by classical Caesarean section.

> A woman at 27 weeks gestation with pneumococcal meningitis following brain death received CPR until the baby could be delivered under optimal conditions. The baby survived.

> A woman at term collapsed during labour as a result of a pulmonary embolism. She was delivered within a few minutes of a liveborn infant which survived.

> Another woman who collapsed during labour had an amniotic fluid embolism. Resuscitation was started immediately and the registrar promptly delivered a live baby by Caesarean section. The mother did not regain consciousness and died 11 days later.

> A woman with a twin pregnancy suffered from idiopathic thrombocytopenia, developed eclampsia and had a subarachnoid haemorrhage. Intubation and CPR were started within minutes of her collapse and living infants were delivered under controlled conditions.

> In another twin pregnancy collapse due to an amniotic fluid embolism occurred during labour. CPR was established within about five minutes and the babies were delivered after 25 minutes. Both were liveborn but one suffered brain damage and died in the neonatal period.

> A suspected drug abuser who had no antenatal care collapsed at home at about 27 weeks gestation and was attended by paramedics. She became apnoeic and was intubated but cardiac function remained normal and her blood pressure was maintained. Soon after admission to the Accident and Emergency unit she was declared brain dead. Consideration was given to deferring delivery and administering dexamethasone to improve the prospects for the fetus but her condition became so unstable that immediate delivery was preferred. The infant was in good condition and survived.

A woman who suffered severe injuries, including intracranial haemorrhage, in a road accident was known to have a dead fetus as the result of traumatic abruptio placentae. She required a craniotomy and a Caesarean section was performed at the same time to facilitate her subsequent management. She failed to regain consciousness and died nine days later.

Another woman with intracranial haemorrhage from an arteriovenous malformation was also delivered by Caesarean section at the time of craniotomy. The baby survived but she did not regain consciousness.

Post mortem

Five Caesarean sections were performed on women already pronounced dead in spite of attempts at cardio-pulmonary resuscitation by paramedics following 999 calls. Three deaths were associated with road accidents. Two women died at home, one following electrocution and the other following unexplained cardiac arrest. The interval from maternal death was not precisely recorded, but the interval from 999 calls to operation was a minimum of 25m in one case and 35m in another.

All the operations were performed in Accident and Emergency units, four of them by obstetric registrars (one of whom had to be called from another hospital). In no case was there any record of the presence of a paediatrician or of facilities for neonatal resuscitation. There were no surviving babies; four were stillborn and the fifth died within two days.

Comment

In previous Reports concern has been expressed about the poor fetal outcome when fetal rescue operations are attempted in understandable but inappropriate circumstances.

The number of perimortem sections in this trimester has fallen compared with the two previous Reports (nine cases compared with 11 and 12 in previous triennia). In this triennium the operation was carried out with adequate staff and facilities in all cases. Also there was a notable improvement in the fetal outcome, with only two of eleven babies being lost. In one of these cases it was known that the baby was dead prior to the operation.

The synopses of the cases have been given to illustrate the circumstances in which successful outcome may or may not be expected. Again following postmortem Caesarean section there were no surviving babies, whereas the fetal results for perimortem sections, performed under optimal conditions, were good.

Table 13.8

Status of the operator and substandard care in Direct and Indirect deaths following Elective and Emergency Caesarean sections; United Kingdom 1991-93 (Peri- and postmortem sections excluded)

	Elective		Planned emergency		Unplanned emergency		Total	
	n	Substandard care	n	Substandard care	n	Substandard care	n (%)	Substandard care
Consultant	7	1	17	5	3	2	27 (29.7)	8 (29.6)
Sr Registrar	1	0	4	2	3	1	8 (8.8)	3 (37.5)
Registrar	4	1	29	12	11	7	44 (48.4)	20 (45.5)
Other	3**	0	7****	0	2*	0	12 (13.2)	0
Total	15	2(13.3%)	57	19(33.3%)	19	10(52.6%)	91	31(34.1)

* One status not recorded

** Two status not recorded

**** Four status not recorded

The need to have clear policies concerning the indications and circumstances in which peri- and postmortem Caesarean section may be appropriate is again emphasised and these should be known to all staff, including Accident and Emergency, who are likely to encounter this problem.

Substandard care

There was judged to be substandard care directly related to the conduct of the Caesarean section and aftercare in 31 (34.1%) of the 91 *Direct* and *Indirect* deaths (excluding peri- and postmortem sections)(Table 13.8).

Consultants or senior registrars performed 38.5% of the Caesarean sections overall. This group included a disproportionate number of high risk cases, such as major life threatening medical and surgical disorders and severe hypertensive complications. Substandard care directly relating to the delivery and post-operative care occurred in 11/35 (31.4%) of these cases. The main substandard aspects of care relating to senior staff included inadequate facilities and support staff for dealing with high risk cases and misjudgement of transfusion requirements.

Over 60% of Caesarean sections were performed by staff below the grade of consultant or senior registrar. Registrars carried out the operation in 48.4% of Caesarean sections overall and 50.9% of emergency procedures. Relevant substandard care was identified in 45.5% of registrar cases. Eleven of the 19 unplanned emergency operations were undertaken by registrars and there was substandard care in seven of these. Deficiencies in care by junior trainees included inappropriate deputising; failure to appreciate the seriousness of the patient's condition with consequent delay in instituting adequate treatment; and failure to seek more senior help.

In most cases with substandard care there were several interrelated contributory factors but it is clear that a number of problems which have been highlighted in the past still pertain, particularly lack of facilities to cope with unanticipated complications and too much responsibility being devolved to or taken by junior staff. Consultants and management should address these problems and look for prompt improvements.

CHAPTER 14

Fortuitous Deaths

Fortuitous deaths are coincidental deaths unconnected with pregnancy or the puerperium. By international definition they are not considered as part of maternal mortality and do not feature in maternal mortality statistics. *Fortuitous* deaths are within the broader defined criteria for reporting to the Enquiry, the final decision on classification being made by the central assessors.

In this triennium 46 *Fortuitous* deaths were recorded during pregnancy or within 42 days of delivery or termination. These are listed in Table 14.1. In addition there were 15 *Late Fortuitous* deaths discussed in Chapter 15. It is interesting to note that an undiagnosed abdominal pregnancy was found at autopsy in one of these cases, although not in any way related to the woman's death.

Neoplastic disease

Ten deaths due to neoplastic disease were considered to be *Fortuitous* in that the pregnancy had no effect on the underlying pathology. In only three cases was the malignancy identified prior to the pregnancy. Three women died undelivered and a further three first presented with symptoms and died in the puerperium. In four cases pregnancy was terminated prematurely. For two the diagnosis of malignancy during pregnancy resulted in premature induction of labour, at 31 and 36 weeks gestation respectively, but only the latter resulted in a live birth. In the other cases elective Caesarean sections were performed, both at 31 weeks, with one baby surviving and the other suffering an early neonatal death from herpes viraemia.

Intracerebral haemorrhage

There were two deaths from intracerebral haemorrhage, one from a traumatic subdural haemorrhage following a skull fracture, the other concerning a woman who collapsed with a subarachnoid haemorrhage secondary to a carotid artery aneurysm five weeks after a normal pregnancy and delivery. It was considered that there were no avoidable obstetric factors in these cases.

Deaths where the cause could not be established

There were four deaths for which no satisfactory cause of death could be established.

> A young multigravida suffered a cardiac arrest at home at 35 weeks gestation in a normal pregnancy. She and the fetus were dead on

Table 14.1

Fortuitous deaths; United Kingdom 1991-1993	
Cause of Death	**Number**
Neoplastic Diseases	
Burkett's lymphoma	1
Acute myeloid leukaemia	1
Osteogenic sarcoma	1
Astrocytoma	1
Malignant pituitary adenoma	1
Carcinoma of colon	1
Cerebral tumour	1
Melanoma	1
Carcinoma of the pancreas	1
Carcinomatosis (unknown primary)	1
Diseases of Nervous System	
Ruptured ventricular cyst	1
Pneumococcal meningitis	1
Intracerebral haemorrhage	2
Diseases of Respiratory System	
Pneumonia[*]	3
Infectious Diseases	
Septicaemia unrelated to pregnancy	2
Cause of death undetermined	4
Unnatural Deaths	
Road Traffic Accident	9
Injecting substance abuse[**]	4
Murder	2
Drowning -suicide/open verdict	3
Burning - house fire	2
Alcohol related	1
Overdose - suicide	1
TOTAL	**46**

[*]   two associated with injecting substance abuse

[**]   one case also mentioned in Chapter 6

arrival at hospital. Autopsy showed pulmonary oedema suggesting that there may have been a dysrhythmia. Although the cause of death was certified as "myocardial fibrosis" the heart was macroscopically normal and no histology was reported from the Coroner's autopsy.

A woman in her second pregnancy collapsed at home at 34 weeks gestation. There was no history of convulsions and she recovered rapidly. She was seen by physicians in hospital and no cause for the collapse was found. She was discharged home. Two weeks later she had another collapse after a heavy meal at home and attempts to resuscitate her for 40 minutes failed. Autopsy showed gastric aspiration and this was the cause of her death but the reason for her collapses is a mystery.

In two other cases the failure to request an autopsy meant no explanation for the death could be established.

A multiparous patient with known inflammatory bowel disease was admitted with pyrexia and chest symptoms under the care of a physician at 26 weeks gestation. Her condition deteriorated and when, many days later, an obstetrician was asked to review her, an intrauterine death was diagnosed. Induction of labour was successful but the patient's condition deteriorated further and she died the same day from multiple organ failure and acute respiratory distress syndrome. The stillbirth was fresh and fetal death was thought to have been secondary to the patients deteriorating condition, not the cause of it.

A multiparous woman developed a puerperal psychosis with paranoia five days after delivery. She was transferred to a psychiatric hospital where she was found dead in bed two weeks later. Autopsy showed only pulmonary oedema and no definite cause of death was established.

Unnatural deaths

There were 23 unnatural deaths, of which 7 are commented on further.

A postmortem Caesarean section was performed on a woman of 38 weeks gestation who had died instantly from multiple injuries sustained in a road traffic accident 45 minutes earlier. The baby was resuscitated and survived for 48 hours but died of cerebral damage due to intrauterine anoxia. This case highlights the poor success rate for fetal survival for postmortem Caesarean sections, which, unless performed immediately following the maternal death, are almost invariably associated with severe fetal anoxia and consequent cerebral damage.

Two women, with known severe psychiatric illness, died from drowning. In one case a verdict of suicide was returned on a known schizophrenic of 34 weeks gestation. In the other an open verdict was returned on a woman with severe manic depressive illness who had been detained for some months under Section 3 of the Mental Health Act.

A third young woman with a long standing history of depressive illness died from an overdose of antidepressants in the first trimester. Although suicide may classified as an indirect cause of maternal death, (see Chapters 12 and 15), the previous medical histories in these three cases make the association with pregnancy in these cases seem unlikely.

A further two women, known injecting substance abusers, and both in early pregnancy, died of aspiration of stomach contents following drug overdoses. One case was associated with the misuse of buprenorphine (Temgesic).

A further puzzling death concerned a known drug addict who collapsed and died at home during the seventh month of her pregnancy. She had excessive levels of Temazepam and methadone in her blood and signs of lobar pneumonia, although the precise cause of her death remains unascertained. As with the first case mentioned in this section, a postmortem Caesarean Section was performed, this time one hour after death, resulting in a stillbirth.

CHAPTER 15

Late deaths

Deaths in women more than 42 days, but less than one year after pregnancy or delivery are defined as *Late* deaths. The current International Classification of Maternal Deaths (ICD9) excludes such deaths but during the collation of earlier Reports it became apparent that strict adherence to this criterion led to the omission of a number of *Late* deaths which were related to pregnancy. This Report includes all deaths occurring up to six months after pregnancy or delivery as well as those occurring between 6 to 12 months if the Regional Assessors considered them to be related to the pregnancy or delivery. Scotland and Northern Ireland continue to collect cases up to one year after pregnancy or delivery. For the next triennium the new ICD10 definition of *Late* deaths will be used and will include all deaths directly or indirectly related to obstetric causes occurring after 42 days but within one year of abortion or delivery. This was discussed in more detail in the Method of Enquiry section of this Report.

A total of 46 *Late* deaths were reported in this triennium compared with 48 in 1988, can be further classified as *Direct*, *Indirect* or *Fortuitous*, although for statistical purposes they are not included under these headings.

Late deaths - *Direct* obstetric causes

Ten of the 46 *Late* deaths were considered to be directly related to maternal causes, despite the time which had elapsed since delivery.

Five of these women died from pulmonary thromboembolism within three months of delivery, all of whom were obese. They are also mentioned in Chapter 4.

> On the ninth day following a Caesarean section and pregnancy associated with appropriately managed mild pre-eclampsia, a woman in her thirties was admitted with a cerebral infarct. Following discharge three weeks later she complained of chest and leg pains and pyrexia for which she was seen on three occasions by separate deputising doctors. After a further week she eventually saw her own general practitioner but died two days later following a pulmonary embolism.

The lack of continuity of care and failure in communication may have resulted in her symptoms not being assessed more accurately and the underlying deep vein thrombosis remained (DVT) undiagnosed. At no time did she receive anticoagulant therapy. A coroner's inquest was held with a verdict of death from natural causes.

The second case concerns a woman who, two months following an uncomplicated pregnancy and delivery, developed pain in her right iliac fossa. Her symptoms were severe enough to require admission to a urology ward where she appeared to be satisfactorily treated for a urinary tract infection. Twelve days following discharge she succumbed to a massive pulmonary embolism. No autopsy was performed but the likely underlying diagnosis of pelvic vein thrombosis was considered to have been extremely difficult to make in view of her considerable obesity.

The third death occurred in a young primigravida who died at home following a premature birth some two months earlier. Her pregnancy had been uneventful apart from mild hypertension. She had not sought medical help since delivery and the autopsy revealed multiple fresh pulmonary emboli and underlying deep vein thrombosis.

The fourth case concerned a woman who had an unremarkable pregnancy apart from a moderate postpartum haemorrhage requiring two units of blood. She was found dead at home some three months after delivery and autopsy revealed the cause to be a pulmonary embolism and underlying DVT.

The fifth death occurred in a very obese woman in her twenties. Her pregnancy was uneventful, apart from a small postpartum haemorrhage. The precise details of her final illness remain obscure but autopsy revealed the cause of death to be a pulmonary embolism consequent to a DVT.

A further woman also had pulmonary emboli but eventually died from septicaemia following resection of infarcted small bowel secondary to mesenteric vein thrombosis.

This young woman suffered from pre-eclampsia and had a family history of hypertension and DVTs. Because of an increasing rise in blood pressure an elective Caesarean section was performed at 28 weeks gestation. She was treated with anti-embolism stockings and subcutaneous heparin until 7 days post delivery. Two weeks later she was readmitted with multiple pulmonary emboli and required a laparotomy to resect infarcted small bowel secondary to mesenteric vein thrombosis. Her condition continued to deteriorate, with further bowel perforations and superior vena cava obstruction. Despite intensive care she eventually died three months after delivery from septicaemia. There was no evidence of substandard care.

Two patients succumbed to postpartum cardiomyopathy and are discussed in Chapter 11.

One death was precipitated by multi-organ failure secondary to acute respiratory distress syndrome (ARDS) and is discussed more fully in Chapter 3.

This complicated case concerned a primigravida who was admitted at 32 weeks gestation and treated conservatively for pre-eclampsia. Before the planned elective Caesarean section could be performed an intrauterine death was discovered on routine ultrasound and labour was induced. A routine screen suggested the possibility of disseminated intravascular coagulation (DIC). It was also considered she might have had abruptio placentae, but this was not finally confirmed. She suffered a blood loss of 3000ml for which she received in total 6 units each of packed cells, cryoprecipitate, whole blood and platelets. She then developed pulmonary oedema followed by ARDS. She was transferred to an ICU where, despite every effort, her condition continued to deteriorate and she subsequently succumbed to multi-organ failure some nine weeks after delivery.

The final direct *Late* death concerns a young woman who died several months after delivery, despite continuing intensive care, of complications from pregnancy induced hypertension and HELLP syndrome. This case is mentioned and discussed in Chapter 2.

Late deaths - *Indirect* obstetric causes

There were 23 cases where the pregnancy may have indirectly contributed to the death. They are listed in Table 15.1, some of which are discussed further.

Suicide

There were five *Late* deaths resulting from suicide considered to be a result of post natal depression and one verdict of accidental death where the case history was suggestive of this. These are in addition to the five cases which occurred before 42 days postpartum which are counted in Chapter 12. Psychiatric difficulties in all but one of the *Late* cases were known to health care professionals; one woman had received a period of inpatient care and two were in mother and baby psychiatric units at the time of death. These cases are discussed more fully in the Annexe to this Chapter.

Unexplained deaths

There were three unexplained deaths.

> In the first case the woman was found dead at home some seven weeks after delivery with no significant preceding medical history. The cause of death was given as aspiration of gastric contents and the autopsy findings were strongly suggestive of gram negative septicaemia. However the source of the putative sepsis could not be identified.

> The second case involved a young woman who died at home two months after a mid trimester spontaneous abortion for which she received prophylactic antibiotics. Although the cause of death was unascertained it is considered possible that this might have been the consequence of a septic abortion.

Table 15.1

Late Deaths - Indirect Causes; United Kingdom 1991-1993	
Causes of death	**Number**
Neoplastic Diseases	
Carcinoma of ovary (clear cell)	1
Carcinoma of cervix	2
Sarcoma of uterus	1
Diseases of the Circulatory System	
Cerebellar capillary haemangioma	1
Mitral valve disease	1
Disease of the Nervous System	
Infantile polydystrophy	1
Disease of Endocrine System	
Diabetic ketoacidosis	1
Disease of Digestive system	
Liver failure	1
Infectious Diseases	
Pulmonary tuberculosis	1
Varicella pneumonia	1
Other	
Haemorrhage following tracheostomy for subglottic stenosis	1
Myotonic dystrophy	1
Unexplained	3
Sudden unnatural deaths - Suicide	
Overdose of co-proxamol[*]	3
Overdose of dothiepin	1
Drowning	1
Jumped in front of train	1
Jumped off bridge	1
Total	**23**

[*] = one case was considered by the coroner to be accidental despite well documented post-natal depression

Table 15.2

Fortuitous Late deaths - unrelated to obstetric causes; United Kingdom 1991-1993	
Causes of Death	**Number**
Diseases of Circulatory System	
Myocardial infarction	3
Subacute bacterial endocarditis	1
Diseases of Respiratory System	
Cystic fibrosis	1
Neoplastic disease	
Malignant melanoma	1
Connective tissue disorders	
Systemic lupus erythematosis	1
Unexplained deaths	
Unascertained*	1
Sudden Unnatural Deaths	
Drug abuse	4
Suicide by hanging	1
Total	**13**

* Despite intensive pathological investigations, the cause for this sudden death remains unexplained but it is not considered related to the earlier pregnancy

Table 15.3

Interval between delivery or abortion and death - Late cases; United Kingdom 1991-1993				
Days after delivery	**Direct**	**Indirect**	**Fortuitous**	**Total**
43-91	8	11	5	24
92-182	1	9	5	15
183-273	-	3	3	6
274-365	1	-	-	1
Total	**10**	**23**	**13**	**46**

The assessment of why the third woman died, an immigrant who had been resident in the country for 10 years, was severely hampered by a singularly unhelpful response from those involved in her care and a grossly inadequate autopsy report which contained several factual inaccuracies. It also proved impossible to locate the notes concerning her final admission to hospital. The woman, who had a history of repeated admissions for chest problems collapsed and died some three months after giving birth, having seen her GP on the day of her death who thought she might have had a chest infection. The cause of death was given as pneumothorax although the autopsy did not reveal any convincing evidence of this. A blood stained pleural effusion was noted but the possibility of a pulmonary embolism was not considered.

Other deaths

A woman died of pulmonary tuberculosis several months after delivery. She was a recent immigrant who failed to gain weight during her pregnancy and although she received full antenatal care the possibility of TB was not considered at this time. In this respect her care was considered to have been substandard.

A young mother died of diabetic ketoacidosis having developed gestational diabetes during pregnancy. It appears that no arrangements were made for follow up post delivery and the GP was not aware of the condition. In the opinion of the assessors this was a case of significantly substandard care.

A woman who had lactation suppressed by bromocriptine following a stillbirth was admitted a month after delivery with jaundice and haemolytic anaemia. Liver biopsy failed to reveal the cause of her hepatic illness but it was considered possible that it may have been due to bromocriptine. Despite continuing medical care she died of liver failure in a supraregional liver unit.

A case of varicella pneumonia was submitted too late for full pathological and intensive care assessment. She developed fulminant varicella infection in the later stages of pregnancy with associated pneumonia and hypoxia. She was delivered by Caesarean section at 35 weeks gestation. She was then transferred to an intensive care unit (ICU) where she required ventilation for seven weeks until she succumbed to her illness. There was no substandard care.

Late deaths - Fortuitous causes

There were 13 such incidental deaths which are listed in Table 15.2. The case of suicide by hanging was considered unrelated to post natal depression because of a long standing psychiatric history.

The interval between delivery and death for all Late deaths is shown in Table 15.3

ANNEXE TO CHAPTER 15

Substance abuse and suicide

Substance abuse

It is disappointing to report that 8 deaths were directly due to injecting substance abuse, 2 in mid trimester, 2 following terminations of pregnancy and 4 occurring between 3 and 6 months after delivery. All these women were known substance abusers and the majority known to the psychiatric and social services. Each case involved the use of heroin, four in association with temazepam, and one each with buprenorphine (Temgesic), carbamazepine or butane gas inhalation.

In addition there were at least two cases where the ingestion of amphetamine or cocaine may have significantly contributed to the cause of death, and three others where this suspicion was raised but not proved because of inadequate autopsies.

Sadly two women died, undelivered, of the consequences of acute alcoholic poisoning. Both were known alcoholics and one also used amphetamines.

Suicide

Apart from three suicides of women with long standing psychiatric histories, and whose deaths were not considered to be related to their pregnancy, there were eleven deaths from suicide associated with pregnancy reported in this triennium. In one of these cases, despite a well documented history of postnatal depression an open verdict was returned on the cause of death.

Suicides associated with pregnancy are counted and discussed in Chapters 12 and 15 depending on when the event occurred. This section aims to bring together the common features of these deaths and points the way to a more detailed psychiatric assessment of such deaths in the next Report. Concerns around the management of post natal depression, which may lead to suicide were expressed in Changing Childbirth (1993), which stated that professionals need to be alert to the possibility of women developing postnatal depression. Some 10-15% of women suffer from postnatal depression and 50-60% experience postnatal blues. The relative risk of admission to a psychiatric hospital with a psychotic illness is 22 times greater in the first month after the birth of a child than in any of the preceding two years (Tilowsky et al 1991). Mental illness is one of the five key areas in the Government's strategy document The Health of the Nation (1992), in which a specific target is a reduction in the number of suicides. The Health of the Nation Key Area Handbook on mental illness (1993) advises that all professional groups would benefit from the development of general and specialist skills in appropriate care of postnatal depression. Any suicide is devastating for the relatives and friends concerned, but is all the more distressing when a young family is concerned. For these reasons it is proposed to include a more detailed specific section on suicides during or following pregnancy in future Reports.

Deaths following termination of pregnancy

Two young women died from drug overdoses following termination of pregnancy.

One woman died five weeks after termination, having taken another overdose three weeks earlier. Following the first overdose the psychiatric registrar phoned the GP to suggest antidepressant medication and psychiatric follow up once she had started the treatment. The GP did not give the medication or arrange for a follow up appointment as the patient did not specifically request it or discuss her personal problems when last seen at the surgery. She died of an overdose sixteen days later.

A woman presented to her GP with depression at 18 weeks gestation. Her request for a termination of pregnancy was refused. She was referred to the psychiatric services but failed to attend for her appointment. She subsequently arranged and had a late termination by evacuation at 20+ weeks in an approved private clinic. She apparently had no follow up counselling and died of an overdose of co-proxamol two weeks later.

Death during pregnancy

One woman with a history of depressive illness which started after an earlier cot death and who lived in poor social circumstances died undelivered in the mid trimester. She was known to the social services and community midwives who supported her as best they could. The woman was under the care of the psychiatrists but was not taking any medication because of her pregnancy. She died following an overdose of paracetamol and alcohol.

Deaths following pregnancy

Eight women died after delivery:

The first, who had already had an episode of postpartum psychosis following the birth of her first child suffered a severe recurrence shortly after the birth of her second. She was informally admitted to a mother and baby psychiatric unit a few weeks following the second birth where, following antidepressant therapy, she improved to the extent that she was able to go out to the shops or take short periods of home leave. Some months later, and although she had not expressed any overt suicidal intentions during the preceding week, she jumped under a train whilst absent on a visit to the local shops.

The second woman first developed signs of post-natal depression two months following a normal delivery. Despite prompt psychiatric treatment and follow-up, her mental state continued to deteriorate and following a drug overdose she was admitted to a specialised mother and baby unit with a diagnosis of a primary bonding disorder. She absconded twice, the second episode resulting in her death by drowning some five months after delivery.

The third death, which, because it occurred two weeks after delivery, is counted in Chapter 12. The GP was called to see the patient at the request of the community midwife because the woman was exhibiting bizarre behaviour and expressing thoughts of suicide. During the visit the GP was sufficiently concerned as to suggest an immediate psychiatric referral. Shortly after the GP left the house to go to the surgery to make the necessary phone calls the woman stabbed herself to death.

A fourth young woman, who had moved to a temporary house in a new area of the country shortly after delivery of her third child died of a drugs overdose. In this case the GP who was initially looking after her, and who had commenced treatment for post-natal depression, did not liaise with the new GP; neither was her condition picked up by the nurse at the new practice who had undertaken a new patient screen the week before. She died four months after delivery. There was no history of postnatal depression in earlier pregnancies.

The fifth woman, who had been treated for post-natal depression both as and in- and out patient for eight months following a difficult Caesarean section, died of monoamine oxidase inhibitor poisoning in conjunction with excessive alcohol. At the time she was being supported by weekly visits from a crisis intervention team. She had a history of post-natal depression in her earlier pregnancies.

The sixth death concerns a young single woman who took an overdose of a relative's antidepressant medication some weeks after delivery. She had not complained of depression and was being fully supported by her family and health care professionals.

The seventh woman, who had been admitted to a psychiatric unit with severe puerperal psychosis shortly after delivery, was discharged after a few days. The next morning she threw herself under a train. This case is counted in Chapter 12 as her death occurred within two weeks of delivery.

The final case concerned a woman with a long standing history of depressive illness who had made several suicide attempts in the past. Following the birth of her child her condition was severe enough to require compulsory admission to a regional secure unit, during which time she appeared to improve and the compulsory order was removed. She continued to remain as a voluntary in patient with less intensive nursing observation. It was during this period that she hung herself whilst in the hospital. It is doubtful whether her illness was due to postnatal depression, but this may have aggravated it.

References

Department of Health. *Changing Childbirth Part 1*; Report of the Expert Maternity Group. London: HMSO; August 1993.

Tilowsky L *et al* (eds) 1991. *Women and Mental Health*. Br J Psychiatry; **158**: Sup 10.

Department of Health. *The Health of the Nation. A strategy for Health in England*. London: HMSO; 1992. (Cmnd 1986).

Department of Health. *The Health of the Nation - Key Area Handbook: Mental Illness*. Department of Health; January 1993.

CHAPTER 16

Pathology

Summary

Of the 320 deaths reported in this triennium, autopsies were performed on 232 cases (73%). The autopsy and report were considered inadequate in 53 (23%). Histology was performed on 143 (62%) of the autopsies and in one case there was a postmortem needle biopsy of the liver without autopsy. In only 105 cases was the histology report considered adequate.

The quality of the autopsy

It is disappointing that the standard of so many autopsies remains inadequate and shows no improvement over those in previous Reports. Because of the poor standard of the initial autopsy a second autopsy was performed in two cases.

> A diagnosis of mediastinal nodular sclerosing Hodgkin's disease was made in a patient three years before death. She was treated with doxorubicin (Adriamycin) and mediastinal radiotherapy with a good response. Two years later she developed a cough and pulmonary fibrosis was diagnosed. The following year, after a normal pregnancy, she was delivered of a full term live baby but one month later the mother developed chest pain and died. The initial autopsy was inadequate, the cause of death being given as hypertensive cardiac failure although the heart was of normal weight and there was no evidence of hypertension during or after the pregnancy. A second autopsy was ordered and this revealed changes of cardiac and pulmonary fibrosis characteristic of doxorubicin/radiotherapy toxicity.

> Four years before delivery the second woman developed a spontaneous dissection of the intracavernous segment of the internal carotid artery leading to caroticocavernous fistula. This subsequently thrombosed with spontaneous resolution. After a normal pregnancy and in view of the previous caroticocavernous fistula labour was induced with 2mg dinoprostone gel followed by elective forceps delivery. There was a third degree perineal tear which was sutured and the vagina packed. Estimated blood loss was 1500 ml. Twenty six hours after delivery the patient had a cardiac arrest. The abdomen was distended and, after cardiac resuscitation, a haemoperitoneum was found at laparotomy. There was no evidence of pelvic or vaginal bleeding, rather the bleeding appeared to come from the upper abdomen. To maintain cardiac output internal cardiac massage was initiated at which stage it was noticed that there was a haemopericardium with

Table 16.1

*Subjective assessment of the adequacy of autopsies in **Direct** maternal deaths; United Kingdom 1991-93*

Chapter	Total Deaths	Autopsies			Histology	
		None*	Satisfactory	Unsatisfactory	Satisfactory	Unsatisfactory*
Hypertensive disorders of pregnancy	20	10	9	1	5	2
Antepartum and postpartum haemorrhage	15	3	8	4	5	1
Thrombosis and thromboembolism						
Pulmonary embolism	30	3	25	2	11	3
Cerebral venous thrombosis	3	3	0	0	0	0
Cerebral arterial thrombosis	1	1	0	0	0	0
Thrombocytopaenia induced by heparin	1	0	1	0	1	0
Amniotic fluid embolism	10	1	7	2	7	2
Early pregnancy deaths	18	2	11	5	8	0
Genital tract sepsis	9	1	5	3	2	1
Genital tract trauma	4	0	3	1	2	1
Deaths associated with anaesthesia	8	0	7	1	3	2
Other *Direct* deaths	9	1	5	3	4	2
Total	**128**	**25**	**81**	**22**	**48**	**14**
Late deaths (*Direct* causes)	11	5	5	1	2	2

* includes cases where there is no record

Note: Histology reports listed as unsatisfactory or no record do not include patients on whom an autopsy was not performed. *Fortuitous* deaths not included.

Table 16.2

Subjective assessment of the adequacy of autopsies in **Indirect** maternal deaths;* United Kingdom 1991-93

Chapter	Total Deaths	Autopsies			Histology	
		None*	Satisfactory	Unsatisfactory	Satisfactory	Unsatisfactory*
Infectious diseases	8	1	5	2	3	4
Neoplastic diseases	1	1	0	0	0	0
Endocrine and metabolic disorders and immune disorders	10	1	7	2	5	4
Blood diseases	3	2	1	0	1	0
Diseases of the central nervous system	25	6	16	3	8	11
Diseases of the circulatory system						
Aneurysms	12	1	1	0	3	8
Air embolism	1	0	1	0	1	0
Cardiac disease	26	4	14	8	14	8
Diseases of the respiratory system	2	1	1	0	1	0
Diseases of the digestive system	6	2	2	2	2	2
Other *Indirect* deaths	6	1	5	0	3	2
Total	100	20	60	20	41	39
Late deaths (*Indirect* causes)	23	10	7	6	5	3

* - includes cases where there is no record
Note - Histology reports listed as unsatisfactory or no record do not include patients on whom an autopsy was not performed. *Fortuitous* deaths not included.

tamponade. There was no spontaneous heart activity and the patient was declared dead. The first autopsy, which was performed in the absence of clinical staff, attributed death to postpartum uterine haemorrhage. Clearly this was not accurate and after a second autopsy it was established that the bleeding had originated from a ruptured dissecting aneurysm of the splenic artery. There was a separate dissection of the left main coronary artery which had ruptured into the pericardium. There was no aortic dissection. The dissected arteries showed cystic medial necrosis. Neither pathologist commented on features of Marfan's syndrome with which this arterial change may be associated although this had been mentioned by the vascular surgeon involved in clinical management.

Both of these cases show a failure of communication between the first pathologist and the obstetrician. It was emphasised in previous Reports that the pathologist must be fully informed of the clinical features before commencing the autopsy.

Autopsies performed at the request of HM Coroners/Procurators Fiscal

Autopsies were performed in 219 cases (94%) on the instruction of HM Coroners/Procurators Fiscal. In an additional 12 cases which were reported no instruction for autopsy was given. Several of these involved intracranial haemorrhage and it has not been possible to identify the cause of the haemorrhage in some of these from the reports of the computerised tomography (CT) scans available.

A patient was admitted at 36 weeks gestation because of hypertension, BP145/100mm Hg. There was no proteinuria. There was a spontaneous vaginal delivery at 39 weeks and she was discharged on the third postpartum day with a normal blood pressure. Three days later she developed a fatal massive haematoma localised on CT scan to the basal ganglia and temporal lobe of the left cerebral hemisphere, with intraventricular spread. It was uncertain whether this was due to a berry aneurysm, an arteriovenous malformation or hypertension. Organs were used for donation but there was no autopsy.

Another patient was admitted in labour at 39 weeks gestation. While in the admission room she had a grand mal convulsion. The blood pressure varied from 140/115 to 170/120mm Hg. A CT scan revealed blood in the ventricles and in the subarachnoid space. A second CT scan 10 days later showed blood only in the posterior part of the lateral ventricles suggesting that bleeding may have originated in the brain rather than the subarachnoid space. Three days later she had a further fatal intracranial bleed. The coroner issued a death certificate without autopsy. The source of bleeding in this case remains in doubt.

On other occasions the cause of death remains in doubt because no autopsy was performed.

A woman was delivered by emergency Caesarean section at 26 weeks gestation because of premature labour, transverse lie and polyhydramnios. After delivery she developed severe disseminated intravascular coagulation (DIC) and multifocal haemorrhage which necessitated hysterectomy. It was presumed she had suffered an amniotic fluid embolus but this could not be confirmed as the coroner did not consider an autopsy was necessary.

In a further five cases the Coroner/ Procurator Fiscal refused to release the autopsy report.

Hypertension

There were 20 deaths directly attributed to pregnancy induced hypertension. Autopsies were performed on 10 cases but in only five of these was there an adequate histological report, of which three showed changes of eclampsia in the liver and kidneys. In a further case there were cerebral vascular changes compatible with eclampsia. The fifth case with adequate histology developed adult respiratory distress syndrome (ARDS) after Caesarean section and survived for 31 days before dying of respiratory failure. In spite of detailed histological examination no changes of eclampsia were found in the liver or kidneys. There were two further cases where the pathologist claimed to have taken tissue for histological examination but no report was issued. In one of these cases it was claimed that there were changes of eclampsia in unspecified tissues.

In nine cases there was clinical evidence of ARDS, which was confirmed by the gross appearance of the lungs at autopsy in five, including histology in two. In a further case without autopsy the diagnosis was established by an open lung biopsy during life. Aspiration of gastric contents was considered clinically to have initiated ARDS in three cases. In one of these there was no autopsy and in the other two no foreign material was demonstrated histologically in the lungs so that gastric aspiration could not be confirmed.

In four cases death was attributed to cerebral haemorrhage, confirmed by CT scan in one and by detailed neuropathological autopsy examination in three. One patient died of a myocardial infarct.

In addition to these 20 cases there were 30 deaths where hypertension was present but not classified as the direct cause of death.

One of these had a blood pressure of 220/130mm Hg at booking at eight weeks gestation and was not considered to have pregnancy induced hypertension. At 17 weeks she had a spontaneous incomplete abortion and two days later she died of a myocardial infarct. This was confirmed at autopsy.

Eight deaths were due to intracranial haemorrhage, five of which were in the brain, (one associated with an arterio-venous malformation), one in the subarachnoid space associated with a berry aneurysm and two where it could not be established whether the haemorrhage had arisen in the brain or the subarachnoid space because there was no autopsy. There were two cases of systemic sclerosis with hypertension one of whom died of cerebral arteritis and the other of pulmonary hypertension associated with pulmonary fibrosis. Of the remaining cases in this group there were five cases of cardiomyopathy, described elsewhere, six cases of pulmonary embolus, two cases each of dissecting aortic aneurysms and pneumonia and one each of cerebral venous thrombosis, acute respiratory distress syndrome (ARDS), myocardial ischaemia and cerebral hypoxia associated with an anaesthetic death.

During the autopsy it is important that pathologists should record the weight of the heart and the thickness of the left and right ventricular walls in these cases of maternal hypertension. Histological examination of tissues should always include the kidneys, liver and placental bed where eclampsia or pre-eclampsia are suspected. If the patient suffered an eclamptic fit then the autopsy should include a detailed examination of the brain by a neuropathologist.

Haemorrhage

There were 15 deaths due to antepartum or postpartum haemorrhage. Autopsies were performed on 12 of these cases. In eight cases the autopsy report was of a high standard but in the remaining four it was inadequate. It is clearly of importance that there should be a detailed description of the genital tract but in one of the reports this description amounted to seven words which were non-contributory. A second report failed to record the placental site although at the time of delivery a cotyledon had been retained and was manually removed. In another case, where total hysterectomy had been performed in an attempt to control bleeding, the surgical specimen was also poorly described. Although a Caesarean section had been performed the pathologist was unable to identify the suture line. The placental bed was described as haemorrhagic but its location was not mentioned. The histology was reported as normal. A fourth patient developed disseminated intravascular coagulation (DIC) but there was a poor description of haemorrhagic foci and no histological confirmation. This patient also had sickle cell trait but in spite of severe postpartum hypoxia there was no comment on the appearance of the renal medulla, which may become infarcted in these circumstances, nor was an attempt made to look for evidence of red cell sickling.

It must be emphasised, as it was in the previous Reports, that there must be a detailed description of the genital tract, including any evidence of obstetric trauma, recording in detail the placental site. There must be an extensive search for DIC in tissues retained for histology.

Pulmonary thromboembolism

As in previous reports pulmonary embolism is one of the most common causes of maternal death and shows little or no reduction in incidence over the past 20 years although there has been some reduction in the rates per million estimated pregnancies. There were 30 in this triennium, with an additional five late deaths. Autopsies were performed on 27 of the 30 cases and in 25 the autopsy report was adequate or excellent. In one case there was no autopsy report but the Regional Assessor in Pathology was able to confirm that an autopsy had been performed and was considered adequate although the source of the thromboembolus was not identified. In another case the autopsy was performed on the coroner's instruction but there was no report although the pulmonary embolus was stated to have arisen in the pelvic veins. In two cases the report was inadequate. In both of these there was no evidence that the leg veins had been examined. In one there was no record that the pelvic veins were examined and in the other the pelvic veins were stated to be clear of thrombus although the cause of death stated that the pulmonary thromboembolus had arisen in the pelvic veins.

The source of the embolus was identified in 19 cases. In 13 of these there was thrombus present in the deep veins of the legs and in 5 cases in the pelvic veins. In one case both the leg veins and the pelvic veins were involved. In a further case left iliac vein thrombosis was confirmed by ultrasound. She was treated with heparin but developed thrombocytopenia. Twelve days later she suffered a cerebral haemorrhage from which she died. In one woman there was a previous thrombotic episode involving the retinal artery; in another there was concurrent thrombosis of the femoral artery.

Cerebral venous thrombosis

There were four cases of cerebral venous thrombosis. In none of these was there an autopsy. Three cases were diagnosed by CT scan; in two there was sagittal sinus thrombosis and in one the site of the venous thrombosis was not specified. In this case, although there was no autopsy, organs were used for donation. In another case no autopsy was performed.

In addition to these cases of cerebral venous thrombosis there was one case of thrombosis of the middle cerebral artery.

Four of these cases had undergone Caesarean section two to sixteen days before the first onset of signs of cerebral dysfunction.

Amniotic fluid embolism

There were 10 cases where death was attributed to amniotic fluid embolism (AFE). Autopsy was performed on all but one of these cases and histology was performed on eight. In all of the latter there was histological confirmation of AFE. In the case without autopsy detailed histological examination of the hysterectomy specimen failed to reveal amniotic fluid in the uterine vessels.

Because of the failure to demonstrate amniotic fluid embolism in a number of clinically diagnosed cases it has been decided by the assessors to relax the criteria for counting these cases. In the past, histological confirmation has been required but this is no longer essential. It seems probable that as more such cases survive for several weeks after delivery evidence of AFE will disappear resulting in a low count. However, great care must be used now and in the future in adopting the relaxed criteria.

For example the case mentioned in Chapter 5 but counted in Chapter 8 under genital tract trauma suffered a ruptured uterus but the speed of collapse suggested AFE. In this case there was a detailed autopsy of high standard and extensive histological examination of the lungs but no evidence of AFE was found.

Another case emphasised the importance of histological autopsy examination of the lungs even in cases of road traffic accidents.

This woman at term, driving a motor car, was involved in an accident with another car. Although her injuries did not appear serious she had a cardiac arrest and the paramedic team called to the scene were unable to resuscitate her. On transfer to hospital a postmortem Caesarean section was performed. Autopsy confirmed that the injuries did not appear sufficient to cause death but pulmonary histology confirmed extensive AFE considered to be caused by rapid deceleration.

Genital tract sepsis

There were nine cases of genital tract sepsis excluding those associated with abortion. Autopsies were performed on all but one of these cases but there was no autopsy report on one and the Regional Assessor in Pathology provided summary findings in this case.

One patient had an antepartum haemorrhage at 33 weeks due to placenta praevia. Caesarean section was performed but post-operatively she developed a wound infection which led to necrotising fasciitis with necrosis of the abdominal wall. A similar incident had occurred in a previous pregnancy. Signs of infective endocarditis were found but all blood cultures were negative. *Candida albicans* was grown from the stool and later from various sites. Immunological screening showed impaired neutrophil activity of an unproven nature. There was a low IgG 3 level and reduced antibody levels to *E. coli* and *C. albicans*. The patient died of fulminating necrotising fasciitis. At autopsy there was endocarditis and myocardial necrosis. *C.albicans* was grown from the mitral valve vegetations but no fungi were seen on microscopy. Postmortem blood culture was negative.

Although *C. albicans* infection in an immunocompromised patient is the probable cause of the endocarditis the failure to demonstrate fungi histologically in the heart and the negative blood cultures raises the possibility of contamination of the mitral vegetations at autopsy and must leave the final diagnosis in doubt.

Of the remaining seven cases there was adequate microbiological investigation in five.

One of these revealed systemic *Herpes simplex type II* infection. This case was thoroughly examined at autopsy and sets a standard for other cases. *Herpes simplex* was shown by culture, immunofluorescence and electron microscopy of the liver. The brain was submitted for specialist neuropathological examination.

Four cases revealed coliform bacterial septicaemia and in one of these cases a *haemolytic streptococcus* and *C. albicans* were also isolated.

Three autopsies were inadequate and there was no postmortem microbiology. The following is an example of an inadequate autopsy report:

> This woman had a forceps delivery nine days after spontaneous rupture of the membranes. She was discharged the following day. A week later she complained of lower abdominal pain. The uterine fundus was tender and a high vaginal swab grew *Proteus mirabilis*. Three weeks later she collapsed and died. There was a presumptive diagnosis of peripartum cardiomyopathy but this was not confirmed at autopsy. The spleen was enlarged compatible with septicaemia, but no blood or uterine cultures were taken and there was no histology report. There remains doubt about the cause of death.

In cases such as this it is inadequate not to undertake extensive histological examination of tissues from many sites including the genital tract but also not to take cultures from tissues such as blood, spleen and genital tract.

Genital tract trauma

There were four cases of genital tract trauma. Autopsies were performed on all four but one was substandard.

> This patient had a vaginal delivery after prostaglandin induction of labour for post maturity. One hour after delivery she complained of chest pain, collapsed and died. A large amount of blood was found in the left pelvic cavity but the volume was not measured. There was rupture of the left lower uterine segment but there was no other description and no record of its size. The placental site was not identified. There was no evidence of pulmonary thromboembolism nor of myocardial infarction. Histological examination was performed but the uterus was described as containing products of conception and there was no comment on trophoblastic infiltration of the myometrium. There was no record that amniotic fluid embolus had been looked for in the lung histology.

The inadequacy of the autopsy leaves unanswered the cause of the ruptured uterus and whether there was any other pathology to account for the sudden death.

> There were two other cases of ruptured uterus, one through a Caesarean section scar with massive haemorrhage from the left uterine artery and the other following syntocinon infusion and forceps delivery. Emergency subtotal hysterectomy was performed through the ruptured lower segment. There was extensive histology which showed no evidence of trophoblastic penetration of the myometrium nor was there evidence of AFE.

The fourth case also followed forceps delivery. There was a spiral tear from the introitus to the fornix communicating with the Pouch of Douglas. There was one litre of blood stained fluid in the peritoneal cavity and 250ml in the left paracolic gutter. There was a detailed histological report and again AFE was excluded.

Cardiac disease

There were 26 deaths associated with cardiac disease in this triennium and to this should be added eight cases of aortic dissecting aneurysm, two cases of dissection of a coronary artery and one of dissection of a coronary vein mentioned later in this chapter. Four other deaths had been certified as due to cardiac disease but three of these have been reclassified as unexplained and one is counted under genital tract sepsis with endocarditis.

Cardiomyopathy

There were four cases of cardiomyopathy, two hypertrophic, one dilated and one associated with myotonic dystrophy. In addition there was a further case of probable cardiomyopathy associated with a phaeochromocytoma. One of the cases of hypertrophic cardiomyopathy had a history of alcohol abuse but there were no pathological stigmata of alcoholism and this aetiology for the cardiomyopathy could not be established. Autopsies were performed on four of these cases.

> In a fifth case the diagnosis of dilated cardiomyopathy was confirmed by echocardiography 35 weeks after delivery. The patient died two months later.

> A sixth case, described in Chapter 7, was diagnosed as peripartum cardiomyopathy but this diagnosis could not be substantiated The heart was little enlarged and there was only slight left ventricular hypertrophy. Histological examination revealed no features of cardiomyopathy.

> Another woman had a spontaneous vaginal delivery at 35 weeks after a normal pregnancy. She died suddenly two months later. The autopsy report was substandard. There was mild left ventricular hypertrophy but neither the heart weight nor the left ventricular wall thickness were recorded. There was no histology of the myocardium.

Ischaemic heart disease

There were nine cases of ischaemic heart disease. All had autopsy confirmation of severe (>90%) occlusion of one or more coronary arteries by atheroma or, in three cases, by recent occlusive thrombosis. One patient had a history of a previous myocardial infarct, one severe hypertension at booking, one supraventricular aortic stenosis from childhood necessitating a Dacron graft, and another had a number of high risk factors including hypercholesterolaemia, hypothyroidism, mesangiocapillary glomerulonephritis, cigarette smoking and a strong family history of myocardial infarction.

Congenital heart disease

In addition to the case of supraventricular aortic stenosis mentioned under ischaemic heart disease, there were eight cases of congenital heart disease. Autopsies were performed on seven of these. The eighth case was diagnosed as having a ventricular septal defect three years before death. She was admitted in cardiac failure and with an intrauterine death. Caesarean section was performed but she died of progressive cardiac failure. Without autopsy it is impossible to establish whether the cardiac failure was due to infective endocarditis or pulmonary hypertension.

There were five cases of septal defects, two atrial, one with pulmonary hypertension (Eisenmenger's syndrome), and three ventricular defects. Of the latter, one was associated with pulmonary hypertension and another with infective endocarditis although the infecting organism was not specified.

There was one case of primary pulmonary hypertension which is described in Chapter 11. There was an excellent autopsy report. Histological sections were submitted to a specialist pulmonary pathologist who confirmed the characteristic features of this disease. The father was known to have died from the same condition.

> A woman with a bicuspid aortic valve and aortic regurgitation developed a dissecting aortic aneurysm and has been mentioned in the section on aneurysms.

> The last case of congenital heart disease was a woman with a 3p+ chromosome abnormality (long arm of chromosome 3). Both her sons had a similar abnormality with speech, heart and kidney defects. The woman collapsed and died at 34 weeks gestation with a cardiac dysrrhythmia. The autopsy was unsatisfactory because there was no specialist examination of the conducting system of the heart. It is desirable that cardiac pathologists should examine the heart in all such cases.

Cardiac infection

There were three cases diagnosed as viral myocarditis.

> In one of these cases there was an excellent autopsy report including coronary angiography. Blood at autopsy showed raised titres of IgG and IgM to *cytomegalovirus*. Cardiac histology confirmed acute myocarditis.

There remains some doubt about the diagnosis in the other two cases.

> The first of these was found dead in bed at 26 weeks gestation. She had undergone in vitro fertilisation and had a multiple pregnancy. For one week before death she had complained of abdominal pain. She was apparently well when seen shortly before death. Although blood was taken at autopsy for viral titres there was no report. Histology confirmed acute myocarditis.

The last of these cases was even less satisfactory. This woman had a cardiac arrest at home at 35 weeks after a normal pregnancy. The autopsy was inadequate and showed multiple foci of subendocardial fibrosis interpreted as due to old myocarditis. The coronary arteries were widely patent. The conducting system of the heart was not examined and no specimens were taken for microbiological examination.

These latter two cases emphasise the necessity of looking for evidence of bacterial or viral infection in cases of sudden unexplained death. If, at a later stage, histological evidence of myocarditis is found, and samples have not been sent for examination the opportunity of identifying the causative agent will have been lost.

There were three cases of infective endocarditis, one of whom had necrotising fasciitis mentioned earlier, another had a ventricular septal defect and the third had mitral valve disease presumed to be of rheumatic fever origin but there was no autopsy in this case nor was the infecting organism identified. In one of the other two cases *Candida albicans* was isolated and in the other there was an *haemophilus* septicaemia.

Aneurysms

Ruptured aneurysms continue to be a relatively common cause of maternal death but it still appears that they are not diagnosed as frequently as they should be. In this Report there were 20 cases of confirmed ruptured aneurysms of which eight were dissecting aneurysms of the aorta, two dissections of a coronary artery, one of the splenic artery and there was one case of dissection of the middle cardiac vein. This was so unusual that the case was presented at a specialist meeting and the diagnosis confirmed.

In addition to these examples of dissecting aneurysms there was one case of massive haemoperitoneum from a ruptured arterio-venous aneurysm at the splenic hilum. This woman had a liver transplant for primary biliary cirrhosis and liver failure three years before death. At 37 weeks gestation she had a spontaneous rupture of the membranes and Caesarean section the following day. Eight hours later she had a cardiac arrest but was resuscitated. Laparotomy for suspected intra-abdominal bleeding revealed six litres of blood in the peritoneal cavity apparently arising in the left upper quadrant. Bleeding could not be controlled and she died. Autopsy revealed features of portal hypertension and a ruptured splenic vein communicating with an arterio-venous aneurysm.

There were eight ruptured saccular aneurysms of the cerebral arteries, four of the middle cerebral, one anterior cerebral, two internal carotid and one basilar. These were diagnosed at autopsy in six and by CT scan during life in two. In two further cases of intracranial haemorrhage the coroner did not order an autopsy and the cause of the haemorrhage could not be established.

Comment

The critcism expressed in previous Reports continues to cause concern. A very high proportion of autopsies are done on the instruction of HM Coroners/Procurators Fiscal. While this ensures an autopsy at higher than that for hospital autopsies the pathologists performing them are often under considerable pressure to complete a large number in a short time. They cannot, therefore, give the time that is required for the detailed examination necessary for the satisfactory investigation of these cases. Furthermore, many of these pathologists are trained in forensic pathology where unnatural and traumatic death demands their expertise. They meet complicated medical and obstetric pathology less frequently. For these reassons it is recommended that Coroners and Fiscals should seek the help of specialist obstetric and gynaecological pathologists. In some ares perinatal pathologists can also provide this specialist help. the Royal College of Pathologists and the Association of Clinical Pathologists are able, and should be requested, to provide lists of suitably trained and qualified pathologists for Coroners/Fiscals to use.

It needs to be emphasised again how important it is to gather all the available evidence for an adequate review. In cases of maternal death it is likely that the information required by obstetricians will go beyond the needs of the Coroner. Clinicians should therefore alert the Coroner/Procurator Fiscal at the earliest opportunity so that, with the Coroner's permission, they may approach the relatives for consent for autopsy which will enable a clinical autopsy to be carried out if the Coroner decides he does not have the legal powers to enquire into the death, or will allow additional investigations or retention of more tissues when the Coroner's autopsy is carried out. Clearly, in either set of circumstances good communication will aalso be required between obstetrician and pathologist if full benefit is to be obtained. Under current Department of Health guidance (FDL(91)127) the costs of tissue retention for clinical purposes should be charged to general hospital overheads or individual clinical specialies.

The Royal College of Pathologists (1993) has produced guidelines for post mortem reports. These guidelines are recommended for use in all maternal autopsies with particular emphasis on the following points which are frequently inadequately reported in cases coming to the attention of the Confidential Enquiries into Maternal Deaths in the United Kingdom.

Although imaging techniques have greatly improved the accuracy of diagnosis there are still cases, especially involving the heart and cerebral vasculature, where a detailed autopsy is required. Where the cause of death is associated withhypertension the autopsy should include a full description of the heart, including its weight and that of the isolated left and right ventricles, the kidneys the liver and the placental bed. Histological sections should be taken from multiple sites in these organs to look for evidence of eclampsia/pre-eclampsia and for pre-existing hypertension.

In cases of death due to maternal haemorrhage there is still a failure in some autopsy reports to provide a detailed account of genital tract trauma, placental site location, and gross and microscopic evidence of intravascular coagulation. Where bleeding has occurred into a body cavity the volume of blood or blood-stained fluid should be measured. Extensive histological examination of the pulmonary vasculature should be undertaken to look for evidence of amniotic fluid embolism.

In previous Reports it has been emphasised that not only the appearance of a thromboembolus in a pulmonary artery should be described but there should be a search of possible sites of origin of the thrombus. There should also be histological examination of the thromboembolus; in this Enquiry one presumed thromboembolus was shown, histologically, to be an embolus of choriocarcinoma.

Because of the failure to identify amniotic fluid embolus in cases where this clinical diagnosis has been made, either because no autopsy was performed, or because it was not identified at autopsy, the criteria for counting these cases have been relaxed. Part of the failure may be due to the inadequacy of the histological examination of the pulmonary vasculature and of pulmonary artery blood using appropriate stains for keratin, mucin and lipid and partly to the survival, sometimes for several weeks, of cases in intensive care. These patients may die from the effects of ARDS after the embolus has been cleared from the pulmonary vasculature. However, the responsibility of pathologists to make a diligent search for AFE whenever suspected must be emphasised.

Cardiac disease continues to be an important cause of maternal death. The diagnosis of peripartum cardiomyopathy must be based on strict pathological criteria. In general it is advisable to refer to a cardiac pathologist for detailed examination of the heart just as it has become common practice to refer to a neuropathologist for detailed examination of the brain. Similarly in cases of congenital heart disease and of cardiac dysrrhythmia the examination of the heart is best conducted by a cardiac pathologist. If an infective agent is suspected of causing either endocarditis or myocarditis then appropriate samples should be taken from the heart, blood, spleen and any other focus of infection at the time of the autopsy. It is distressing to find histological evidence of myocarditis when it is no longer possible to identify the causative organism.

The importance of clinico-pathological correlation in these autopsies cannot be over-emphasised. Consultant obstetricians must ensure that the pathologist performing the autopsy is fully briefed and is informed of the points which are of clinical interest so that they can be highlighted in the examination.

Reference

The Royal College of Pathologists. *Guidelines for Post-mortem Reports*. The Royal College of Pathologists; London: 1993.

CHAPTER 17

Intensive Care

There were 104 maternal deaths where there was a recorded need for intensive care, either immediately for resuscitation or as the patient deteriorated. This means that 40% of all *Direct* and *Indirect* maternal deaths (including *Late* deaths in these categories) required some intensive care facility although in some cases only resuscitation was possible before the patient died.

It is logical to broadly define main categories of admission to an intensive care unit (ICU) in terms of the physiological disturbance necessitating the admission. This includes such categories as respiratory (including acute respiratory distress syndrome (ARDS)), neurological, cardiovascular, sepsis, multiple organ failure and haematological.

However, specific questions relating to the treatment in the ICU are not included in the Enquiry form so, for this triennium, the Tables at the end of this chapter will relate to only to cases counted in other Chapters of this Report. The new form, MDR (UK)1 contains a specific section relating to intensive care.

In only a limited number of cases were intubation/ventilation or resuscitation mentioned in the case reports. Very few cases were recorded as having a tracheostomy or as having a pulmonary artery (PA) catheter. Obviously more treatment was prescribed but not recorded on the form because there was no request for it. However, supplementary reports were often provided by the anaesthetist or ICU consultant.

Table 17.1 shows the numbers of admissions for intensive care required by the patients reported in each Chapter and the duration of the treatment received within the limitations stated above.   Intensive care was required for a wide variety of conditions and therapies for 66 *Direct* and 38 *Indirect* deaths. There was 42 cases in which the duration of intensive care was two days or less and 27 in which duration of stay was seven days or more.   There were five *Late* deaths amongst the latter.   One of these is discussed in Chapter 9 where there was a considerable delay in admission to ICU and a lack of high dependency facilities.   These patients consume a great deal of resources and mostly die of multiple organ failure.

Comments

Previous reports have highlighted the additional risk that pregnancy and childbirth present to a mother with co-existent disease. However even identification of the risk factors does not eliminate the additional need for intensive care for unexpected emergencies. Obesity, cardiac disease and asthma are common problems.

Table 17.1

Number and percentage of cases counted in each Chapter requiring intensive care and duration of treatment; United Kingdom 1991-93			
Principal disorder	Number of cases	% of cases counted in Chapter	Duration of intensive care (days)
Hypertensive disorders	16	80%	1-30
Haemorrhage	9	60%	1-4
Thrombosis/thromboembolism	5	14%	1-35
Amniotic fluid embolism	5	50%	1-14
Early pregnancy	10	56%	1-2
Sepsis	7	77%	1-2
Genital tract trauma	2	50%	<1
Anaesthetic	2	25%	10-42
Other *Direct* deaths	8	88%	1-25
Cardiac deaths	14	39%	1-14
Other *Indirect* deaths	18	19%	1-42
Fortuitous deaths	3	7%	1-7
Late deaths	5	11%	1-165

Pregnant patients may develop critical illness as a direct result of their pregnancy or coincidentally. The requirement for or availability of intensive care world-wide for obstetric patients has been variously reported as 1-9 per 1000 deliveries (Kilpatrick and Matthay 1992). A 10 year survey from Australia reviewed the requirement for mechanical ventilation in a large obstetric hospital (Stevens 1991). One third of deliveries required some form of anaesthesia of which one third was provided by general anaesthesia and two thirds as regional anaesthesia. There were 126 ICU admissions from 61,435 patients who delivered. Sixteen of the admissions followed anaesthesia. The incidence of a major complication after general anaesthesia was 1 in 932 and of regional anaesthesia 1 in 4177 when these were given for delivery.

Most authors believe that critical illness in obstetric patients should be managed on a general ICU in the same way as other patients with similar conditions (Hinds and Watson 1995). It is clear that good liaison is required between the intensivists, obstetricians and physicians, with easy access to fetal monitoring (Phelan 1991).

Acute respiratory distress syndrome (ARDS)

Acute (adult) respiratory distress syndrome was reported in the last triennial report. Its incidence in pregnancy is now better recognised by pathologists and may be increasing as patients are kept alive for longer as organ support defers death and ARDS becomes established. The major predisposing factors are haemorrhage and sepsis but hypertensive disorders of pregnancy, inhalation of gastric contents, dead fetus and amniotic fluid embolism are all aetiological factors and the use of beta-adrenergic agents for patients in premature labour contributes. Patients who require high ventilatory pressure or volume may develop further acute lung injury indistinguishable from ARDS. Development of pneumonia in these patients worsens the prognosis. ARDS is frequently the prelude to development of multiple organ failure.

Cardiac disease

Patients with underlying cardiac disease may be expected to have complications during pregnancy and delivery. However in some the cardiac disease was not diagnosed until delivery and many had unpredictable requirements for intensive care. Congenital heart disease is usually diagnosed and recognised to be a problem in pregnancy but ischaemic heart disease is becoming more prevalent.

Amniotic fluid embolism (AFE)

In patients who survive the initial collapse caused by AFE, acute right heart failure with profound hypoxia does occur but there is often associated left ventricular failure. About 75% of those who do survive the original collapse develop increased alveolar-capillary permeability and ARDS. AFE is a condition with a very high mortality (80%) which makes considerable demands upon intensive care facilities particularly if unevaluated measures such as haemofiltration are instituted. The initial hypoxia may be sufficient to produce severe neurological damage and even brain stem death (Clark 1990; Vanmaele et al 1990).

Provision of Intensive Care

In this triennium seven patients required to be transferred to another hospital for intensive care. Another eight had their ICU admission delayed because of lack of availability of a bed. In one case this was related to lack of consultant availability. It was the opinion of the assessors that in five cases the distance of the intensive care unit from the maternity unit was a major factor in the demise of the patient. In two cases the inability of an ICU to accept the patient had a significant adverse effect. Deficiencies in the provision of essential services and facilities have been noted in relation to the surgical specialities generally in the last three NCEPOD reports and obstetrics is no exception to this. Obstetricians and anaesthetists must have immediate access to essential services. It is clear that intensive care and high dependency facilities must be readily available for obstetric patients in the same hospital as the maternity unit. There is good evidence that provision of intensive and high dependency care reduces morbidity (Sage et al, 1986; Franklin et al, 1993). It is easier to achieve physiological stability if patients are treated earlier in their illness.

References

Kilpatrick SJ, Matthay MA. Obstetric patients requiring critical care. A five year review. *Chest* 1992; **101**; 1407-1412.

Stephens ID. ICU admissions from an obstetric hospital. *Canadian Journal of Anaesthesia* 1991; **38**: 677-87.

Hinds C, Watson D. Obstetric intensive care. In: *Intensive Care a concise handbook* 2nd edition 1995; London: Saunders pp 395-406.

Phelan JP. Critical care obstetrics: management of the fetus. *Critical Care Clinics* 1991; **7**: 917-928.

Clark SL. New concepts of amniotic fluid embolism: a review. *Obstetrical and Gynaecological Survey* 1990; **45**: 360-368.

Vanmaele L, Noppen M, Vincken W, DeCatte L, Huyghens L. Transient left heart failure in amniotic fluid embolism. *Intensive Care Medicine* 1990; **16**: 269-267.

National Confidential Enquiry into Perioperative Deaths. Campling AE, Devlin HB Hoile RW, Lunn JN. 1992-93. London 1995.

Sage WM, Rosenthal MH, Silverman JF. Is intensive care worth it? - An assessment of input and outcome for the critically ill. *Critical Care Medicine* 1986; **14**: 777-782.

Franklin CM, Rackow EC, Mandani B. Decreases in mortality on a large urban medical service by facilitating access to critical care. *Archives Internal Medicine* 1993; **148**: 1403-1405.

CHAPTER 18

Substandard Care

Summary

Assessment of substandard care has been a feature of all three United Kingdom Reports. As cases are judged on the basis of contemporary good practice standards have altered over the years, so that figures for different triennia are not statistically comparable.

In the period covered by the three United Kingdom Reports (1985-93) substandard care was identified in 288 (44.6%) maternal deaths. There were deficiencies in hospital care in 33.1%, in general practitioner care in 5.6% and in the compliance or actions of the patient in 11.3%.

In this triennium substandard care occurred in 93(40.1%) deaths, with deficiencies in hospital care in 31.1%, of general practitioner care in 7.0% and of the mother and/or family in 11%. Substandard care was most common in deaths due to hypertensive disorders (80%) and haemorrhage (73.3%). There were eight deaths directly attributable to anaesthesia and seven were associated with substandard anaesthetic care. Substandard anaesthetic care was identified as a contributory factor in a further 6 cases and in ten cases the anaesthetist bore some responsibility for substandard perioperative management.

Specific problems have been addressed in the appropriate preceding chapters but recurrent common features include diagnostic errors, inappropriate treatment and failure to refer patients to senior staff or other disciplines.

Many of the deficiencies identified are amenable to correction at little cost. However, an underlying but common problem is the availability and utilisation of staff to cope with major clinical problems. Previous recommendations for dedicated consultant sessions for delivery unit supervision have yet to be fully implemented but this is a key factor in providing an efficient and safe service. Although new appointments will correct this deficiency in time there is an immediate need to review contracts in order to hasten the change.

Introduction

During the first 30 years of the Enquiries the maternal mortality rate fell by approximately 50% each decade but there was been a levelling off in the two triennia preceding this Report. This has led some obstetricians to the complacent belief that we are approaching the irreducible minimum. However, more detailed study of the principal causes of maternal death, particularly in relation to substandard care, shows that this is without justification. For a variety of reasons improvements in some areas, such as infection, abortion and anaesthesia, have been far greater than in others and the hard core of major conditions requires more critical analysis, particularly in relation to standards of care.

From the outset the Confidential Enquiries into Maternal Deaths sought to identify deficiencies in the quality of patient care which might have contributed to the demise of the patient. Initially these deficiencies were referred to as *avoidable factors.* This was interpreted as some departure from the generally accepted standards of satisfactory care during the triennium which may have contributed to the fatal outcome. It did not mean that death could have been prevented, or that a factor identified as avoidable was the direct cause of the mother's death. The incidence of avoidable factors in the first England and Wales Report, for 1952-54 was approximately 45% and by 1976-78 had increased to nearly 60%.

In the England and Wales Report for 1979-81 the term *avoidable factor* was replaced by *substandard care* and this was continued when the United Kingdom Reports started in 1985-87. The change was introduced because the term *avoidable* was sometimes misinterpreted as meaning that avoiding these factors would necessarily have prevented the death. *Substandard care,* in the context of the Reports means that the care which the patient received, or the care that was made available to her, fell below the standard which the assessors considered should have been provided. It does not *per se* imply professional negligence.

Substandard care is judged by the assessors in relation to contemporary standards of good practice, so that criteria have tended to become more rigorous in succeeding Reports and the interpretation of the incidence of substandard care must be seen in this light. In some cases substandard care may be mentioned but it is not included in the statistics unless it contributed to the outcome of the case. The assessors consider the following features:

- clinical management,

- staffing,

- physical resources,

- support services,

- administrative factors, and

- the cooperation and actions of the patient herself and her relatives if appropriate.

The England and Wales Report for 1976-78 contained a detailed discussion of *avoidable* factors for the whole period covered by the Reports but a similar analysis of *substandard care,* either by triennia or longer periods, has never been undertaken and earlier Reports do not contain sufficient information to make this possible. Data abstracted from the first two United Kingdom

Reports is presented here, together with comparable data from the current Report. Only *Direct* and *Indirect* deaths are considered. There are fluctuations in numbers between the triennia which may reflect variations in standards of subjective assessment as well as chance variations and changes in clinical practice.

In the current enquiry the following criteria for substandard care were used:

Major - Contributed significantly to the death of the mother, ie different management would reasonably have been expected to alter the outcome.

eg Lack of availability of blood. Fluid overload and poor blood pressure control in eclampsia.

Minor - Relevant contributory factor. Different management might have made a difference but survival was unlikely in any case.

eg Severe cardiac disease, Caesarean section, inexperienced anaesthetist, poor fluid / electrolyte management.

Irrelevant - Elements of substandard care were identified but did not influence the outcome.

eg Delay in expert treatment and poor control of blood pressure in pregnancy induced hypertension, but death from pulmonary embolism.

Only major and minor factors are included in the present analyses. Identification of deficiencies in care which did not contribute to the outcome may give some indication of overall standards of care in the unit but these have not been specifically asked for to date and only six cases were reported. This aspect will be pursued in subsequent Reports.

Responsibility for substandard care

In 1991-93 there were 93 *Direct* and *Indirect* deaths (40.8%) in which substandard care was implicated; it was judged to be a major contributory factor to the demise of the patient in 71 cases and a minor factor in 22. In many of these cases more than one person or persons was implicated.

Overall, during the three triennia of the UK Reports there were 288 deaths associated with substandard care, an overall incidence of 44.6%.

Table 18.1

Responsibility for substandard care in Direct and Indirect deaths; United Kingdom 1985-93

	1985-87 n(%)	1988-90 n(%)	1991-93 n(%)	1985-93 n(%)
Hospital only	47 (26.1%)	84 (35.3%)	55 (24.1%)	186 (28.8%)
GP only	5 (2.8%)	3 (1.3%)	11 (4.8%)	19 (2.9%)
Patient only	19 (10.6%)	16 (6.7%)	11 (4.8%)	46 (7.1%)
GP + Hospital	2 (1.1%)	6 (2.5%)	2 (0.9%)	10 (1.5%)
GP + Patient	1 (0.6%)	3 (1.3%)	-	4 (0.6%)
Hospital + Patient	1 (0.6%)	8 (3.4%)	11 (4.8%)	20 (3.1%)
Hospital + GP +Patient	-	-	2 (0.9%)	2 (0.3%)
Hospital +/- other	50 (27.8%)	98 (41.2%)	71 (31.1%)	214 (33.1%)
GP +/- other	8 (4.4%)	12 (5.0%)	16 (7.0%)	36 (5.6%)
Patient +/- other	21 (11.7%)	27 (11.3%)	25 (11.0%)	73 (11.3%)
Overall	75/180*(42%)	120/238* (50%)	93/228 (40.1%)	288/646 (44.6%)

* Not all cases were available for analysis

Table 18.1 identifies who was responsible for substandard care in the three triennia. It is seen that hospital staff were wholly or partly implicated in about one third of all deaths, or about three quarters of cases with substandard care. In 11% deaths the actions of the woman herself contributed and in about 6% deaths there were deficiencies in management by the general practitioner. It is notable that in the most recent triennium there were 16 cases in which a general practitioner was implicated but in seven of these the doctor concerned was a locum tenens or was deputising.

Hospital care

Deficiencies in hospital care were principally in five areas, but in many cases a combination of factors operated:

- too much responsibility was taken by, or was delegated to, inexperienced staff,

- there was a lack of guidelines for the immediate management of acute emergencies,

- treatment was inadequate, inappropriate or started too late,

- there was lack of cross-discipline collaboration, especially in the management of medical disorders,

- deliveries and care took place inappropriately in units with inadequate resources or were not reasonably sited in relation to high dependency or intensive care facilities.

Obstetric staff

During 1991-93 substandard care was ascribed to obstetric staff in 71 cases, 32 cases to consultants, six to senior registrars and 33 to other grades (including midwives). The main deficiencies in consultant and senior registrar cases were equally divided between errors in diagnosis, failure to appreciate the severity of the condition and inappropriate treatment. The main deficiencies with junior staff were similar but multiple deficiencies were more common and there were thirteen cases in which the failure to inform the consultant was considered to be a contributory factor to the demise of the patient.

The midwife was mentioned as contributing to substandard care in only four cases, in each of which she had undertaken work for which she was not appropriately trained.

Anaesthetic staff

In this triennium anaesthetic staff were responsible for, or contributed to, sub-standard care in 23 cases. Eight deaths were directly attributable to anaesthesia and substandard care occurred in seven of these, whilst in a further six cases substandard anaesthetic care contributed. In addition there were 10 cases in which the anaesthetist was at least in part responsible for substandard resuscitation and perioperative management. Inappropriate treatment was the main fault for both consultant and non-consultant anaesthetic staff, but there was failure of junior staff to inform a consultant of problems in six cases.

General practitioners

General practitioner failings were relevant in 16 deaths during 1991-93. These were most commonly related to failure of diagnosis or failure to recognise the seriousness of a condition, leading to delay in referral. In seven of the 16 cases a deputising or locum doctor was involved.

Patients

In many cases it was difficult to evaluate the rôle of the woman herself, but in 25 cases it was judged that she failed to accept or comply with treatment. Some women chose not to seek or to accept professional advice, or failed to maintain their prescribed treatment. In other cases personal convictions dictated a course of action contrary to clinical judgement and advice, such as withholding blood transfusion. Communication problems, especially related to language, sometimes resulted in misunderstandings or misinterpretations.

Apparent failings on the part of the patient should be critically appraised in relation to the quality of counselling and whether advice offered is realistic and fully comprehended. Every effort must be made to improve the quality of information provided and to ensure that it is presented in appropriate forms. Special attention must be given to the needs of patients who are not fluent in the English language and managers should ensure that appropriate interpreters and literature are readily accessible to these groups.

Substandard care related to the principal causes of death

The numbers of deaths and death rates from the principal causes for the three triennia, together with the incidences of substandard care, are shown in Table 18.2. In the triennium 1985-87 the incidence of substandard care for pulmonary embolism was not available.

Table 18.2

Principle causes of Direct and Indirect maternal deaths, with rates/1,000,000 maternities and incidence of substandard care; United Kingdom, 1985-93

Rank	1985-87		1988-90		1991-93		1985-93	
	Deaths n (Rate)	Substandard care n(%)	Deaths n (Rate)	Substandard care n(%)	Deaths n (Rate)	Substandard care n(%)	Deaths n (Rate)	Substandard care n(%)
Direct								
Hypertension	27 (11.9)	23 (85.2)	27 (11.4)	24 (89.0)	20 (8.6)	16 (80.0)	74 (10.7)	63 (85.1)
Pulm. Embolism	29 (12.8)	N.K.	24 (10.2)	6 (25.0)	30 (12.9)	5 (16.7)	83 (12.0)	11/54* (20.4)
Haemorrhage	10 (4.4)	7 (70.0)	22 (9.3)	14 (63.6)	15 (6.5)	11 (73.3)	47 (6.8)	32 (68.1)
Ectopic gestation	16 (7.1)	7 (43.8)	15 (6.4)	7 (46.6)	8 (3.5)	8 (100)	39 (5.6)	22 (56.4)
Indirect								
Cardiac disease	23 (10.1)	14 (60.9)	18 (7.6)	16 (88.9)	37 (16.0)	10 (27.0)	78 (11.2)	40 (51.3)

* 1988-93 only

Hypertensive disorders

For the period 1985-93 substandard care was identified in 85.1% deaths. However in the period covered by the current Report both the number of deaths(20) and the incidence of substandard care (80%) were lower than previously.

The high frequency of substandard care in relation to hypertensive disorders was mainly due to delays by the general practitioner or the hospital staff in making clinical decisions; inadequate consultant involvement or failure to involve a consultant with special expertise; and/or inappropriate therapy. However, in many cases the consultant was culpable. In half the cases the postpartum management was deficient, particularly in relation to fluid and electrolyte control. Many of these problems would have been overcome by the provision and use of a regional advisor.

Pulmonary embolism

The relatively low incidence of substandard care in deaths from pulmonary embolism (25% for 1988-90, 16.7% for 1991-93) possibly reflects the absence of generally agreed assessment criteria, particularly in relation to prophylaxis. There is clearly a need for a more aggressive approach to solving the underlying problems relating to thromboembolism and proposals for improved prophylaxis are outlined in the annexe to Chapter 4.

Haemorrhage

Substandard care occurred in 73.3% deaths from haemorrhage in the recent triennium, a higher proportion than in the preceding triennia, but three of the deaths were attributable to the patient refusing blood transfusion for religious reasons. Deaths were approximately equally divided between ante- and postpartum haemorrhage. The main substandard features were failure of adequate supervision and monitoring and failure to recognise coagulation disorders. The lack of high dependency and intensive care facilities, and of adequate immediate blood supplies were also significant factors.

Ectopic gestation

The number of deaths from ectopic gestation fell in the last triennium. There were only eight deaths but all were associated with substandard care. Misfortunes frequently stemmed from lack of awareness and failure of diagnosis but there were also deficiencies in post-operative management. The importance of access to adequate diagnostic facilities is discussed in Chapter 6.

Cardiac disease

Cardiac disease remains the main cause of indirect death but the distribution of disorders has altered, the chief causes of death in this triennium being ischaemic heart disease, cardiomyopathy and ruptured thoracic aortic aneurysm. Nevertheless substandard care was found in over one quarter of the cases, usually because the diagnosis had been missed or the severity of the disorder had not been appreciated. These included five patients in which senior help was not sought in spite of known cardiac disease or who were acutely ill. In particular, in three of the nine cases with aortic aneurysm no radiological examination was performed in spite of the patient complaining of chest pain. The patient herself played a significant part in several cases of substandard care, with failure to heed advice to avoid pregnancy or for termination of pregnancy, although this problem was less in the last triennium than formerly.

Caesarean section

Deaths associated with Caesarean section are counted in the chapters relating to the primary pathology but in many cases there was substandard care relating to the operation itself, or to the preparatory and/or immediate aftercare. In the current triennium such factors were identified in 31 (34.4%) cases. The main deficiencies were lack of supporting facilities and staff when dealing with high risk cases; misjudgement of the severity of the patient's condition, and of transfusion requirements and fluid balance; and inappropriate deputising or assumption of responsibility.

Clinical facilities

Lack of appropriate facilities and staff for dealing with complications were highlighted in the last Report and were further discussed by Hibbard and Milner (1994,1995) - see Table 18.3. All the recommendations studied had appeared in previous Reports but in a significant number of cases even those such as management guidelines and the development of expert advisory facilities, which could be easily and quickly established, had not been implemented. Other deficiencies which require capital expenditure, such as split and isolated units, and the absence on site of adequate support services are less easy to remedy quickly but remedial plans should have the highest priority in budgets.

Autopsies

The assessors endeavour to verify the clinical facts and supporting evidence from laboratory and autopsy evidence but autopsies frequently do not provide the information desired for the Confidential Enquiries. Although deficiencies in autopsies have not been counted as substandard care lack of adequate information about the cause of death means that it is often not possible to allocate the case with confidence, particularly in relation to such *Direct* causes as amniotic fluid embolism and in many cases of sudden death. The quality of autopsies has been an ongoing matter of concern and the number and quality of the autopsies is shown in Table 18.4. In particular, because a high proportion of autopsies are carried out on the instruction of the coroner or fiscal, whose requirements are different from those relevant to the Enquiry, and by pathologists without special expertise in maternal deaths important information is often lacking, especially histological examination.

Table 18.3

Responses to questionnaire on facilities and protocols in National Health Service consultant obstetric units (Data from Hibbard and Milner 1994)

Region	Units	Responses	Unit on Acute General Hospital site		ICU on site		Blood bank on site		Massive Haemorrhage Protocol		Eclampsia Protocol	
			n	%	n	%	n	%	n	%	n	%
Northern	18	18	15		16		15		17		17	
Yorkshire	18	18	16		13		16		15		16	
Trent	16	15	14		11		13		11		13	
East Anglia	8	8	7		7		7		6		7	
NW Thames	15	12	12		10		12		12		12	
NE Thames	15	15	9		11		11		13		15	
SE Thames	17	17	15		15		16		16		15	
SW Thames	15	12	11		9		10		11		11	
Wessex	10	10	9		7		9		9		9	
Oxford	10	10	9		9		9		9		10	
South Western	11	9	8		7		7		9		9	
West Midlands	21	20	20		17		20		17		19	
Mersey	7	7	4		4		6		7		7	
North Western	21	19	19		15		16		18		19	
Country												
England	202	190	168	88	151	79	167	88	170	89	179	94
Wales	17	17	14	82	13	76	15	88	15	88	17	100
Scotland	24	24	15	63	13	54	19	79	15	62	18	72
N.Ireland	17	17	16	94	11	65	15	88	4	24	11	65
United Kingdom	260	248	213	86	188	76	216	87	204	82	225	91

Table 18.4

	1985-87	1988-90	1991-93
Autopsies performed and quality of report. All reported deaths 1985-93			
Autopsies performed	**215 (81%)**	**265 (82%)**	**232 (73%)**
High standard	91 (42%)	91 (34%)	} 179 (77%)
Adequate	64 (30%)	117 (44%)	
Histology available	113 (53%)	124 (47%)	143 (62%)*

* Adequate in 105 cases (45%)

The deficiencies do not rest solely with the pathologists. There is sometimes a reluctance on the part of the clinical staff to seek permission for autopsy but in several cases organ donation has occurred and yet even a limited relevant autopsy has not been performed. Also there is often failure of the clinical staff to provide adequate information to the pathologist or to attend the autopsy.

Conclusions

Changes are needed to ensure that the momentum for improvement, evident over such a long period continues, and that the previous favourable trends in reduction of maternal mortality and general improvements in maternity care are not lost.

The rôle of the Confidential Enquiries requires reappraisal, particularly in regard to audit and innovative studies of specific problems, and the dissemination of information and authoritative guidelines.

Many of the deficiencies identified are amenable to correction at little or no cost, such as improved communication the provision of guidelines and organisation of staff duties and responsibilities.

A recurring theme is the availability and utilisation of staff to deal with major problems and it is evident that the establishment of consultant sessions for delivery unit supervision still falls far short of needs.

The number of consultant units on sites away from acute hospitals and without appropriate and adequate facilities is now in a significant minority and they should be regarded as substandard. There should be renewed efforts on the part of the authorities to correct these deficiencies and any reversal of this policy would be viewed with concern.

References

Hibbard BM, Milner D. Reports into Confidential Enquiries into Maternal Deaths: an audit of previous recommendations. *Health Trends* 1994; **26:** 26-28.

Hibbard B, Milner D. Auditing the audit - the way forward for the Confidential Enquiries into Maternal Deaths in the United Kingdom. *Contemporary Reviews in Obstetrics and Gynaecology* 1995;7:97-100.

UK Health Departments. *Report on Confidential Enquiries into Maternal Deaths in the United Kingdom 1985-1987*. London: HMSO, 1991.

UK Health Departments. *Report on Confidential Enquiries into Maternal Deaths in the United Kingdom 1988-1990*. London: HMSO, 1994.

CHAPTER 19

Recommendations

Introduction

The purpose of this chapter is to identify the principal factors contributing to maternal deaths, the lessons which can be learnt and clinical and administrative actions which are needed to improve care. Below we set out some of the problems and highlight the most important recommendations. General issues are considered first, followed by comments on specific clinical problems.

Many of the general issues identified as contributing to maternal mortality are not peculiar to this Enquiry. The more recently established National Confidential Enquiry into Perioperative Deaths (NCEPOD) has identified similar problems, which reinforce many of the recommendations made in this Report.

Standards need to be monitored by both purchasers and providers and particular attention should be paid to the recommendations shown in bold print in the following sections.

Method of enquiry and reliability of data

The method of enquiry has hardly changed through its long history but continues to be highly effective in identifying and investigating maternal deaths. It is of note that the system, through its various channels, identified 228 *Direct* and *Indirect* deaths, compared with 140 deaths recorded by the Registrars General. For this Report enquiries were completed on 320 of the 323 identified cases, for which no data were available for three.

In the last Report reference was made to increasing problems in collecting data and this has continued. Thanks to the considerable efforts of the secretariat, members of the Editorial Board and Regional Assessors reports have been completed for 98% of identified deaths. Some of the problems are consequent on the administrative reorganisation of the NHS but the quality of clinical information provided has continued to deteriorate. It is hoped that the introduction of a new report form (MDR(UK)1), as recommended in the last Report, will help to correct the latter deficiency.

The methods of initiating enquiries and retrieval of data are no longer efficient and if the high standards are to be maintained an early review of the system, particularly in regard to assistance for the Regional Assessors, is recommended.

In many cases the investigation was hampered by the standards of, and retrieval systems for, medical records. Accurate record keeping is essential. In some cases the enquiries were hampered by the assessors' inability to obtain the original medical records of the cases and we recommend that these records be made available, in strict confidence, to all assessors on request.

There is still evidence of under-reporting of maternal deaths through the statutory system, estimated as at least 39% for *Direct* and *Indirect* deaths in this triennium. Enactment of legislation to alter the death certificates for England, Wales and Northern Ireland, as previously recommended, has not been possible so far but a question relating to pregnancy status has been added to the reverse side of the certificate for Northern Ireland and a limited pilot study has been initiated in England and Wales.

It is recommended that the necessary legislation be expedited in conformity with the previous recommendation and with the revised International Classification of Diseases (ICD 10) which will be used for following Reports.

As in previous Reports the constraints imposed by national statistical analyses, particularly in relation to denominators, have meant that some analyses in this Report are not as complete as would be desirable. Thus, for example, the parity distribution is based on estimates because parity is only recorded for married mothers; there are no reliable denominators for ethnicity; there are no readily available or reliable figures for clinical procedures such as Caesarean sections, obstetric anaesthesia and analgesia.

A collaborative approach is needed to collect and make available denominator data which are regarded as necessary for evaluation of clinical care on a national basis.

Provision of services

The review of substandard care reveals continuing problems on several fronts.

Staffing

Improvements have occurred and will continue to occur in staffing structures, especially in relation to out of hours cover. A recurring theme is the non-availability of consultant staff to deal promptly with major problems because of competing commitments elsewhere and it is recommended that appropriate arrangements are made to ensure that consultants in charge of the delivery unit can attend at short notice.

Previous recommendations for dedicated consultant sessions for delivery unit supervision have yet to be fully implemented but this is a key factor in providing an efficient and safe service. Although new appointments will correct this deficiency in time there is an immediate need to review contracts in order to hasten the change and ensure full 24 hour consultant cover.

Inappropriate delegation and assumption of responsibility

Junior staff continue to have inappropriate responsibility deputed to them, or assume it without reference to senior colleagues, for the care of seriously ill patients. This is often because clear unit guidelines have not been drawn up.

The need for consultants to draw up local policy and managerial guidelines in conjunction with professional colleagues and to bring these to the attention of all staff concerned, especially in relation to consultation with senior staff, is reiterated. We support the NCEPOD recommendation that it is no longer acceptable for basic specialist trainees to work alone without suitable supervision and direction by their consultant.

Substandard care was identified in a significant number of deaths in which a doctor was deputising for a general practitioner or was a locum tenens in a hospital post. Inexperience, lack of continuity of care and lack of familiarity with local practice all contributed to the problems.

In 1990 NCEPOD advised that the supervision of locum appointments at all grades in anaesthesia and surgery needed urgent review. This is at present being considered by the Department of Health and the General Medical Council.

Split sites and essential services

Deficiencies in the provision of essential services and facilities have been noted in relation to acute surgical specialties generally (NCEPOD) and obstetrics is no exception to this. Split sites increase the problems of providing adequate staffing as well as such facilities as high dependency, intensive care and on site blood banks.

The number of consultant units on split sites, away from acute hospitals and without appropriate facilities is now in a significant minority and there should be continuing efforts on the part of those authorities which have not achieved unification of services to rectify this deficiency.

Patient information and education

Communication problems, especially related to language, sometimes result in misunderstandings or misinterpretations. In some cases religious or personal convictions dictated a certain course of action contrary to clinical opinion, such as withholding blood transfusion or, for some women, to refuse examination even by a female professional involved in their care.

Apparent misunderstandings on the part of the woman should be critically appraised in relation to the quality of counselling available and whether advice offered is realistic and fully comprehended. Every effort must be made to improve the quality of information provided and to ensure that it is presented in appropriate forms. Special attention must be given to the needs of patients who are not fluent in the English language and managers should ensure that appropriate interpreters and literature are readily accessible to these groups.

Hypertensive disorders of pregnancy (Chapter 2)

Although there was a fall in the number of deaths from hypertension and its complications, there is still room for improvement. In spite of previous recommendations there were clear deficiencies within some units in adopting a team approach to management involving all relevant medical and midwifery staff. In no death from hypertensive disorders was there any record of help being sought either from a Regional consultant with special expertise or another expert in the field.

In the nine years covered by the UK Reports there was substandard care in 85% deaths from hypertensive disorders, the highest proportion for any of the major causes of death and, although this had fallen to 80% in this triennium, it is a deficiency which still requires urgent attention. Apart from heeding previous recommendations, clinical policies should be reviewed by every unit, particularly in the light of the findings and recommendations of the BEST survey and of the UK Collaborative Trial. All units should have a lead consultant, clear guidelines for management of severe pregnancy induced hypertension, including eclampsia, and ready access to a Regional advisory service led by a consultant with special expertise.

Antepartum and postpartum haemorrhage (Chapter 3)

Although there has been a slight improvement, the number of deaths from haemorrhage remains unacceptably high. It is still thought that inappropriate deputing of responsibility plays a significant part in these misfortunes.

Of particular note in this Report is that four deaths were due solely to the patient, supported by her relatives, refusing to allow blood transfusion on religious grounds. Such cases, in which staff are unable to implement available treatment, cause considerable distress to all concerned.

Support should be available for staff who are required to care for patients whose personal beliefs or convictions may put their lives in jeopardy. All staff likely to be involved in the management of such cases should be familiar with, or know where to obtain, immediate advice on the steps to be taken and the best alternative management strategies. The particular situation of management of severe haemorrhage in cases where blood transfusion is refused is discussed in the guidelines annexed to Chapter 3.

Thrombosis and thromboembolism (Chapter 4)

Thrombosis and thromboembolism remains the biggest cause of maternal death, the principal factors being inadequate use of prophylactic measures in vulnerable women, lack of recognition of warning symptoms and signs, and inadequate use of ancillary investigations.

Close attention should be paid to any woman with chest symptoms who is currently pregnant or recently delivered, to exclude the presence of deep vein thrombosis or small pulmonary embolism.

Caesarean section is clearly a risk factor for development of venous thrombosis. Prophylaxis has been a controversial issue but its value has been shown in major surgery (NECPOD) and it is now widely accepted in relation to Caesarean section.

The recommendations of the Working Party of the Royal College of Obstetricians and Gynaecologists on prophylaxis, which are summarised as an Annexe to Chapter 4, should be adopted and incorporated in the clinical policies of all obstetric units.

Early pregnancy deaths (Chapter 6)

There was a significant fall in the number of deaths in early pregnancy. However, overall they rank third in the *Direct* causes of maternal death. There were only eight deaths from ectopic gestation, compared with 15 in the previous Report. The main problem is lack of awareness of the possible diagnosis of ectopic gestation in women presenting with abdominal pain, particularly when first seen by general practitioners or in Accident and Emergency Departments. Also, appropriate diagnostic techniques are often not used. The importance of the availability of sensitive ßhCG tests and of ultrasound facilities was emphasised previously but requires repetition.

Attention is drawn to "Guidance on Ultrasound Procedures in Early Pregnancy", and in particular to the section on organisation of services, published by the Royal Colleges of Radiologists and of Obstetricians and Gynaecologists.

Deaths following legal termination of pregnancy continue to occur. It is important that all units have adequate facilities to deal with unexpected complications. The arrangements for after care, especially for day care cases, must be clearly defined and understood by the staff, patients and general practitioners.

Anaesthesia and intensive care (Chapters 9 and 17)

A large number of the women detailed in this report required high dependency or intensive care. Facilities should therefore be conveniently sited and readily available.

In seven of the deaths in this series transfer to another hospital for intensive care was required and in a further eight cases admission to an ICU was delayed because of lack of facilities.

All obstetric patients should be regarded as high anaesthesia risks, especially when emergency procedures are required, and there should be early involvement of consultant anaesthetists in the management of complex deliveries. Siting of essential services, staffing and management should reflect this.

Ready access should be available to appropriate monitoring equipment and training provide in their use.

Extra care needs to be taken with patients with darker skin where careful assessment and monitoring is required since cyanosis may go undetected. Pulse oximetry must be provided both intra- and postoperatively.

Other *Direct* deaths (Chapter 10)

Three deaths resulted from persistent vomiting and in two of these Wernicke's encephalopathy was suspected. Persistent vomiting can result in severe electrolyte and nutritional disturbances as well as behavioural disturbances and the risk of aspiration of vomitus.

Fluid and electrolyte balance and control of anti-emetic drug therapy in cases of hyperemesis gravidarum require expert management. In all cases where an intravenous infusion is required thiamine should also be administered.

The use of ß agonists to inhibit labour continues to pose therapeutic problems and two deaths in this series illustrate the difficulties which can arise, particularly from fluid overload.

The RCOG Guidelines for the use of ritodrine indicate circumstances in which the drug may be useful and emphasise the need for carefully controlled administration and monitoring. These guidelines should be adhered to unless there are pressing reasons for deviating from them.

Medical and surgical disorders (Chapters 11 and 12)

Indirect deaths associated with medical and surgical disorders now account for 45% of *Direct* and *Indirect* maternal deaths. The number of deaths from cardiac disease is comparable with those from thromboembolism and is greater than those from haemorrhage or from hypertensive disorders. Whilst deaths from structural heart disease have diminished those from ischaemic heart disease and aneurysm of the thoracic aorta have increased. Substandard care occurred most commonly in cases of aneurysm, usually because of failure to take heed of chest pain and failure of adequate examination, including radiology.

The need to refer all known or suspected cases of heart disease for expert assessment and for shared care is again emphasised. The use of chest X-Rays in these cases is fully justified.

Other medical and surgical conditions which are significantly influenced by pregnancy or create special problems for the pregnancy itself require team management with experienced physicians or surgeons, and there is a need for more physicians with a particular interest in medical problems of pregnancy.

Caesarean section (Chapter 13)

In most cases with substandard care there were several interrelated contributory factors but it is clear that a number of problems which have been highlighted in the past still pertain, particularly lack of facilities to cope with unanticipated complications and too much responsibility being devolved to or taken by junior staff.

Deficiencies in care by junior staff included inappropriate deputising; failure to appreciate the seriousness of the patient's condition, with consequent delay in instituting adequate treatment; and failure to seek more senior help.

Over half of the Caesarean sections were carried out by registrars. Eleven of the 19 unplanned emergency operations were undertaken by registrars and there was substandard care in seven of these.

Many of the deaths were in high risk patients with medical or surgical disorders. Even when the management of these cases was undertaken by consultant obstetricians substandard care was common and frequently stemmed from lack of a team approach and adequate communication between specialists.

Many of the deficiencies in management of patients undergoing Caesarean section, and of their aftercare, could be resolved by attention to the recommendations made earlier in this chapter under 'Provision of services'.

The number of perimortem Caesarean sections was slightly fewer than in previous Reports, and with improved fetal outcome. This reflects the fact that these procedures are being carried out in better and more controlled circumstances.

In spite of previous recommendations there continues to be a small number of postmortem Caesarean sections performed in hopeless circumstances and with no fetal survivors.

It is again emphasised that the decision to undertake Caesarean section in moribund or recently dead patients should be made at consultant level after careful assessment and preferably after discussion with the relatives. As the intention is fetal salvage appropriate neonatal resuscitation facilities must be immediately available.

Pathology (Chapter 16)

Once again the number of substandard autopsies is disappointing.

Attention is drawn to the "Guidelines for Maternal Autopsy" published by the Royal College of Pathologists and wherever possible the autopsy should be performed by a pathologist with specific experience in obstetric pathology.

Monitoring of recommendations

There is some published and anecdotal evidence of improvements in the provision of facilities which were reviewed in relation to the last Report (see Chapter 18) but a more formal review of these and other recommendations should be the subject of continuing audit.

It is recommended that a further review of clinical facilities be undertaken for publication in the next Report. This should include the elements of the review by Hibbard and Milner(1994) which was referred to in the last Report so as to provide some measure of progress towards the objectives on which that survey was based but it should be conducted on a broader front.

ACKNOWLEDGEMENTS

This Report has been made possible by the help and work of the District Directors of Public Health in England and Northern Ireland and the Chief Administrative Medical Officers in Wales and Scotland who initiated case reports and collected the information, and the consultant obstetricians, anaesthetists and pathologists, general practitioners and midwives who have supplied the detailed case records and autopsy reports.

Considerable assistance has also been given by procurators fiscal who have supplied copies of reports of autopsies, and by coroners who have supplied autopsy reports and sometimes inquest proceedings to the assessors.

The staff of the Medical Statistics Division of the Office of Population Censuses and Surveys in England have worked with the information and Statistics Division of the Common Services Agency in Scotland and Departmental statisticians in Wales and Northern Ireland to process the statistical data and prepare the Tables and Figures.

The Editorial Board would like to express their thanks to all these people and also in particular to the consultant obstetricians, anaesthetists, pathologists and midwives listed below who have acted as Regional assessors in England and assessors in Scotland and helped in the preparation of this Report. All assessors for Wales and Northern Ireland are members of the Editorial Board who are listed in the front of this report.

I. ENGLISH REGIONAL ASSESSORS IN OBSTETRICS

Northern Region	Professor J M Davidson MD FRCOG
Yorkshire Region	Mr P S Vinall FRCOG
Trent Region	Miss H J Mellows FRCOG
East Anglian Region	Mr P J Milton MA MD FRCOG
North West Thames Region	Mr H G Wagman FRCSE FRCOG
North East Thames Region	Mr M E Setchell FRCS FRCOG
South East Thames Region	Prof L D Cardozo MD FRCOG
South West Thames Region	Professor G V P Chamberlain MD FRCS FRCOG
Oxford Region	Mr M Gillmer MD FRCOG
South Western Region	Professor G M Stirrat MA MD FRCOG
West Midlands Region:	Mr H Oliphant Nicholson FRCSE FRCOG
North Western Region	Mr P Donnai MA FRCOG
Mersey Region	Mrs S H Towers MD FRCOG (to January 1994) Miss A Garden FRCOG (from February 1994)
Wessex Region	Mr C P Jardine Brown FRCS FRCOG

II. ENGLISH REGIONAL ASSESSORS IN ANAESTHESIA

Northern Region	Dr M R Bryson FRCA
Yorkshire Region	Professor F Richard Ellis PhD FRCA
Trent Region	Dr A Caunt FRCA
East Anglian Region	Dr B R Wilkey FRCA
North West Thames Region	Dr M Morgan FRCA
North East Thames Region	Dr Miriam Frank FRCA
South East Thames Region	Dr P B Hewitt FRCA
South West Thames Region	Dr H F Seeley MSc FRCA
Oxford Region	Dr L E S Carrie FRCA
South Western Region	Dr T A Thomas FRCA
West Midlands Region	Dr A M Veness FRCA
North Western Region	Dr J M Anderton FRCA
Mersey Region	Dr T H L Bryson FRCA
Wessex Region	Professor John Norman PhD FRCA

III. ENGLISH REGIONAL ASSESSORS IN PATHOLOGY

Northern Region	Dr A R Morley MD FRCPath
Yorkshire Region	Dr I N Reid FRCPath
	Prof M Wells MD FRCPath
Trent Region	Dr A Shirley Hill FRCOG FRCPath (until Nov 1993)
	Dr L J R Brown MRCPath (from Nov 1993)
East Anglian Region	Dr P F Roberts MRCP FRCPath
North West Thames Region	Dr I A Lampert FRCPath
North East Thames Region	Dr R G M Letcher FRCPath
	Dr J Crow MB BS FRCPath (from Nov 1992)
South East Thames Region	Dr N Kirkham MD FRCPath
South West Thames Region	Dr M Hall FRCPath
Oxford Region	Dr W Gray FRCPath
South Western Region	Professor P P Anthony FRCPath
West Midlands Region	Dr D I Rushton FRCPath
North Western Region	Professor H Fox MD FRCPath (until 1993)
	Dr H Buckley MD FRCPath (from 1993)
Mersey Region	Dr I W McDicken MD FRCPath
Wessex Region	Dr G H Millward-Sadler BSc MB ChB FRCPath

IV. ENGLISH REGIONAL ASSESSORS IN MIDWIFERY

Northern Region	Miss L Robson MA SRN SCM ADM PGCAE
Yorkshire Region	Miss W Robinson RN RM QIDNS
Trent Region	Miss I Cooper RN RM
East Anglian Region	Miss E Fern RGN RM MTD
North West Thames Region	Miss C Nightingale BA RN RM RSCN DipN

North East Thames Region	Mrs M Grant RN SCM
South East Thames Region	Ms I Bryan RN SCM
South West Thames Region	Mrs M Wheeler RN RM ADM
Oxford Region	Mrs C Osselton RN SCM
South Western Region	Mrs V Beale RN SCM
West Midlands Region	Miss J Goulding RN RM ADM MSC
North Western Region	Mrs J Bracken RN SCM
Mersey Region	Miss C Whewell RN RM ADM MTD
Wessex Region	Mrs J Duncan RGN RM

V. SCOTTISH ASSESSORS TO THE CEMD NOT SERVING ON THE UK CEMD EDITORIAL BOARD

Dr M H Hall MD FRCOG
Dr N B Patel FRCOG
(until mid 1993))
Dr J G Donald FRCOG
(from mid 1993))
Dr J B Scrimgeour FRCS FRCOG
(until mid 1993)
Dr W A Liston FRCOG
(from mid 1993))
Dr K S Stewart MD FRCS FRCOG
Dr H P McEwan MD FRCS FRCOG
Dr J Thorburn FRCA

Printed in the United Kingdom for HMSO.
Dd.0302629, C110, 5/96, 569516, 5673, 352403.